Notable Quotes/Quotable Notes

- "Two Doors" Analogy - pg. 63
- Kim's Sermon on Ex. 17:1-7 - "Rock of Ages" pg. 90
- Categories + Functions of Law passages pg. 117

Preaching the Whole Counsel of God strategically blends an emphasis on proclaiming Christ as the unifying Hero of the entire Bible with insights drawn from recent communications research into the ways that listeners attend to and process what they hear (or not!). Among various recent books on Christ-centered preaching, a distinctive strength of Dr. Kim's work is his well-informed, practical coaching on sermon structure, illustration, and delivery, helping preachers bring God's Word home to hearers' hearts in dependence on the Holy Spirit. I highly recommend this book.

—**Dennis E. Johnson,** Ph.D., Professor of Practical Theology,
Westminster Seminary California

Julius Kim's many years of teaching and modeling biblical preaching combine with a keen mind and a caring heart to provide this excellent and highly accessible resource for preaching the whole counsel of God. Among the book's many fine features are its commitment to seeing the whole Bible as a revelation of God's redemptive message and its great suggestions for communicating these truths to contemporary culture.

—**Bryan Chapell,** Pastor, Grace Presbyterian Church, Peoria, IL;
President Emeritus, Covenant Seminary

If Christ is the one "in whom and for whom" everything has been created, faithful sermons ought to illuminate this reality. They ought to manifest the ways in which all of life is held together "in Christ" and the manner in which the great story of Scripture is likewise glued together "in Christ." Julius Kim has done a marvelous job in bringing this conviction to life and making it so practical that no preacher worth their salt will miss it. And every listener of sermons will see why these matters are of such great importance.

—**Richard Lints,** Vice President for Academic Affairs, and Andrew Mutch
Distinguished Professor of Theology, Gordon-Conwell Theological Seminary

A wonderful blend of hermeneutics and homiletics! Kim takes the reader from the text to the pulpit in a clear and concise way. Here preachers will learn how to think about the text and how to package those thoughts into a compelling sermon. A great textbook for a preaching class, and a revitalizing read for seasoned preachers!

—**Mark D. Futato Sr.,** Robert L. Maclelland Professor of Old Testament,
Reformed Theological Seminary, Orlando, FL

Only a thorough knowledge of Christ at the center of all Scripture, years of teaching preachers, laborious research, and a pastor's heart could produce a book as useful as this to the church.

—**George Robertson,** Ph.D, Senior Pastor, First Presbyterian Church,
Augusta, GA

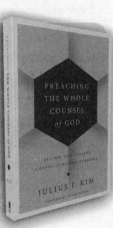

PREACHING THE WHOLE COUNSEL *of* GOD

DESIGN AND DELIVER
GOSPEL-CENTERED SERMONS

JULIUS J. KIM

ZONDERVAN

Preaching the Whole Counsel of God
Copyright © 2015 by Julius J. Kim

This title is also available as a Zondervan ebook.

Requests for information should be addressed to:

Zondervan, 3900 *Sparks Drive SE, Grand Rapids, Michigan 49546*

Library of Congress Cataloging-in-Publication Data

Kim, Julius J.
    Preaching the whole counsel of God : design and deliver gospel-centered sermons / Julius
J. Kim.
        p. cm.
    Includes bibliographical references.
    ISBN 978-0-310-51963-8 (hardcover)
    1. Preaching. I. Title.
BV4211.3.K55 2015
251—dc23   2015023624

All Scripture quotations, unless otherwise indicated, are taken from the ESV® Bible (The Holy Bible, English Standard Version®). Copyright © 2001 by Crossway, a publishing ministry of Good News Publishers. Used by permission. All rights reserved.

Other Scripture versions quoted in this book are listed on page 18.

Any Internet addresses (websites, blogs, etc.) and telephone numbers in this book are offered as a resource. They are not intended in any way to be or imply an endorsement by Zondervan, nor does Zondervan vouch for the content of these sites and numbers for the life of this book.

Cover design: Christopher Tobias / tobiasdesign.com
Interior design: Matthew Van Zomeren

Printed in the United States of America

---

17 18 19 20 21 22 23 24 25 /DCI/ 23 22 21 20 19 18 17 16 15 14 13 12 11 10 9 8 7 6 5 4 3

To

My wife, Ji Hee,

Thank you

for your faith, hope, and love;

my heart is full.

CONTENTS

PART ONE: DISCOVERING THE TRUTH OF THE TEXT
ACCORDING TO THE HUMAN AUTHOR

CHAPTER 1

CHAPTER 2

PART TWO: DISCERNING CHRIST IN THE TEXT
ACCORDING TO THE DIVINE AUTHOR

CHAPTER 3

CHAPTER 4

CHAPTER 5

PART THREE: DESIGNING THE SERMON ACCORDING TO TRUTH, GOODNESS, AND BEAUTY

PART FOUR: DELIVERING THE SERMON FOR ATTENTION, RETENTION, INTEGRATION, AND TRANSFORMATION

FOREWORD

People in the pews, especially younger generations, are tired of much of what passes for preaching today. They are tired of preachers trying too hard, dangling carrots that have nothing to do with the Bible to entice them back next week. They are tired of the constant "how-to," the glitz-and-glamour of a choreographed presentation. Many pastors, caught up in pleasing the crowds, have little time left — and sometimes insufficient expertise — to truly unpack the text.

On the other hand, some preachers have the opposite problem. I know of a few (okay, maybe more than a few) on the other side of the spectrum who spend hours in the study. There, focused solely on the text, they hope that their study will cover over a multitude of other homiletical sins. They say with conviction: "Content is everything: it doesn't matter *how* you deliver it. When you preach the Word, it's *supposed* to hurt." Sadly, they often succeed in their goal of making the congregation uncomfortable. But the pain people experience under their preaching is not always a work of God.

As heralds of God's Word, must we choose between these two extremes? Between being faithful expositors and relevant communicators?

Preaching: Who Cares?

Many in our churches today are losing confidence in the power of God's Word. They wonder, can it truly bring life to the dead? The apostles were convinced that the Spirit works his greatest miracles through his Word, particularly through the gospel — the "power of God unto salvation for everyone who believes ..." (Rom 1:16). In Romans 10, Paul unfolds the logical argument for why we must preach and why we need preachers:

> But how are they to call on him in whom they have not believed? And
> how are they to believe in him of whom they have never heard? And

how are they to hear without someone preaching? And how are they to preach unless they are sent? As it is written, "How beautiful are the feet of those who preach the good news!" But they have not all obeyed the gospel. For Isaiah says, "Lord, who has believed what he has heard from us?" So faith comes from hearing, and hearing through the word of Christ (vv. 14-17 ESV).

Yes, gimmicks can attract momentary interest. But Paul is very clear: *People will only believe and call on the Lord if they hear the gospel, and the gospel is a message that must be preached.* Do we, today, share the apostles' confidence in the uniqueness of proclaiming God's Word as the Spirit's means of bringing the new creation into this present evil age?

A Bewildering Complex of Contexts

The basic message of Scripture is not complicated. It's simple enough to be summarized by a child. Yet the Bible is truly more of a library than a single book. Written over millennia, through prophets from various contexts and walks of life, Scripture is a collection of narratives, laws, songs, wisdom sayings, apocalyptic, and teaching. Faithful preachers must learn how to respect the particular genre, the human writer, and the context of a particular passage while interpreting it within the larger story of the Triune God and his saving and gathering grace. Then the preacher must take these ancient texts and deliver them to people living in vastly different times and places. No one said this would be easy.

Yet our Christian growth depends on a lifetime of such sermons, and we need the full counsel of God's Word to help us grow and mature in our obedience to Christ. God is the ultimate speaker in all of this, but he has seen fit to use weak and sinful vessels to bear this treasure to his people. So how do we do this? How do we interpret and apply the whole counsel of God in ways that appreciate the distinct regimes or covenants in which God spoke to our forebears in the faith? How do we preach Leviticus? Or the Sermon on the Mount? And how can we hear these words of our Lord today in a way that is faithful to their original meaning?

What Is Different about This Book?

There are many useful textbooks on preaching available, but among them, this book stands out. It is evenly balanced between theory and practice, hermeneutics and homiletics. Julius Kim insists that God's herald must *discover* the truth, *discern* Christ in the text, *design* a sermon that is "good, true, and beautiful," and *deliver* sermons that dwell richly in the hearts of their hearers. Kim not only insists on this point, but shows us how to do it well.

Anyone who does this work week after week knows that the work of preaching is challenging. Julius Kim is aware of the challenge. As a seminary professor, he listens to hundreds of student sermons, offering critique and encouragement, and he sees how preachers develop from their first exposition to being ready to enter the harvest field. He is experienced and uncompromising and extraordinarily patient, kind, and constructive.

In addition, his treatment is unashamedly committed to seeing Christ in all the Scriptures, the promise-fulfillment pattern of God's unfolding drama from creation to consummation. This is no small thing in a day when "relevance" is so often sought outside of Christ, the one in whom the Father has placed all spiritual treasures.

Finally, by my reckoning at least, this is the only book on preaching that takes ample account of the most recent studies in brain research. There is always a danger to think of our parishioners as "brains on a stick," as James K. A. Smith puts it. If some ignore the "renewing of the mind" by God's Word, others wrongly assume that preaching addresses the intellect alone. Yet, as Professor Kim points out, the brain is far more interesting and complex, and how we hear—and hide God's Word in our heart—must be a crucial aspect of the preacher's concern.

God created us and redeems us as *whole* people through his *whole* Word, which delivers the *whole* Christ to his people in every time and place. If sharing with God in that sacred ministry is the burden of your heart, then this resource will richly repay repeated exploration. If your experience is like mine, you will come away with a much greater appreciation for both the serious challenges and joyful blessing of being counted a herald of God's unspeakable wealth.

Michael Horton
J. Gresham Machen Professor of Systematic Theology
and Apologetics at Westminster Seminary California

ACKNOWLEDGMENTS

No book is the result of just one person. It is the product of many lives, interwoven by God's masterful hand, coming together to form a beautiful mosaic of wisdom and beauty. So while all the errors and problems in this book are entirely mine (especially omitting special people in these acknowledgments), all that is true and good is a result of many people whom I must now thank.

First I'd like to thank the formidable and fantastic team at Zondervan and HarperCollins for their faith and hope in this book. I especially want to thank my editor, Ryan Pazdur, for both his professional skill and his pastoral grace in the entire process. Ryan, I thank God for you and the unique talents you are using for God's glory.

I also want to thank the faculty and students at Westminster Seminary California who have helped me understand what it means to preach the whole counsel of God. Fellow professors, thank you for allowing me to participate with you in this grand adventure of training the next generation of servant leaders for the church of Jesus Christ. I especially want to thank two colleagues. Dennis Johnson, thank you for modeling what a true pastor-scholar looks like. Since the day I joined you in the Practical Theology department, you have generously revealed to me how to humbly and diligently work hard to shepherd students through my research, teaching, counseling, and mentoring. Mike Horton, thank you for helping me grow a theology that is faithfully biblical, robustly confessional, and eminently practical. I am indebted to your scholarship and friendship. Students, thank you for letting me refine my ideas on preaching over these years and letting me hear and evaluate your sermons. In many ways, this is your book!

I would be remiss if I did not mention my former professor and friend from Westminster California, the late Dr. Edmund Clowney. Through his insightful teaching and faithful mentoring, Ed taught me most what it means to be a steadfast and devoted herald of the King. He lived to know Jesus more and to make him known. He sought ways to serve others more than himself. He cared neither for acclamation nor commendation. For Ed, his life and ministry was always about one person: Jesus. This, then, is what he passed on to me: to preach Christ in word and in deed, to die to myself daily for others, and then, to be forgotten.

I am also deeply grateful for my past and present ministry colleagues, the pastors, elders, and deacons at New Life Presbyterian Church in Escondido. Each of you has played a crucial role in my development as a pastor, professor, preacher, and friend. While many of you deserve special mention, space limitations prevent me from thanking all of you personally. I hope I can remedy that by thanking you all privately with a copy of this book! I would like, however, to thank Ted Hamilton, Senior Pastor at New Life. Thank you for faithfully and tirelessly preaching the gospel of Jesus Christ week in and week out with such breathtaking clarity and life-transforming cogency. We would not be the Christians we are today were it not for your shepherding ministry of making Christ known from every part of Scripture to every part of our lives. Thank you for loving and leading, knowing and feeding, protecting and providing. My family and I are forever grateful.

I want to thank my parents, Gwan Hae and Sook Ja Kim. This book is a product of your years of faithful support and constant love. *Appa* and *Umma*, you have not neglected to pray for me daily since the day I was born. You have endured much hardship and heartache, coming to a foreign land so that we would have a better life. What words can do justice for your selfless sacrifice for us? Thank you for embodying and exemplifying the life of a gospel pilgrim, dying to self and living for others while constantly looking forward to the great day when you shall see Jesus face-to-face.

Finally, I want to thank the three most important people in my life. To my daughters, Emma and Phoebe: Thank you for helping me become the father and man that I am today. Your love and devotion cannot be described by words alone. But God knows all that you have

ACKNOWLEDGMENTS

done and continue to do to make my heart so full of joy and gratitude. Again, please accept my apology that this book is not a picture book about our family. To my wife, Ji Hee: You know me better than anyone else on this planet, and yet still decided to marry me and stick with me all these years. The words on this page cannot express what you mean to me. You are light to my dark, warmth to my cold, joy to my sorrow. Though this is woefully inadequate for all that you are to me, I dedicate this book, with breathless adoration, to you, my love and my life.

ABBREVIATIONS

BDB   Brown, F., S. R. Driver, and C. A. Briggs, eds., *A Hebrew and English Lexicon of the Old Testament* (1907; reprint, Peabody, Mass.: Hendrickson, 1994).

BDAG   Danker, F. W., W. Bauer, W. F. Arndt, and F. W. Gingrich. *A Greek-English Lexicon of the New Testament and Other Early Christian Literature.* 3rd ed. (Chicago: University of Chicago Press, 2000).

CFC   Christ-focused connection

FCF   fallen-condition focus

ISBE   *International Standard Bible Encyclopedia.* Rev. ed. Edited by G. W. Bromiley. 4 vols. (Grand Rapids: Eerdmans, 1979–1988).

JETS   *Journal of the Evangelical Society*

NT   New Testament

OT   Old Testament

PCPMW   Clowney, Edmund P., and Timothy Keller. *Preaching Christ to a Post-Modern World.* Unpublished syllabus, Reformed Theological Seminary.

PNAS   *Proceedings of the National Academy of Sciences*

TDNT   *Theological Dictionary of the New Testament.* Edited by G. Kittel and G. Friedrich. Translated by G. W. Bromiley. 10 vols. (Grand Rapids: Eerdmans, 1964–1976).

WCF   Westminster Confession of Faith

WSC   Westminster Shorter Catechism

WTJ   *Westminster Theological Journal*

BIBLE VERSIONS

In addition to the *English Standard Version*, the following Scripture versions are quoted in this book:

Scripture quotations marked CEV are taken from the *Contemporary English Version*. Copyright © 1995 by American Bible Society. Used by permission.

Scripture quotations marked NASB are taken from the *New American Standard Bible*. Copyright © 1960, 1962, 1963, 1968, 1971, 1972, 1973, 1975, 1977, 1995 by The Lockman Foundation. Used by permission.

Scripture quotations marked NIV are taken from The Holy Bible, *New International Version*®, *NIV*®. Copyright © 1973, 1978, 1984, 2011 by Biblica, Inc.® Used by permission. All rights reserved worldwide.

INTRODUCTION

Preaching is a glorious calling. What other calling allows you to represent the King of Kings and the Lord of Lords? What other calling allows you to speak words of life, joy, and peace? What other calling allows you to see dead people come to life through mere words? What other calling allows you to see God at work in the lives of people, transforming them, renewing them, maturing them? Preaching is a glorious calling. But it isn't easy.

Having preached for almost thirty years and having taught preaching for the last fifteen, listening to and evaluating thousands of sermons, I find that preaching is still quite challenging—and not just for me! Over the last several years of teaching young preachers how to interpret and communicate the truths of God's Word, one particular image has helped and encouraged me. In the Bible, one of the primary images used to convey the identity of a preacher is the *herald*. Specially chosen by a king to proclaim his decrees—be it to his loyal subjects or even to his enemies—a herald had a unique character and calling. Let's examine this person and see what it teaches us about the preacher and his preaching.

The Herald/Evangel

Trained at an early age, the herald became the voice of the king. Though the words that he spoke came from his own mouth, the words represented another, more powerful one, whose words had authority. People listened when he spoke, for often the news that he brought on behalf of his king could change their lives drastically.

In the NT, preachers of the gospel, or the good news of Jesus Christ, were called heralds (*kerux*, or *evangel*). A herald was one who was specially trained and tested to represent his king, whatever the need. The herald had to ensure that the message he was to proclaim on behalf of his king was accurate and persuasive not only in its content but also in its delivery. The herald's task wasn't easy, but it was glorious. The words he spoke had the power to change lives.

Several writers in the NT used the word *herald* to describe the nature and task of the preacher of the gospel. Heralds may not be common today, but the image conveys some wonderful truths.

During the first century, an evangel was a herald or messenger that brought news of such historical significance that life would be forever different for those who heard it. Whether the news was positive or negative, it could have a profound effect. It could comfort and inspire or warn and frighten. Usually serving under the direct command of the king, heralds were carefully trained and chosen to represent the authority of the king. A modern-day analogy would be the Secretary of State of the United States, who is granted the power to communicate diplomatic news to the leaders of other nations.

Heralds brought life-changing news to people. Based on the Greek literature during the time the NT was written, heralds proclaimed something had transpired that had transformational consequences. For example, evangels proclaimed victory in war or the ascension of a new king. With the news of victory or coronation, a new era of peace and joy broke out in the lives of those blessed to hear the good news.[1]

The herald not only proclaimed good news to the king's loyal subjects but also delivered severe warnings to the king's enemies. Gordon Hugenberger notes the Greek practice of officially sending a herald deep into enemy territory prior to the outbreak of war. He writes that the herald had the authority and protection of the king to "warn the enemy of certain destruction unless they accepted the terms for peace."[2]

The herald had the majestic privilege as well as formidable responsibility to represent his king with clarity, cogency, and conviction,

---

1 One scholar lists many examples of the classical and Hellenistic uses of the "evangel" and "herald" word groups that may have influenced the NT authors' usage of these words (Gerhard Friedrich, *TDNT* 2:707–737; 3:683–694).
2 Gordon P. Hugenberger, *ISBE* 3:942.

whether delivering good news or bad. On the one hand, the herald was part of the king's court, with direct access to the king and all the benefits associated with that kind of proximity. On the other hand, misrepresenting the king would lead to a speedy punishment, usually death.

While the analogy to the modern-day preacher does not correspond in every way, the image of the herald is a helpful one as we begin thinking about the preacher and his preaching. As a herald of the King of Kings, everything we think, do, and say must align with the King's mind, heart, and will. The preacher's King has revealed himself in the Bible, and it is the herald's great privilege and awesome responsibility to proclaim his will. Nothing else matters but to communicate the King's wishes and will to the best of our ability so that those who hear the King's voice, through the herald, would find comfort and courage. This is essentially the preacher's character and calling: to bring all that we are and have to bear upon the glorious task of speaking for the King.

This book functions to help current heralds and future heralds as they train and prepare to speak for the Lord. Be it from the pulpit or in a Bible study, heralds can use this book to help them not only understand the words of the King (interpretation) but also convey his message well (communication). With this image in mind, we will explore through the course of this book the work of a faithful herald. The herald's task, and this book, has four integral parts.

1. The herald must *discover* the truth of the text according to the human author.
2. The herald must *discern* Christ in the text according to the Divine Author.
3. The herald must *design* a sermon that is true, good, and beautiful.
4. The herald must *deliver* the sermon for attention, retention, integration, and transformation.

A preacher is a herald, called and appointed by God, to proclaim God's message of the gospel from his revealed Word, with truth, goodness, and beauty, so that the hearer would be transformed by his grace.

PART ONE

DISCOVERING THE TRUTH *of* THE TEXT ACCORDING *to* THE HUMAN AUTHOR

CHAPTER 1

PRAYING, SELECTING, READING, AND MEDITATING

We begin this book by examining several preliminary steps that are important to the overall sermon preparation and delivery process. The four steps of *praying*, *selecting*, *reading*, and *meditating* provide an indispensable foundation for the herald of the King as he discovers, discerns, designs, and delivers gospel-centered sermons. We shall look at these four preliminary yet foundational steps in turn.

Praying

The Bible records that the first Christian leaders of the fledgling NT church devoted themselves to two primary tasks: preaching and prayer (Acts 6:4). Following the example set by their rabbi, Jesus, they knew that prayer was an essential part of their ministry. They remembered how Jesus would often wake early in the morning, while it was still dark, to pray to his heavenly Father before his preaching and teaching (Mark 1:35–39). Early Christian believers included prayer as an essential part of their life together (Acts 2:42).

The apostle Paul also understood the necessity of prayer for his ministry. His letters reveal the priority he placed on prayer not only for the growth and maturity of the believers (Eph 1:15–23) but also for his own ministry of preaching (Col 3:2–4). He knew that without the power of God, his preaching ministry would be fruitless. He prayed and asked others to pray with him and for him. He prayed that the gospel would transform believers (Eph 3:14–21; Col 1:9–10) and prayed that his preaching would be bold and effective (Eph 6:19–20; Col 4:3–4). After all, prior to sending his disciples out on their preaching ministry, Jesus said, "Apart from me you can do nothing" (John 15:5). As preachers of the Word, we follow in the pattern of Jesus and the apostles: praying is a necessary part of our sermon preparation and delivery.[1]

We pray before, during, and after the process of preparing a sermon. We will not grasp the truth, goodness, and beauty of God's Word apart from the Holy Spirit's work of conviction, illumination, and regeneration (John 16:8–10, 13–16; Titus 3:5). This is what we pray for ourselves as we prepare and for our church as they hear. We pray for comprehension and integration, application and transformation.

Every effort in sermon preparation is worthless without the accompanying work of the Holy Spirit's work. Prayer is not simply one important step in the sermon preparation process. It is the most important step in the process of sermon design and delivery. We pray throughout our sermon preparation efforts—before we read, as we interpret, when we write, and while we preach. Pray for wisdom, knowledge, and understanding, both for yourself and for your hearers. Pray for protection, provision, and power. Pray that unbelievers and believers would trust and obey the gospel of Jesus Christ to the glory of God.

---

1. What is prayer? The Westminster Shorter Catechism (WSC) provides a helpful summary: "Prayer is an offering up of our desires unto God, (1) for things agreeable to his will, (2) in the name of Christ, (3) with confession of our sins, (4) and thankful acknowledgement of his mercies" (Q&A 98). The proof texts are Ps 62:8; 1 John 5:14; John 16:23; Ps 32:5–6; Dan 9:4; Phil 4:6.

Selecting

Part of the process of preparing to preach is selecting your text and/ or topic. While this may seem self-evident, there are some important factors to consider when selecting a text to preach, not the least of which is discerning the spiritual state and needs of your unique congregation.

As heralds, we don't speak truth in the abstract. We speak truth to a particular audience at a particular time in a particular place. Knowing your audience is an important component in selecting your text and speaking to your audience. It is both a science and an art. A preacher can learn more about his audience by doing a demographic analysis of such traits such as age, gender, educational level, and so on. Moreover, some of the cultural values and sensibilities of the group can also be discerned through analysis. The art of audience analysis gives consideration to how those demographics and values shape the thinking and feelings of one's audience in response to the truths and implications of the gospel. Richard Lints has been helpful in showing the theological link between the art and science of preaching. He states that our task is essentially a theological one, as we move out from our understanding of God and his Word and preach it to particular people in their time, space, and history.[2]

The apostle Paul understood this intersection between the timeless truths of God and the time-bound nature of his different audiences. Take, for example, his preaching ministry at a synagogue in Pisidian Antioch (Act 13) and his presentation evangelism in Athens (Acts 17). While the nonnegotiable elements of his gospel proclamation remained the same, his selection of material and his presentation were drastically different due to the audience. To the primarily Jewish audience in Acts 13, he strategically employed several OT texts and argued that Jesus was the promised Messiah who had come to die for sin yet was raised for their justification. In Acts 17, however, his approach was remarkably

---

2. Richard Lints, *The Fabric of Theology: A Prolegomenon to Evangelical Theology* (Grand Rapids: Eerdmans, 1993), 9.

different. To this group of biblically illiterate philosophers on Mars' Hill, he constructed a biblical worldview starting with creation and then proclaimed Christ's resurrection from the dead. While much more can be said about these texts, it's clear that Paul engaged in careful audience analysis to discern his listeners' spiritual and cultural state so as to present the gospel of Jesus more effectively.[3] Knowing your audience influences the text you select.

For many preachers, however, selecting a text occurs on the Monday or Tuesday prior to the upcoming Sunday. Unfortunately, this is not helpful or wise. Because of the limited amount of time available, you will not have the time you'd like and need for important factors such as studying the text and context, meditating on its truths for you and your hearers, finding compelling illustrations, and identifying meaningful applications. Furthermore, the last thing you need is to be stressed because you may not be sure if the text or topic you've chosen is the right one at the right time. To offset this tendency and temptation, you need to explore the concept weeks or even months ahead. I offer three words of advice when it comes to selecting a text to preach: pray, pattern, and pastor.

Pray

Spend time seeking the Lord through prayer for wisdom on the decision of which text to preach. Wise pastors know that discerning the needs of their congregation to determine what to preach requires help from the Lord God of all wisdom. We cannot discern the hearts of our hearers without the aid of the Holy Spirit, who searches hearts. Go to the Lord in prayer and ask for wisdom and insight into the portions of Scriptures your congregation needs to hear. Some pastors may want to spend some intentional time alone, praying and reflecting, while others may want to pray with fellow leaders in the church. Some pastors may want to spend a few days in prayer and planning as they map out their sermon series

---

3. For more on Paul's approaches in Acts 13 and 17, see D. A. Carson, "Athens Revisited," *Telling the Truth: Evangelizing Postmoderns*, ed. D. A. Carson (Grand Rapids: Zondervan, 2000), 384–98.

for the entire year. Others may want to use a day each quarter to pray and discern. Whatever method you choose, be intentional in setting aside time to pray as part of selecting which texts or topics to preach.

Pattern

There are three patterns that may help you determine what portions of Scripture to preach: the *lectio continua*, the topical/textual, and the lectionary.

1. *Lectio Continua*: Literally meaning "reading continuously," this pattern of text selection essentially follows the biblical text as it has been given. For most preachers this means preaching through an entire biblical book or smaller sections of a longer book. Many preachers in the history of the church have followed this pattern so that their congregations would be able to hear and be fed from the whole counsel of God. There are many benefits to this method, not the least of which is that the upcoming Sunday's preaching text has been preselected for you, as it were, minimizing your stress of selecting the "perfect" text. While you still need to wisely determine the length of the portion of Scripture based on issues such as genre, this method also provides a helpful model for your congregation as they read, interpret, and apply Scripture for themselves.[4] Further, issues and topics emerge naturally from the text rather than making it seem that you have specific theological "axes to grind" or "hobbyhorses to ride."

This pattern allows you to present all that the Bible has for your congregation as you faithfully preach week by week and year by year. The challenge, of course, is the possibility that certain series may become too long and unwieldy. Pastors need to wisely determine when and if a break from a series is needed to address an urgent need in the congregation. Also, make sure you provide enough context for those who are new and did not have the benefit of sitting through the series thus far.

2. Topical/Textual: Another pattern to use in the selection of what to preach is the topical/textual approach. In this pattern, the preacher focuses

---

4. Chapters 4 and 5 will cover issues related to genre.

on an idea or topic and preaches that topic from a text or several texts of Scripture that address it. With this pattern, the wise preacher has the ability to focus on certain topics and issues the congregation may be facing in their own lives or in society at large. It is crucial, however, that the preacher does his best to ensure that he is being faithful to the text(s) and allowing the primary truths to be communicated and not twisting texts and their meaning to somehow "fit" the chosen topic. Thus, if after studying the text the preacher discovers that the selected text does not address the desired topic, he will need to find another text that is germane to the topic.

This method has many advantages. First, it allows the preacher flexibility in choosing topics from scriptural texts that will ultimately meet the unique needs of his congregation. Second, it provides a built-in unity to the sermon, as the main topic will hopefully be the emphasis and focus of the entire sermon. Third, it helps the congregation see how the Bible as a whole addresses topics of importance for its spiritual life.

Preachers need to take care, however, that they don't allow certain topics to dominate their preaching emphases and series. One can easily fall into the temptation of constantly preaching specific topics that are of interest only to him. Furthermore, strictly using the topical approach may not allow the congregation to mature through a balanced diet of the whole counsel of God. A balanced approach of using multiple patterns of selection can offset this.

3. Lectionary: This approach to selecting texts or topics to preach emerged from the Jewish synagogue worship context. It refers to a book or listing that contains preassigned Scripture readings for worship. For every worship service, Jewish rabbis and preachers referred to the listing of verses for that particular worship day. In the Jewish synagogue context, usually two texts were chosen for each Sabbath day worship: a passage from the Law (the five books of Moses) and the Prophets (the major and minor prophets). An example of this is found in Jesus' "Bread of Life" sermon in John 6. He utilized the given lectionary passages that were assigned for that day as the primary texts for his sermon.

Today, when pastors decide to do a series of Christmas sermons during December, they are following this lectionary pattern during the season of Advent. Using this approach has certain benefits. It focuses the preaching texts and topics for the year on the redemptive work of Jesus, his life, death, and resurrection. It also means the preacher doesn't have to decide which texts or topics to preach, as it has already been decided for him. And the topics that are addressed emerge naturally from the texts that were preassigned so as to remove the potential charge that the preacher chooses to speak on his "hobbyhorse" topics.

Pastor

In addition to praying and considering different patterns of selecting texts and topics, you will also want to think *pastorally* regarding your unique congregation and the parts of Scripture that the Lord is calling you to bring to them. Like parents who carefully discern the best foods to give their children for their physical growth and development, pastors need to wisely determine congregational needs for spiritual nurture and maturation. Pastors thus need to analyze factors such as their congregants' various levels of biblical education and prior knowledge, general needs, and specific problems to come up with a schedule of preaching texts and topics that are beneficial for them. Since every congregation has unique characteristics and needs, this pastoral task is both an art and a science. Every pastor is called to "know, feed, lead, and protect" the flock entrusted to his care.[5] To help with the process, here are some questions that may be beneficial.

- What parts of the Bible have been preached before? What parts have not?
- Has there been a balance of preaching from the OT and the NT?
- Has there been a diversity of genres (narrative, poetry, etc.)?
- Are there any specific topics that may be helpful for the congregation right now (e.g., suffering, stewardship)?
- Are there sinful patterns emerging from your counseling ministry that may require a special series?

5. See Timothy Z. Witmer, *The Shepherd Leader: Achieving Effective Shepherding in Your Church* (Phillipsburg, N.J.: P&R, 2010).

- Is there a balance of topics regarding exaltation of God (worship), edification of believers (discipleship), and evangelism to unbelievers (witness)?
- Is there a balance of doctrinal topics covering the major loci of theology?
- What texts or topics do your fellow leaders recommend?

Reading

After having selected the text and/or topic and prayed over it in light of your congregation, you are ready to *read* the text. What follows are some suggestions for reading the text in preparation for interpretation and communication.

First, read the text. Do this several times and you will pick up on prominent features and characteristics that might otherwise go unnoticed. Then, read the text in its context. Read at least one chapter before and one chapter after. After these initial readings, try to formulate the main idea of the text and its purpose. Answer these two questions: What is the text primarily about? What kind of response is it calling for? While this step of formulating a sermon proposition will be discussed in more detail in the following chapter (and in chapter 6), attempt a two-part preliminary statement after this initial stage of reading the text in its context.

There's a simple formula that is immensely helpful in capturing the main point and purpose of a text for preaching. Bryan Chapell suggests writing a two-part statement that begins with an indicative statement about God and finishes with an imperative statement about our response.[6] You can start the first half of the statement with the word "Because" and the second half of the statement with "then." So it will look something like this: "Because God (fill in the rest according to what your text says), then we should (fill in the rest with the appropriate response)." You will undoubtedly modify this sermon proposition as

---

6. Bryan Chapell, *Christ-Centered Preaching: Redeeming the Expository Sermon*, 2nd ed. (Grand Rapids: Baker Academic, 2005), 143–49.

you progress in your sermon preparation, but it's helpful to start shaping the central idea and specific purpose of the text at this stage.

Meditating

In addition to the work of praying over, selecting, and reading the text humbly, *meditating* on the text and topics that you are preparing to preach is vital. From his study of the meaning of meditation in the Bible, Ed Clowney has argued that meditation is a spiritual discipline whereby one centers the mind in reflection on God through his Spirit-given Word, for the purposes of worship and wisdom.[7] Since God is the source of all wisdom, and since God has revealed his wisdom in both his written Word and living Word (the Bible and Jesus), meditation on his Word through the Holy Spirit is one way to attain wisdom, which leads to worship.[8] Thus, meditation is not just a mantra; it is reflection on God's wisdom for God's glory and our good. For preachers, this spiritual discipline is a key part of the overall process of wise sermon preparation. When we meditate, God's Word intersects with our hearts, and wisdom results in worship.

Meditation is fundamentally part of our praise of God. The meditation practices of Eastern religions (e.g., Zen Buddhism, Transcendental Meditation) lead one inward, into themselves. Christian meditation leads one outward to God as he is revealed in his Word. In describing the blessed man, the psalmist in Psalm 1:2 states that "his delight is in the law of the LORD, and on his law he meditates day and night." Thus, when a Christian, or more specifically, a preacher, meditates, he does so by "going out," to the objective God revealed in this Word as part of his praise and worship. This outward activity is what distinguishes Christian meditation from the inward focus of religious mysticism.

Augustine, a great father of the early church, wrote his *Confessions* primarily as an exercise of meditation and not as a theological treatise.

---

7. Edmund P. Clowney, *CM: Christian Meditation* (Nutley, N.J.: Craig, 1979), 19–22.
8. Ibid.

He writes about his own relationship to God devotionally and doxologically. Psalm 119:15 – 16 says, "I will meditate on your precepts and fix my eyes on your ways. I will delight in your statutes; I will not forget your word."

The wisdom of God found in his own revelation ultimately centers on wisdom personified, Jesus Christ. Clowney states,

> Christian meditation is not and cannot be unmediated access to God, far less an experience of identity with God. Not ecstasy but wisdom marks the path of Christian meditation. To seek the face of the living God the Christian does not launch a voyage in inner space nor does he center on abstract infinity. Rather, he meditates on the Christ of Scripture and on the Scripture of Christ.[9]

Thus, when we meditate on God's Word during our sermon preparation, "learning of Jesus is personal communion, not just textual instruction. A lover cherishes every word in a letter from his beloved; he does not just examine it as a document or file it for information. The Spirit of Jesus who inspired the Scripture is the Spirit who dwells in our hearts to bring living communion with the Lord."[10] The apostle Paul in his letter to the Philippians makes it clear that Jesus is the focal point of our meditation, the center that holds all that God has revealed in the Word.

Christian meditation starts and ends with Jesus. Indeed, he is the Word made flesh, who became like us in his incarnation, yet was without sin so that through his sacrificial death on the cross and vindicating resurrection, we might be able to make sense of our sin-cursed lives and world. The preacher's thoughts regarding the sermon text must find its way to Jesus. Through him, the preacher and the people have life and hope, comfort and courage. Knowing Jesus helps us to make him known with more clarity and compassion.

Here are some tips to help you meditate during your sermon preparation.

---

9. Ibid., 29.
10. Ibid., 30.

- Read the Scripture text in its context quietly several times. Try reading the text out loud.
- Try memorizing several key phrases and verses by reciting them aloud and writing them down.
- Praise God in light of what the text says about God and you.
- Reflect especially on what this passage says about God's works of creation and redemption.
- Pray to God, asking what you can learn from this text about God, you, and your congregation.
- Reflect especially on how God would want you to respond in light of the truths of this text.
- Praise God for his presence, provision, and power as you meditate on his Word.
- Share the preaching text's message with others during the day and week as you have opportunity. Use it as part of your personal devotions and your family's devotions during the week.
- Meditate during the entire process of the sermon — especially when you are thinking about how to apply the truths of the passage to your heart and to the hearts of your listeners.

CHAPTER 2

INTERPRETING THE TEXT: LINGUISTIC, LITERARY, LIFE-SETTING ANALYSIS

Once you've prayerfully selected a text, you have to discover the truth it contains. Part of discovering the truth of the text according to the human author is to engage in the interpretation of the text itself. Before we examine the steps to analyze the text that you will be preaching, several preliminary comments are necessary.

First, you must approach this task as one who believes that the Word of God is trustworthy because it is inspired by God.[1] The Bible is a divine book. Though written over many years, by various authors, in multiple languages and cultures, the Bible is the most unique literature in all of world history because it was supernaturally authored by the living God so that mankind would know God and reach out to him.[2]

---

1. The best summary of my understanding of and commitment to the Scriptures is found in the Westminster Confession of Faith (WCF), written by a group of pastors and scholars that met in Westminster Abbey in 1643–48. Under the orders of the English parliament, they were called to produce a document summarizing the main doctrines of Scripture. Many of the Reformed and Presbyterian churches worldwide use the WCF as their standards of doctrine, subordinate to the Scriptures. It can be accessed online at http://www.reformed.org/documents/wcf_with_proofs/.
2. 2 Tim 3:16–17; Acts 17:27.

Some important implications that emerge from the conviction that God's words are trustworthy and inspired are that they are authoritative and relevant—ultimately calling us to trust and obey. For preachers, this has tremendous value. If the words of the King of Kings are divinely authoritative and eternally relevant, heralds can speak with self-forgetful boldness and confidence.

Second, though the Word of God is characterized by perspicuity (that the ideas of salvation in Jesus found in Scripture can be understood through normal means), careful interpretation is still necessary.[3] This is because no one reads anything without engaging in interpretation. Whether we know it or not, when we read the Bible to discern its meaning we also bring along our unique history, experiences, knowledge, culture, and values. Furthermore, the Scriptures are human words written in history. This means that every word is influenced by language and culture. So while the Bible is a divine book, inspired by God, it is also a human one, with historical particularity and literary artistry.[4] Thus, we must attempt to understand the text as it was written and received, not only in its unique historical context but also in its unique literary genre, be it prose, poetry, prophecy, or parables. In addition to all this, it's important to remember two other principles of interpretation: (a) the interpreter is only able to interpret the Word of God through the Holy Spirit (1 Cor 2:13–16), and (b) the Scriptures interpret Scripture.

Third, this chapter is an overview of the exegetical process, that is, the analysis of the Scripture to discover the original meaning intended by the author to his audience.[5] Like a detective gathering evidence at the scene, observing suspects and their actions, conducting interviews of witnesses, and examining the circumstances of the crime, the interpreter of the Scripture engages in a process of discovering all the elements

---

3. WCF 1:7.
4. Gordon D. Fee and Douglas Stuart, *How to Read the Bible for All Its Worth* (Grand Rapids: Zondervan, 1982), 19.
5. As an overview, this chapter cannot cover all the intricacies involved in this process. Hopefully readers will supplement their understanding of and skill in exegesis through supplemental reading and/or taking courses at a seminary or Bible college. For another helpful approach, see Dennis E. Johnson, "From Text to Sermon: A Step-by-Step Guide to Biblical Interpretation in Sermon Preparation," in *Him We Proclaim: Preaching Christ from All the Scriptures* (Phillipsburg, N.J.: P&R, 2007), 397–407.

related to the text: the author and recipients, occasion and purpose, language and culture, literary form and theological truths, and how it has been interpreted throughout the history of the church. This is done ultimately to help our hearers discover the meaning and significance of the text for their own lives, as they find connection to the original truths of the text through the gospel of Jesus Christ. Thus, this first layer of interpretation, of discovering the truths of the text, is followed by the second layer of discerning Christ and the gospel in the text and context (see chapter 3). To these two layers of interpretation are added the third layer, finding meaning and significance to the contemporary hearer. Examples of these three layers will be seen in chapters 4 and 5.

Fundamentally, the key to discovering the truth of the text by the original author for the original audience is "to learn to read the text carefully and to ask the right questions of the text."[6] With that in mind, there are three stages of interpretative analysis that will help you carefully read and interpret the text. Please note that there is not only overlap between the different stages of interpretation but also a dynamic moving back and forth between the stages. In what follows, the process is dynamic and nuanced, involving both inductive and deductive methods of interpretation.

Discovering the truth of Scripture involves three types of analysis: linguistic analysis, literary analysis, and life-setting analysis. Or put in question format, What does the text actually say? How does it say it? When and why is it being said?

Linguistic Analysis: What Does the Text Actually Say?

In determining what the text says, six steps of linguistic analysis are suggested.

---

6. Fee and Stuart, *How to Read the Bible*, 23. Fee and Stuart helpfully recommend reading Mortimer Adler's *How to Read a Book* (New York: Simon & Schuster, 1972). Another helpful book is T. David Gordon's *Why Johnny Can't Preach: The Media Have Shaped the Messengers* (Phillipsburg, N.J.: P&R, 2009).

1. *Pray* for understanding and transformation. Prayer is vital not only for your own present comprehension but also for your future communication. The Bible teaches that the Holy Spirit helps us understand God's Word. Pray for the Spirit's illumination throughout the entire process. In addition to comprehension, we also pray for transformation. That is, we pray that the message of the passage would change us first — in our head, heart, and hands.

2. *Read* the passage several times. Read the preaching passage in its context several times in the language with which you are most comfortable. As you are reading, keep these preliminary questions in mind: What is the main idea that the author is emphasizing? Why does he seem to be emphasizing these ideas (or what are the issues and problems, either explicit or implicit)? How does this all connect with the gospel of Jesus Christ and with my hearers? Even at this point, it is helpful to meditate on the answers to these questions. Jot down some preliminary ideas. The main idea of the passage can often be found through a specific statement in the passage, the context of the passage, repeated ideas, or a combination of these.

3. *Formulate* a preliminary sermon proposition.[7] Though this statement will inevitably change, attempt a sermon proposition statement that has two parts: the first half identifies the main *what* of the text, namely, an indicative statement about God, his person, and work, that the author is communicating; and the second half identifies the *so what* of the text, namely, an imperatival statement describing the desired response to this truth. Try devising this sermon proposition in a consequential format: Start the first half of the proposition with the word "Because," followed by what this text may be stating regarding God.[8] Finish the second half with the word "then" followed by the response we ought to have. Here is an example from 1 John 3:11–24: *"Because God loved us first, then we ought to love one another."*

4. *Translate* your preaching passage.[9] Translate your passage from

---

7. See chapter 6 for more on the sermon proposition.
8. See Bryan Chapell, *Christ-Centered Preaching: Redeeming the Expository Sermon*, 2nd ed. (Grand Rapids: Baker, 2005). See also chapter 7.
9. I'm assuming here that the reader will have familiarity and a level of facility with the original languages of the Bible, Hebrew and Greek. For helpful books on interpretation

the Hebrew or Greek, parsing all the words and paying careful attention to anything that stands out (unique words, purpose statements, theological ideas, connections to other passages you know). Inspect the verbs and their tenses. Consider the nouns and their semantic range, that is, the ways in which the words were used by the author and audience in their day. At this point, it may be helpful to consult reference tools, such as dictionaries,[10] grammars, concordances, and so on, jotting down notes on words or phrases that will help you formulate the meaning and significance of this passage.[11]

5. *Identify* the syntax and structure of your passage. Take note of the genre of your passage (narrative, poetry, wisdom, epistle, etc.) as this determines the way an author organizes his ideas. While genre analysis will be examined in the next section, it's important at this stage to analyze the main movements of ideas in the preaching passage. For example, does the arrangement of the words and phrases within the sentences reveal anything?[12] What about the main movements of thought in the passage? Is anything significant in the relationship between the main movements and subordinate ideas? Do they reveal anything about the author's main ideas and intentions? Again, jot down the ideas you are discovering.

6. *Reformulate* your sermon proposition statement. Based on what you've newly discovered from your linguistic analysis thus far, clarify your

---

without knowledge of the biblical languages, see the following: Fee and Stuart, *How to Read the Bible*; Dan McCartney and Charles Clayton, *Let the Reader Understand: A Guide to Interpreting and Applying the Bible* (Wheaton, Ill.: Victor, 1994); Daniel M. Doriani, *Getting the Message: A Plan for Interpreting and Applying the Bible* (Phillipsburg, N.J.: P&R, 1996); and Dennis E. Johnson, *Walking with Jesus through His Word: Christ-Centered Bible Study* (Phillipsburg, N.J.: P&R, 2015).

10. Useful Hebrew dictionaries include the BDB; William L. Holladay, ed., *A Concise Hebrew and Aramaic Lexicon of the Old Testament* (Grand Rapids: Eerdmans, 1972). For Greek, consult the BDAG; Johannes P. Louw and Eugene A. Nida, eds., *Greek-English Lexicon of the New Testament Based on Semantic Domains*, 2 vols. (New York: United Bible Societies, 1989).

11. Note well that *using* these language tools (including computer ones) can be very different from *knowing* the language itself. Not knowing how a foreign language works can lead to erroneous interpretations and false teaching. Even a beginner's level study of the languages can be very advantageous (e.g., the equivalent of one year of study of both Hebrew and Greek). For self-study, I would recommend Gary Pratico and Miles Van Pelt's *Basics of Biblical Hebrew: E-Learning Bundle* (Grand Rapids: Zondervan, 2014) and William Mounce's *Learn Biblical Greek Pack* (Grand Rapids: Zondervan, 2013).

12. See Moisés Silva, *Biblical Words and Their Meanings: An Introduction to Lexical Semantics* (Grand Rapids: Zondervan, 1983).

sermon proposition by including more key ideas from the text. Remember that your goal is to articulate the author's intended message regarding God and the subsequent response. You will simplify and condense your proposition later, so at this point utilize the main themes and words that this text uniquely states to hone the author's intended message.

Literary Analysis: How Does the Text Say It?

As you engage in the literary analysis of the text, examine your preaching text in light of the following three contexts: the chapter and book, other books of the Bible, and its genre.

1. Examine the passage in light of *the chapter and book*. Like concentric circles that form when a pebble is dropped in still water, you want to move out from your preaching passage and examine its surrounding literary contexts. First, examine the narrow literary context, that is, the passages before and after your preaching passage, looking for corresponding themes. Often, the preceding and following literary contexts offer insights into how to read and interpret the author's intention. For example, many of the narratives stories in the Gospels seem to be grouped together by the author around a central theme. Take, for instance, Mark 4:35–5:43, where a collection of four miracle stories reveals Jesus' increasing power and authority over natural and supernatural obstacles. Preaching one of these sections requires keeping in mind the surrounding contextual themes.

Moving further out, examine your passage in light of the entire book, looking for key themes related to your text's occasion and purpose. Are there similar problems being addressed and similar solutions being offered? Examine also how the entire book is structured. Does the book's larger structure have any significance to its purpose and meaning? If so, what is it and how does your preaching passage fit in that overall purpose? For example, the book of Mark can be divided into two parts between the prologue/introduction (1:1–15) and the conclusion (16:1–20). The two halves of the book answer two questions: Who is Jesus (1:16–8:26)? What did Jesus come to do (8:30–15:47)? Peter's confession that Jesus is the Christ forms the hinge between the two parts (8:27–30). Thus, preaching a passage found in the first half of the book will be influenced by Mark's desire to answer the larger question of Jesus' identity, whereas passages located in the latter half deal with Jesus' mission.

Lastly, does the author have any other writings in the Bible? If so, are there any similar words, themes, and ideas? What makes the themes in this book similar or different from that book? For example, the apostle John utilizes the themes of light and darkness in both his gospel and his epistles. How does his usage of these themes in the gospel influence how he uses it in his letters? These clues will aid your overall interpretation and preaching of the text.

2. Examine the passage in light of *other books in the Bible*. After having examined the way the author composed his ideas in his unique literary style, you want to examine how the rest of Scripture communicates similar ideas and themes. Mentioned earlier, this principle of interpretation involves utilizing all of Scripture to help discover the meaning and significance of your passage. If God the Holy Spirit inspired the entire Bible, then there is a unified mind and meaning to all that was revealed. Though this is not an easy task, this step is crucial in ensuring that your interpretation coheres with the rest of biblical teaching.[13] What does the Bible principally teach? That the triune God is creator, redeemer, and consummator, desiring to save a people for himself, through the person and work of Jesus Christ. All the books of the Bible must be seen under this story of redemption wrought within history.

3. Examine the passage in light of *its genre*. In addition to examining all the contexts of your passage, both narrow and broad, it is also important to examine the unique literary genre of your text. Genre is "a group of texts that bear one or more traits in common with one another."[14] Thus, works in a particular genre have similar literary characteristics—such as

13. Here theological dictionaries can be helpful: *TDNT*; Colin Brown, ed., *New International Dictionary of New Testament Theology*, 4 vols. (Grand Rapids: Zondervan, 1986); Xavier Léon-Dufour, ed., *Dictionary of the New Testament*; trans. P. Joseph Cahill (New York: Seabury, 1973); Leland Ryken, James C. Wilhoit, and Tremper Longmann III, eds., *Dictionary of Biblical Imagery* (Downers Grove, Ill.: InterVarsity Press, 1998).
14. Tremper Longman III, *Literary Approaches to Biblical Interpretation*, vol. 3 (Grand Rapids: Zondervan, 1987), 76.

style, form, techniques, and tone—in the way it communicates. Poetry, for example, is a genre that is characterized by parallelism and figurative language. As such, when one writes or reads poetry, certain rules govern the way it is conceived and received. All poetry will exhibit a similar kind and degree of artistry in getting the message across.

Genre analysis becomes important to the interpreter since it helps to first *classify* the type of literature it is (historical narrative, prophecy, epistle, etc.), which then helps *clarify* its meaning based on the conventions of that genre. Genre thus provides the interpreter with strategies to read and interpret the text. Consciously or not, readers make genre classifications that help them comprehend what they are reading. For example, when a father reads Dr. Seuss's *Green Eggs and Ham* to his child, he will approach that text differently from when he later reads the stories found on the front page of his local newspaper. Thus, genre establishes *rules* for writing and for reading; it works as an unspoken contract between the writer and reader. Otherwise, communication would be impossible.

The genre of the text may also contribute to the way you outline your sermon. Though this will be discussed in chapter 6, whether your preaching passage is narrative, poetry, or law, for example, will influence how you may want to structure your sermon. There are two general ways to outline your sermon, either *textually* or *topically*. Textual sermon outlines essentially follow the flow of the biblical passage. As the passage moves from one main idea to the next, so the sermon outline will follow the pattern already laid out in text. Narrative texts often work well with textual sermon outlines. Topical sermon outlines reorganize the data discovered from the text according to the main topics in the text. Poetic passages of Scripture usually work well with a topical approach since key ideas are often repeated in the poem. Keep in mind that no one approach is better than the other. Often it will depend on the particular passage and how it is structured. Either way, your ultimate goal is for your sermon to be understood with clarity and cogency.

In sum, the interpreter must study and learn the various literary forms found in the Bible. While some disagreement exists over how many genres are found in the Bible, the generally recognized ones include the following: historical narrative, law, wisdom, poetry, prophecy, apocalyptic, discourse, gospel, parable, and epistle. The major genres of the Bible and how to preach them will be discussed in later chapters.

Life-Setting Analysis: When and Why Is It Being Said?

You have spent some quality time examining both the text and its surrounding literary context to discover the original meaning and purpose of the original human author for the original audience. At this point you will want to revisit your sermon proposition. Continue to hone both what you are trying to communicate regarding the unique truths about God from this text as well as how your hearers should respond. You can shorten it later to make it more memorable to your hearers. For now, you want to ensure it passes the test of clarity, conviction, and compassion. Is it comprehensible to the mind, credible to the heart, and applicable to life?

Now we turn to the last layer of textual analysis to discover the truth of the text according to the human author: life-setting analysis. Two main areas of analysis take place at this point: the general historical and cultural backdrop (when?), and the specific occasion and purpose (why?).

1. Examine *the general historical and cultural backdrop*. Knowing the historical and cultural backdrop of the time of writing can be crucial in understanding the meaning and significance of the author's words. For example, geographic locations as well as particular customs are often taken for granted by biblical authors since they know their readers will understand the reference. You will want to consult various resources that provide background information regarding the history and culture of the time in which the author was writing to this audience.[15] We saw

---

15. Some helpful resources are Everett Ferguson, *Background on Early Christianity*, 3rd ed. (Grand Rapids: Eerdmans, 2003); Clinton E. Arnold, ed.: *Zondervan Illustrated Bible Backgrounds*, 4 vols. (Grand Rapids: Zondervan, 2002); Raymond B. Dillard and Tremper Longman III, *An Introduction to the Old Testament* (Grand Rapids: Zondervan, 1994); D. A. Carson, Douglas J. Moo, and Leon Morris, *Introduction to the New Testament*, 2nd ed. (Grand Rapids: Zondervan, 2005).

earlier that the Bible refers to preachers as heralds. Investigating the history and culture of the original audience enables us to understand the analogy of preachers as heralds.

2. Examine *the specific occasion and purpose.* In addition to general information regarding historical and cultural backdrop, you will want to discover data regarding the original life context of the author, recipients, and circumstances, specifically, the occasion and purpose that prompted this text. What were some of the situational factors that caused the author to write? Were there specific sins, problems, and/or issues in the lives of the recipients that needed to be addressed? After examining this, you will want to make the "turn" to the present. Do my hearers face similar sins, problems, and issues today? As humans affected by sin and sin's effects in the world, both the original recipients and my hearers need the grace and wisdom of God found in the revealed Word of God.[16]

At this point, you are attempting to discover what Bryan Chapell has helpfully called the original "fallen-condition focus" (FCF) of the text.[17] In his helpful book on preaching, he states that the FCF "is the mutual human condition that contemporary believers share with those to or about whom the text was written that requires the grace of the passage for God's people to glorify and enjoy him."[18] Determining the FCF is vital, for it not only clarifies the meaning of the text for the original recipients but also conditions the significance of the sermon for our current hearers. The "problem" of sin and sin's effects that need a "solution" in the gospel of Jesus Christ gives the entire sermon its unity and focus.[19]

---

16. Check your work by consulting helpful commentaries. To determine which commentaries to use, see the excellent annotated survey of commentaries for both the OT and the NT: Tremper Longman III, *Old Testament Commentary Survey*, 4th ed. (Grand Rapids: Baker, 2007); D. A. Carson, *New Testament Commentary Survey*, 6th ed. (Grand Rapids: Baker, 2007). The use of commentaries is purposely listed here at this point in the process so that you have had time to examine the text without too many preconceived ideas from other scholars. Nonetheless, checking your work against other scholars is an important safeguard against unintended errors. In addition to the principle that Scripture interprets other Scripture, we should also read the Scripture in the way the Christian church has read and interpreted Scripture for over 2,000 years.
17. This section is adapted from Chapell, *Christ-Centered Preaching*, 48–55.
18. Ibid., 50.
19. Chapell notes that specific sins that are explicitly addressed in the text are often the FCF on which the sermon will focus. Any of the prohibitions found in the Ten Commandments or in Jesus' Sermon on the Mount, e.g., would be examples of sin that needs the grace of

There are three questions to ask of the text to determine the FCF for both the original audience as well as our present ones.

What does the text say?

What spiritual concern(s) did this text address (in its context)?

What spiritual concerns do listeners share in common with those to (or about) whom the text was written?[20]

Examining and identifying the specific occasion and purpose that gave rise to the words of the author is thus key in discovering the text's purpose for not only the original hearers but also for ours. Remember, this includes the preacher. How are my concerns or fears like the concerns and fears of the people in the text? What do I have in common with those being addressed in this text? How does this text comfort and/or challenge me? What is one thing the text is calling my hearers and me to do right now? The FCF is a helpful principle to draw connections between then and now in the application of scriptural truth.

As you formulate the FCF and its relationship to your sermon proposition, be cautious in determining parallels between the issues of the original recipients and the challenges our hearers face today. There will certainly be many areas of continuity since we share the same humanity in this sin-cursed world. There will also be discontinuity in the way the FCF manifests itself in unique cultural contexts.

Hopefully at this point, discovering the FCF of the text will propel you to discern the solution that only God's grace in the gospel can provide. Start thinking about the Christ-focused connection (CFC) of the text. How does the gospel of Jesus Christ solve the problem(s) introduced by the FCF? This will be discussed more in the next chapter. If the Bible is a unified story of God's grace found in the gospel of Jesus Christ for humans who are faced with the problem of sin and

---

God. But sin's effects on our lives and world can also be the FCF, e.g., issues such as the grief we experience because of the death of a loved one or the sickness many of us face. He states, "An FCF need not be something for which we are guilty or culpable. It simply needs to be an aspect or a problem of the human condition that requires the instruction, admonition, and/or comfort of Scripture" (ibid., 50–51).

20. Ibid., 52.

sin's effects, then every sermon needs to resolve in the gospel. This is done through the CFC. The CFC reveals how the good news of what Jesus accomplished through his life, death, and resurrection has radical implications to all of life's problems and concerns.

Conclusion

The goal of this chapter was to provide a framework to help discover the truths of the text according to the human author. Three layers of interpretation are utilized to discover the original author's meaning and purpose for his audience. Through linguistic, literary, and life-setting analysis of the text, you are now able to determine the primary problem of the text that will require a solution in the gospel of Jesus Christ.

So let's return to your sermon proposition and attempt another revision. Up to this point, the first half of this proposition was essentially God-centered, stating the main truth about God, who he is or what he has done (indicative). Let's rephrase it so that it is Christ-centered, focusing on who Christ is or what Christ has done. Earlier we used the example of 1 John 3:11 – 24 to determine a preliminary sermon proposition: "*Because* God loved us first, *then* we ought to love one another." We can now modify this to become, "Because God loved us by sacrificing his Son, then we ought to love one another." In this way, the truth of the good news of Jesus becomes the reason we should respond rightly.

The gospel thus provides the grounds, the motivation, and the power to think, feel, and live differently. Gospel-centered preaching is Christ-centered preaching. Every sermon from the whole counsel of God will have this focus. We turn now to learn how to discern Christ in the text according to the Divine Author.

PART 2

DISCERNING CHRIST *in* THE TEXT ACCORDING *to* THE DIVINE AUTHOR

CHAPTER 3

WHY SHOULD WE "PREACH CHRIST"? BECAUSE IT'S FOUNDATIONAL, BIBLICAL, AND PRACTICAL

I t seems so obvious. Every Christian preacher would wholeheartedly agree with the proposition that they should preach Christ in their sermons. After all, they would be following a long line of preachers in history who modeled their ministry after the apostle Paul, who stated so unequivocally, "But we preach Christ crucified" (1 Cor 1:23) and "For I decided to know nothing among you except Jesus Christ and him crucified" (1 Cor 2:2). Sidney Greidanus, in his book *Preaching Christ from the Old Testament*, cites diverse preachers from various Christian traditions who advocate preaching Christ—from the Eastern Orthodox to the Baptist.[1] Yet upon hearing the sermons from these preachers in

---

1. Sidney Greidanus, *Preaching Christ from the Old Testament: A Contemporary Hermeneutical Method* (Grand Rapids: Eerdmans, 1999), 1–2.

various Christian traditions, there often emerges some significant differences as to what exactly "preaching Christ" entails, especially with sermons from the OT.

To some preachers, "preaching Christ" entails spending the entire sermon explaining and teaching the unique linguistic and life-setting issues of the text except for the last five minutes, which would then be devoted to a five-minute gospel presentation without any obvious connection to the sermon text. To others, "preaching Christ" involves showing how every linguistic and life-setting issue of the text reveals some aspect of the person and work of Jesus without much discussion of the unique traits of the text as given to a unique people in a unique time and place (e.g., the Israelites during the exodus in the wilderness of Sinai).

Making the issue even more challenging, not all preachers are convinced that "preaching Christ" is something that should be done in every sermon at every occasion from every portion of Scripture. To bring some clarity, then, this chapter explores three reasons *why* preachers should interpret and preach Christ from all the Scriptures: because it's biblical, foundational, and practical. The following chapters will then demonstrate *how* this is done from various genres found in the Bible, providing a model of Christ-focused interpretation that leads to gospel-centered communication. We've examined how to discover the truth of the biblical text, and now we set out to discern how the text points us to Christ.

"Preaching Christ" Is Biblical

One of the most compelling reasons preachers should interpret and preach Christ from all the Scriptures is because Jesus and the apostles did it. Jesus and his disciples interpreted the Scriptures — which for them was the Hebrew Bible (the OT) — in light of the person and work of Jesus Christ, the Messiah-King. They modeled a particular pattern for preachers to follow. Early Christian preaching had a central controlling *message* and a specific evangelistic *purpose*.

The message and purpose of the NT was essentially what the apostle Paul wrote to the church in Corinth.

> For I delivered to you as of first importance what I also received: that Christ died for our sins in accordance with the Scriptures, that he was buried, that he was raised on the third day in accordance with the Scriptures (1 Cor 15:3–4).

The apostle Peter stated with the same force,

> Let it be known to all of you and to all the people of Israel that by the name of Jesus Christ of Nazareth, whom you crucified, whom God raised from the dead—by him this man is standing before you well. This Jesus is the stone that was rejected by you, the builders, which has become the cornerstone. And there is salvation in no one else, for there is no other name under heaven given among men by which we must be saved (Acts 4:10–12).

These two great apostles of the NT—arguably the two most important leaders at the beginning stages of the Christian church—spoke with unanimity regarding their message and purpose: Christ crucified and raised is the only hope for sinful humanity. This message and purpose, however, did not originate with them; they learned it from their rabbi, Jesus.

At the end of Luke's gospel, a story is recorded that would forever change the way readers and preachers understand the central message of the Bible. In chapter 24, Luke describes the risen Jesus appearing to two discouraged disciples on the road to Emmaus (Luke 24:13–49). These disciples had recently witnessed with much amazement the life and ministry of Jesus of Nazareth—a man they thought was the promised Messiah, the one who had the power to redeem them from their sin. What confused and troubled them, however, was what had just happened three days earlier: this Jesus, who was condemned to die and then was crucified like a common criminal, was reported to be missing from his tomb. They were not only discouraged, but also perplexed.

Jesus begins to explain that what transpired over the last three days as well as over his entire life and ministry, was all foretold in the Bible—in this case, the thirty-nine books of the Hebrew Bible. Probably to the shock of these two disciples, Jesus states,

> "O foolish ones, and slow of heart to believe all that the prophets have spoken! Was it not necessary that the Christ should suffer these things and enter into his glory?" And beginning with Moses and all the Prophets, he interpreted to them in all the Scriptures the things concerning himself (Luke 24:25–27).

Jesus utilizes a common designation for the entire corpus of the Holy Scriptures to make his case that all the Scriptures revealed him: "Moses and all the Prophets." Later in the story, Luke records Jesus again signaling that all the Scriptures spoke of him.

> Then he said to them, "These are my words that I spoke to you while I was still with you, that everything written about me in the Law of Moses and the Prophets and the Psalms must be fulfilled" (Luke 24:44).

Here Jesus uses the three-fold designation that is still used today to refer to the canon of the Hebrew Bible, the *Tanakh*. This name is an acronym *(TNK)* of the first Hebrew letter of the Hebrew Scripture's three traditional divisions: the *Torah* ("Teaching"; the first five books of Moses), the *Nevi'im* ("Prophets"), and the *Kethuvim* ("Writings"). Essentially here in Luke, Jesus is stating that *all* of the Holy Scriptures had a central message and purpose—to proclaim the person and work of Jesus, the promised prophet, priest, and king of not only Israel but of all mankind. It's important to note that during the time of Jesus' ministry, the NT canon had not been written or compiled. As such, he utilized the only Scriptures available to him in order to proclaim the gospel, the *Tanakh*—what Christians now call the Old Testament.

The Preaching of Jesus: John 6

That Jesus viewed the Scripture through this Christological lens is demonstrated in a record of one of his early sermons. The gospel writer John records for us an abridged version of one of Jesus' sermons in John 6:25–59. Commonly referred to as the Bread of Life discourse, this passage reveals Jesus' own preaching method. After performing the miracle of feeding a crowd of more than 5,000 people with five loaves of bread and two fish (John 6:1–12), Jesus preaches a sermon utilizing a form and structure that would have been familiar to those who frequented the worship services in Jewish synagogues. What was unfamiliar and probably shocking to this Jewish audience, however, was Jesus' interpretation of the two OT texts that he used to frame his sermon.

While the origins of synagogue worship are unclear, the Bible reveals various elements that constituted the kind of worship services that Jesus and his disciples would have experienced in the synagogues of their day.[2] Of particular importance was the establishment of the lectionary, or a system of appointed readings from the Torah and the Prophets for synagogue services. Though this system of reading specific Scripture texts was codified by the Middle Ages, we see evidences of this practice in Jesus' day (e.g., Luke 4:16–21). After the Scripture readings, the rabbi or teacher for the day would then commence interpreting and applying the texts that were read, starting with the primary text, usually from the *Torah*, which was further explained by the use of the secondary text from the Prophets. It is this rabbinical sermon pattern that Jesus uses in John 6.

Jesus begins his sermon with the primary text from the *Torah*, Exodus 16:4 (John 6:31). After explaining and applying this text, he expands his points through the use of a secondary text from the Prophets — Isaiah 54:13 (John 6:45). Though this pattern of preaching would have been familiar to the listeners, the meaning and purpose would not be. Jesus proclaims that the historical event of God providing manna for the Israelites has a connection to what had just occurred, namely, the miraculous feeding of the 5,000. The same God that nourished the Israelites during their wilderness wanderings is the same God who feeds them now. In fact, Jesus is the nourishment that God provides, because he is the bread of life (John 6:35). To the shock of those listening, Jesus

---

2. See Ezra 7:10, 25 and Neh 8:1–8. Hughes Oliphant Old demonstrates how Ezra formed the basic shape of the liturgy of the Word found in the synagogue (*The Reading and Preaching of Scriptures in the Worship of the Christian Church*, vol. 1 [Grand Rapids: Eerdmans, 1998], 94–105).

proclaims that to truly live, they must partake of him. He thus gives new covenant meaning to this old covenant story, as he did in Luke 4:21 when he stated so clearly, "Today this Scripture has been fulfilled in your hearing." It is this Christological interpretation and application that not only advances the redemptive historical story line of the Bible's central message, but also provides the pattern for every Christian preacher after Jesus—like the apostles Peter and Paul.

The Preaching of the Apostles

The heart of apostolic preaching was Jesus Christ.[3] In the NT, there are multiple Greek verbs used for the preaching ministry of the apostles, variously translated into English words such as "preaching," "teaching," "witnessing," "proclaiming," and "evangelizing."[4] What is interesting to note, however, are the direct objects for these verbs used for "preaching." The following is a list of *what* the apostles preached: Jesus, Lord Jesus, Christ, Christ Jesus as Lord, Christ crucified, Christ as raised from the dead, Jesus and the resurrection, good news about the kingdom, Jesus as the Son of God, the gospel, the gospel of God, the gospel of Christ, the gospel of peace, the Word of the Lord, the forgiveness of sins, the unsearchable riches of Christ, and Christ in you—the hope of glory.[5] As the objects of these verbs demonstrate, there is no doubt that Christ was the heart of apostolic preaching.

One of the earliest apostolic sermons recorded in the Bible is found in Acts 2: Peter preaching at Pentecost. Peter addresses the crowd after the supernatural event of the disciples speaking in other known

3. See Dennis E. Johnson, *Him We Proclaim: Preaching Christ from All the Scriptures* (Phillipsburg, N.J.: P&R, 2007), for a thorough defense of apostolic preaching that is "Christ-centered, redemptive-historically structured, missiologically communicated, and grace-driven" (16).

4. Klaas Runia summarizes the thirty-plus times "preaching" is used in the NT in these six main word groups: *keryssein*—"to proclaim"; *euangelizestai*—"to herald joyful news"; *marturein*—"to witness"; *didaskein*—"to teach"; *propheteuein*—"to prophesy"; and *parakalein*—"to comfort/admonish" (*The Sermon under Attack: The Moore College Lectures, 1980* [Exeter, U.K.: Paternoster, 1983], 26). See also Gordon P. Hugenberger, "Preach," *ISBE* 3:940–43.

5. Here are some examples from the NT: Acts 5:42; 8:5, 25, 35; 9:20; 11:20; 14:7; 15:35; 17:18; 19:13; 20:25; 28:31; Rom 1:15; 10:8, 15; 1 Cor 1:23; 9:18; 15:12; 2 Cor 1:19; 4:5; Eph 3:8; Phil 1:15; Col 1:27; 1 Thess 2:9; 2 Tim 4:2.

languages, glorifying and praising God. Though the onlookers thought these disciples were drunk, Peter preaches a sermon in which his main text is a passage from the OT prophet Joel.[6] In so doing, he interprets Joel in light of Christ's person and work. He does so in light of the new covenant context that he is in — for new Israel.

How does he do this? In verse 22 he recites redemptive history, answering questions such as, Who is this Jesus? What happened to him? And ultimately, why did this need to happen? Then he applies this message to his hearers, urging them to repent and believe the good news of salvation found in Jesus Christ alone. The sermon thus begins with a recounting of God's deeds in the history of Israel, moves on to the fulfillment of God's promises to Israel in Jesus Christ, and then concludes with this application to repent and believe the Christ. Peter preached Christ.

Peter was not the only apostle following the sermonic pattern set by Jesus. The preaching of the apostle Paul also provides us with much insight into what it means to preach Christ. Although his sermons are often recorded in brief outline format, we can with confidence "fill in the blanks" of his sermons with the teaching found in his epistles.[7] One such sermon is the one found in Acts 13:16–41. Here we find the apostle Paul in a Jewish synagogue at Pisidian Antioch, with Jews and Gentile converts to Judaism as his audience. Given the opportunity to speak to the gathered audience, Paul crafts a sermon interpreting several OT passages and how they find fulfillment in Christ. He explains these texts in light of what they proclaim about Christ and then applies it directly to those that are present. Here is a model of exegesis in the original human author's intention, interpretation of the Divine Author's intention in Christ, and then gospel application for the lives and hearts of his hearers.

Why should we preach Christ from all the Scriptures? Because it's

---

6. Joel 2:28–32.
7. NT scholars have shown how Paul's "sermon" in Athens (Acts 17:16–34) can essentially be reconstructed using the themes and ideas found in his epistle to the Romans (e.g., D. A. Carson, "Athens Revisited," in *Telling the Truth: Evangelizing Postmoderns* [Grand Rapids: Zondervan, 2000], 384–98).

biblical. Jesus and the apostles did it. Jesus and the apostles saw Christ as the center of the entire biblical story line. Without Christ, the overall structure of biblical revelation has no coherence or purpose. Every part of the Bible is about the historical unfolding revelation and accomplishment of gospel salvation through Jesus Christ. Thus, there is a story within all the Bible stories. God in his grace is redeeming a people for himself in the face of human rebellion and human desire for a religion of good works. This interpretive method is foundational for preaching the whole counsel of God.

"Preaching Christ" Is Foundational

The second reason we should preach Christ from all the Scriptures is because it is foundational to our understanding of the entire story of the Bible. Simply put, the Bible makes no sense without Jesus Christ. As we have seen, Jesus and his apostles understood this overarching paradigm that the life, death, and resurrection of Jesus was the key to unlocking the *mystery* of the grand narrative of the Bible.[8] Rather than being a loose collection of historical narratives, poetry, and other types of literature, the Bible has one central story, from beginning to end: God and redemption.

God, as the divine author of all the Scriptures, was involved in the process, supernaturally inspiring all the human authors to communicate his purposes for his creation. Though written by many human authors spanning time, geography, and culture, "All Scripture is breathed out by God and profitable for teaching, for reproof, for correction, and for training in righteousness, that the man of God may be complete, equipped for every good work" (2 Tim 3:16–17). As such, reading and understanding different portions of the Bible requires this foundational paradigm, namely, that God is the divine author of the Bible, with a divine purpose.

The story of the Bible, authored by God, then, is not just a nationalistic epic describing the successes and failures of one Middle Eastern

---

8. The apostle Paul equates being a steward of the mysteries of God with his preaching of Christ (Rom 11:25; 16:25; 1 Cor 2:7; 4:1; Eph 1:9; 3:1–13; 6:19; Col 1:26–27; 4:3).

people group. Rather, it is a grand narrative that has repercussions to all of humanity. It is an epic story of a creator God who redeems and saves his own people from the death sentence of sin, through the sacrifice of his very Son, the sinless God-man Jesus Christ, freely offering them pardon of sin and the promise of eternal life through faith. These foundational themes of sin and death, salvation and redemption, found throughout the entire Bible, cannot be understood apart from the story of Jesus.

Only Jesus, his eternal presence, prophetic promise, virgin birth, sinless life, atoning death, vindicating resurrection, and glorious ascension, resolves all the redemptive themes of the Bible, from Genesis to Revelation. Regardless of the story, the poem, or epistle found in the Scriptures, God had a redemptive purpose in revealing himself and his purposes in Christ to sinful humanity. Our preaching, then, must take into account this redemptive paradigm when we approach any portion of the Bible. Thus, *preaching* Christ presupposes *interpreting* Christ from all the Scriptures. Edmund Clowney states unequivocally,

There are great stories in the Bible ... but it is possible to know Bible stories, yet miss the Bible story.... The Bible has a story line. It traces an unfolding drama. The story follows the history of Israel, but it does not begin there, nor does it contain what you would expect in a national history.... The story of the Bible is real history, wrought in the lives of hundreds and thousands of human beings. In a world where death reigned, they endured, trusting the faithfulness of God's promise. If we forget the story line of the Old Testament, we will also miss the witness of their faith. That omission cuts the heart out of the Bible. Sunday school stories are then told as tamer versions of the Sunday comics, where Samson substitutes for Superman. David's meeting with Goliath then dissolves into an ancient Hebrew version of Jack the Giant Killer. No, David is not a brave little boy who isn't afraid of the big bad giant. He is the Lord's anointed.... God chose David as a king after his own heart in order to prepare the way for David's great Son, our Deliverer and Champion.[9]

9. Edmund P. Clowney, *The Unfolding Mystery: Discovering Christ in the Old Testament* (Phillipsburg, N.J.: P&R), 11–14.

So, the OT contains redemptive "tensions" that need resolution. Only in Christ can these themes be ultimately resolved and fulfilled. Timothy Keller says,

> There are quite a number of what Don Carson calls "inter-canonical" themes that "cut across" the entire Biblical corpus. Alec Motyer points out that the Old Testament asserts truths in *apparently irreconcilable tension* with each other. Thus these themes have "thickening plots" as the Old Testament goes on. In other words, like all good stories, there is *dramatic tension* within the themes that seems almost insoluble. Only in Christ, however, are the "tensions" in these themes resolved and fulfilled. With this approach, rather than only looking for "types" we should look for *questions* the text raises to which only Jesus can be "the answer in the back of the book."[10] ✷

Thus, every part of the Bible points to Christ. Jesus fulfills the writings of the prophets (1 Peter 1:11). Jesus fulfills all the ceremonial law and writings (Heb 10). Jesus fulfills the moral law (Matt 3:15). Jesus fulfills all the characters of history (Adam, 1 Cor 15; Moses, Heb 3). Jesus fulfills the history of Israel (Gal 3:16–17; Hos 11:1/Matt 2:15).

The historical study of these interconnected themes of Scripture culminating in Jesus is called biblical theology. Not to be confused with systematic theology, which is a study of the major doctrines taught within Scripture, biblical theology attempts to read and interpret the Scriptures as an unfolding story of redemption, progressively unveiling God's plan to save a people through Jesus. What this means practically is that when reading the OT, for example, one must not only discover the truths of God—expressed through the human author as different people, places, and redemptive truths are presented—but also discern how those redemptive truths find ultimate fulfillment in Christ.[11]

---

10. *PCPMW*, 36; emphasis his.
11. Some excellent resources for the study of biblical theology and its implications for preaching are: Geerhardus Vos, *Biblical Theology: Old and New Testaments* (1948; repr., Grand Rapids: Eerdmans, 1988); Edmund P. Clowney, *Preaching and Biblical Theology* (Grand Rapids: Eerdmans, 1965; repr., Phillipsburg, N.J.: P&R, 2002); Sidney Greidanus, *Sola Scriptura: Problems and Principles in Preaching Historical Texts* (Toronto: Wedge, 1970); Frances Foulkes, "The Acts of God: A Study of the Basis of Typology in the Old Testament," in *The Right Doctrine from the Wrong Texts? Essays on the Use*

This foundational way of understanding the unity of the Bible was established by the apostles in the NT. Their way of seeing the Scriptures, especially the OT, was through an interpretive method called *typology*.[12] In this approach, they saw in OT symbols (or types) both a preliminary meaning for the original writers and recipients but also further significance and fulfillment (or antitype) in the NT. Christ becomes the key to unlocking the mystery to what OT shadows and symbols prefigure. For typology to work, however, three components need to be present: (1) There must be a *corresponding analogy* between the OT symbol and the NT fulfillment. (2) There must be *historical reality* in both the OT symbol and the NT fulfillment—whether persons, actions, or institutions. (3) There must be *increased escalation* between the OT symbol and the NT fulfillment.[13] Typology thus sees Christ in OT historical symbols through the principles of analogy and escalation.[14]

Having seen that "seeing" Christ, and thus "preaching" Christ, in all of Scripture is both biblical and foundational, we turn to our last point: preaching Christ is practical.

"Preaching Christ" Is Practical

The last reason we should preach Christ from all the Scriptures is because it is eminently practical. We cannot become a Christian or

of the Old Testament in the New, ed. G. K. Beale (Grand Rapids: Baker, 1994); Graeme Goldsworthy, *Preaching the Whole Bible as Christian Scripture: The Application of Biblical Theology to Expository Preaching* (Grand Rapids: Eerdmans, 2000); Edmund P. Clowney, *Preaching Christ in All of Scripture* (Wheaton, Ill.: Crossway, 2003); Sidney Greidanus, *The Modern Preacher and the Ancient Text: Interpreting and Preaching Biblical Literature* (Grand Rapids: Eerdmans, 1988); Johnson, *Him We Proclaim;* Jason Meyer, *Preaching: A Biblical Theology* (Wheaton, Ill.: Crossway, 2013).

12. Leonhard Goppelt, *Typos: The Typological Interpretation of the Old Testament in the New*, trans. Donald H. Madvig (Grand Rapids: Eerdmans: 1982), 198. Goppelt's work is arguably the seminal book on this topic. For a good summary on the main proponents and their respective views on typology, see W. Edward Glenny, "Typology: A Summary of the Present Evangelical Discussion," *JETS* 40, no. 4 (December 1997): 627–38.

13. Goppelt, *Typos*, 17.

14. Typology is admittedly a complex method. It is nonetheless an important process of interpretation for those who see that God has a unified design of Scripture and Scripture's story. For more on typology and its impact on Christ-centered interpretation, see Clowney, *Preaching Christ*, 20–44; Johnson, *Him We Proclaim*, 199–238; Dennis E. Johnson, *Walking with Jesus through His Word: Christ-Centered Bible Study* (Phillipsburg, N.J.: P&R, 2015), ch. 3.

grow as a Christian without the grace that Christ provides. The good news is that Christ has done something in space, time, and history that can change lives. This is the "gospel"—the good news that something has transpired that can transform your life.

The NT authors recognized this when they chose the word to describe their unique message. The use of the word "gospel" (*euangelion*) distinguished the Christian message from other religions.[15] Other possible words available at that time included those used by other religions of that period—such as "illumination" (*photismos*) and "knowledge" (*gnosis*). Also available were words that Judaism used at that time, such as "instruction"/"teaching" (*didache*) or "wisdom" (*Sophia*). But with the use of this unique word, "gospel," the Christian message was not only distinguishable from all other religions but also revealed its practical character. And while all of the words from the prevailing Hellenistic and Jewish religions were used to describe some aspects of Christianity, none of them achieved the centrality and importance of "gospel."

First, the Bible presents the gospel as good news about what God has already done for you, rather than instruction about what you are to do for God. Every other religion presents a system in which we must somehow find and earn our own salvation. In Christianity, however, we discover what God has already achieved for us—preeminently in the person and work of the God-man Jesus Christ. Thus, the gospel is primarily an announcement of good news that must be received and believed.

Second, the Bible presents the gospel as news that has a public character. Keller states, "It identifies the Christian faith as news that has significance for all people, indeed for the whole world, not merely as esoteric understanding or insight."[16] Compared to other religions, Christianity stands or falls depending on whether or not Jesus actually was sinless, died, and rose from the dead. Whether or not Buddha or Mohammed had special powers or miraculous events does not impact whether or not the system of Buddhism or Islam is viable. If Jesus was

15. *PCPMW*, 56–57.
16. Ibid., 57.

not sinless, did not die as our substitute to appease God's wrath over sin, and did not rise again from the dead, then as the apostle Paul said, our faith is in vain. The gospel is that Jesus did die and rise again for us. Thus, the word "gospel" means that something has transpired in history that can transform everything.[17]

In summary, the gospel is an announcement that Jesus Christ's life, death, and resurrection in history has achieved our salvation. Unlike the founders of other religions, who could be said to bring good news, Jesus is the good news.

This is important because many Christians think the gospel is only needed for the two "doors" of life that we need to walk through to have the assurance we will be with God forever. That is, we first become a Christian by believing in the good news that Jesus died for us — the first door. After we get through that portal, we don't have to worry about the gospel until the end of our life, when we need the assurance that we'll have access to heaven. That's when we need the gospel to get us into that portal to heaven — the second door. In between those two portals, however, many Christians don't think they need to hear and believe the good news of what Jesus has done for them and all the benefits they receive by faith through their union with him. Thus, much of what passes for Christian preaching is nothing more than moral advice or moving storytelling that leads to some form of good moral advice.

Michael Horton has rightly said, "The Gospel is not good instructions, not a good idea, and not good advice. The Gospel is an

---

17. This public, historical aspect of the gospel is especially seen when the term "the gospel of Christ" or "of Jesus Christ" is used. Often the word "gospel" and the life and work of Christ are essentially synonyms. Particularly significant is how Luke links "gospel" to "Jesus." In Acts 5:42, it reads, literally, "they never stopped ... evangelizing Christ Jesus." Obviously, Jesus is not the *object* of their evangelism (they were not trying to convert him!). But the word *euangelizomenoi* means, all by itself, "to preach the gospel" or literally "to gospelize." So in the places in Acts where it says, literally, "they evangelized Jesus," the English translations have to render it "they told the gospel about Jesus Christ" or "they told the good news that Jesus was the Christ" (cf. Acts 5:42 NIV). But the Greek construction clearly has a stronger meaning than that. Its intentional redundancy aims to say that the good news they preached *was* Jesus. His very life, and all his works, *is* what saves us. To declare Jesus and to declare the gospel is the same thing. Jesus does not bring the gospel; he *is* the gospel, because the gospel is that God has broken into history and accomplished everything necessary for our salvation.

announcement of what God has done for us in Jesus Christ."[18] What Christians may not realize is that <u>the gospel is not just the *portal* to get in and get out, but is also the *power* for living in between</u>. You see, without the knowledge and faith that Christ's presence in our lives actually transforms us and renews us day by day after the image of Christ, we don't need to declare what Christ has done and what he continues to do in our lives. Tim Keller helpfully summarizes:

> Not only must we read the Bible Christocentrically to understand its meaning, we must read it Christocentrically in order to grow from it personally. <u>There are, in the end, only two ways to read the Bible: is it basically about me or basically about Jesus? In other words, is it basically about what I must do, or basically about what he has done?</u> Until I see that Jesus fought the real giants (sin, law, death) *for* me, I will never be able to fight the giants in my life. Unless I see that Jesus made the big sacrifices *for* me, I will never be able to make the normal sacrifices in life. Unless I can see him as forgiving *me* on the cross, I won't be able to forgive others. As a model, Jesus and the rest of the Bible is a crushing, terrible burden. So reading "Christocentrically" is not just a trick of interpretation, but the key to new life.[19]

Whether the gospel is the *portal* or the *power*, preaching the grace that only God in Christ provides is eminently practical.

When we preach Christ from every passage of Scripture, we are preaching some facet of his person and/or work. Though this will be described in more detail in the following chapters, every text will somehow illuminate the grace of Jesus, which is practical and pertinent for every hearer. "Finding" Christ in the text will differ from text to text, but the CFC will be found in one or more of the following aspects of Christ.

- Christ the Penalty Payer: Many texts will find their connection to Christ through his penalty-paying sacrifice on the cross, enduring the covenant curse for us. As sinners, we deserve death

---

18. Michael S. Horton, "Christ at the Center," *Christianity Today* (November 2009): 48.
19. *PCPMW*, 57.

(Rom 6:23), but by God's grace, Christ pays the penalty for us by offering himself as a substitutionary sacrifice for our sins. Though sinless and undeserving of death, Jesus takes our place on the cross and he receives the punishment of death for our sins. But those who repent of their sins and put their trust in him receive the benefits that he earned—forgiveness of sins and the promise of eternal life.

- Christ the Probation Preserver: Here the emphasis of the text points to how Jesus never sinned, perfectly preserving the covenant in our place. Christ faithfully keeps all the holy requirements of God where we could not. Yet God in his great love and faithfulness provides his only Son, who in spite of our disobedience and rebellion perfectly obeys every single law of God. As a result, he earns the righteousness we need. This is demonstrated in his resurrection from the dead. Those who repent of their sins and put their trust in Christ receive the merits that Christ earned—the imputation of his righteousness, making us simultaneously sinless yet justified.

- Christ the Power Provider: Other texts and sermons will focus on how Jesus provides the power through his Spirit, re-creating us into covenant keepers. As those who trust in Christ, believers are given the promise that Christ not only defeats the power of sin but also sanctifies us day by day with his grace so that our lives are living sacrifices to God's glory and for the good of those around us.

- Christ the Passion Producer: This CFC is often used with the others. It emphasizes how Christ's penalty-paying sacrifice and probation-keeping sinless life motivates us to love God with all our hearts, souls, minds, and strength and to love our neighbors more than ourselves. Our goal as preachers is to faithfully present the truth, goodness, and beauty of Christ from every text and in every sermon. Revealing who he is and what he's done for us will compel and transform hearers. No other motivation will do.

Conclusion

Preaching Christ is biblical, foundational, and practical. As the apostles before us, we have the great privilege and responsibility of presenting before a needy world the only hope of this life and the life to come. The apostle Paul said it best when he addressed the church elders in Ephesus.

> But I do not account my life of any value nor as precious to myself, if only I may finish my course and the ministry that I received from the Lord Jesus, to testify to the gospel of the grace of God. And now, behold, I know that none of you among whom I have gone about proclaiming the kingdom will see my face again. Therefore I testify to you this day that I am innocent of the blood of all, for I did not shrink from declaring to you the whole counsel of God (Acts 20:24–27).

CHAPTER 4

PREACHING CHRIST FROM THE OLD TESTAMENT

The task of reading, interpreting, and preaching Christ from the OT involves many challenges. Aside from the obvious fact that Jesus is rarely mentioned explicitly in the OT, other obstacles loom large—not least of which is the fact that the OT is an elaborate book. It is filled with various types of literature, describing the experiences of numerous people and nations, spanning thousands of miles of geography, and taking place over hundreds of centuries. Is it conceivable that these Scriptures—filled with thousands of people, places, and years—are essentially one story?

The Bible is like other epics, a long story with a coherent unifying plot, involving multiple characters, taking place over a span of many years (think *War and Peace* by Leo Tolstoy or the Harry Potter series by J. K. Rowling). While the Bible has some unique differences from these novels, part of interpreting the Bible is to recognize that it is essentially one story with one main character. An important way to grasp that understanding is to examine the Bible's redemptive and historical contexts.

Redemptive and Historical Contexts

Genesis to Revelation is at its core a historical story of redemption over time and space involving God, the creator and sustainer of the universe, through the primary agent involved in redemption, Jesus Christ. This is an important reality to keep in mind: the Bible is a story about God and his redemptive purposes. God creates and sustains all things, including the pinnacle of creation, mankind. Yet in spite of mankind's rebellion in sin, God redeems a people for his own purposes and glory through the person and work of Jesus Christ. Every passage in both the OT and the NT must be seen in light of this broad, overarching, ultimate context. Thus, whatever passage we may be reading and interpreting for the purposes of preaching, be it prose, poetry, or prophecy, we keep this *ultimate* redemptive context in mind. After all, the Bible is God's story of revealing himself and his plan of salvation for his people.

Furthermore, as we approach the OT specifically, we recognize that God accomplishes his *ultimate* purposes through the *narrow* history of Israel. Much of the OT, especially with the introduction of Abraham in Genesis 12, is written in light of the history and experiences of this single nation. The triumphs and tragedies of this narrow group of people serve the ultimate purpose of telling God's story of redemption. Israel is chosen from all the other nations to display God's providential power, provision, and purposes. Thus, every passage, be it a narrative from Exodus or a poem in Psalms, needs to be read and interpreted in light of the history of Israel's relationship to their Redeemer God. Thus, this *narrow* historical context is vital in our reading, interpreting, and preaching the OT.

Reading, interpreting, and preaching Christ from any *specific* passage in the OT needs to keep these two concentric contexts in mind: the *narrow* history and experience of Israel and the *ultimate* redemptive story of God in the gospel of Jesus Christ. The Bible, however, is more than just a theological treatise on redemption or a national history of Israel. It is first and foremost literature — creative and sublime compositions by skilled artisans of language. Whether the genre is prose, poetry, or prophecy, the Scriptures need to be not only read and interpreted with consideration of its redemptive and historical contexts but also appreciated and extolled for its truth, goodness, and beauty.

As literature, then, the Bible's literary contexts, or genres, also need to be examined. The rest of this chapter will address how to read, interpret, and preach Christ from two main OT genres: prose (narrative) and poetry (especially Psalms).[1] Some of these genres will overlap with similar ones found in the NT. For example, the literary features found in OT historical narratives have commonalities with the NT gospels. Furthermore, doctrinal and ethical literature in the NT has much in common with the law genre found in the OT. This chapter will examine each genre (prose and poetry) through two parts: first some of the features of each genre will be explained, and then some strategies for preaching Christ from them will be offered.[2]

Preaching Christ from OT Prose/Narrative Genre

Approximately 60 percent of the Bible is written in narrative genre. Why do stories form the largest percentage of literature in the Scriptures? While the exact answer will ultimately remain a mystery, we can venture some guesses. First, we have all experienced the power and poignancy of good stories. From the tales we heard as children to the movies that we watch in theaters, stories are simple yet profound. They not only stimulate our minds but also stir our souls. Perhaps more than any other genre, stories have a way of touching our entire being. As such, they make truths arresting and memorable. I still remember certain sermons I heard as a child because of the unforgettable stories that complemented biblical truth.

Second, stories help make abstract ideas understandable and concrete.

1. See Dennis E. Johnson, *Him We Proclaim: Preaching Christ from All the Scriptures* (Phillipsburg, N.J.: P&R, 2007), 272–330, for insight into understanding and preaching OT literary genres, such as historical narratives, law, wisdom, song, and prophetic vision.
2. This chapter introduces the reader to some of the foundational issues involved in interpreting and preaching Christ from various OT genres. It is suggestive, not exhaustive. As such, it can and should be supplemented by other resources found in the footnotes and bibliography.

The Bible is full of important doctrinal truths that must be understood and believed. But while some of these truths are simple, others can be quite complex. Regardless of the truth, stories have a way of imparting truth in ways that are vivid and tangible to the mind, heart, and will. This is why a truth like "Love your neighbor" is much more concrete when told through the story of the good Samaritan (Luke 10:25–37). The Bible is full of these unforgettable stories that possess powerful truths.

How do we preach these great stories in the Bible without essentially repeating the narrative and adding some universal moral lessons at the end? How do we find Christ in these stories that don't mention him explicitly? How do we do justice to the biblical truths, literary art, and covenantal purpose in Christ that is inherent in these stories? How do we preach the good news of Jesus to our hearers while doing justice to the unique biblical truths and literary beauty of these stories? Let's first review some of the unique features of OT narrative genre that will help us uncover the text's meaning and significance and then examine some strategies for preaching Christ from this genre.

Features of OT Narrative Texts

Let's examine four main features of OT narrative texts that are important for interpretation and communication: people, plot, places, and particulars.[3]

1. People: What types of *people* are found in biblical narrative texts, and why are they important? The characters present in the stories of the Bible are typically human, divine, or demonic. Sometimes animals (e.g., serpent, donkey) that supernaturally exhibit personal characteristics (speech, emotion, will, purpose, etc.) are found. All of these characters function within biblical stories in three main ways.

---

3. Other features of narrative exist that cannot be fully developed here (e.g., narrator and point of view). For more information on these features of biblical narrative, see Tremper Longman, *Literary Approaches to Biblical Interpretation*, Foundations of Contemporary Interpretation, vol. 3 (Grand Rapids: Zondervan, 1987), 83–88. Adele Berlin also provides helpful insights into biblical literary features in *Poetics and Interpretation of Biblical Narrative* (Winona Lake, Ind.: Eisenbrauns, 1994), 23–82.

- The first character is the *protagonist*, the primary character involved in the main conflict of the plot. The main action of resolving the conflict of the story will involve this hero figure. Being the protagonist does not necessarily mean that this character possesses positive spiritual or moral qualities. In the estimation of the inspired narrator, who is often omniscient in his storytelling capabilities, this figure may be evil (i.e., an antihero), or most likely, a person with mixed integrity. Regardless of the protagonist's spirituality or morality, this is the central character experiencing the main action of the plot (e.g., the Israelites in Ex 17:1–7; the paralytic in Mark 2:1–12).
- The second character is the *antagonist*, the primary character that opposes the protagonist. This villain figure can be an individual or a group (Pharisees), personal or impersonal (the storm in Mark 4:35–41). The antagonist is often inextricably linked to the conflict that poses a threat or obstacle to the protagonist in the story. Thus, resolving the main problem of the story usually involves overcoming the antagonist or what the antagonist may represent (e.g., thirst symbolizing death in Ex 17:1–7; paralysis symbolizing death in Mark 2:1–12).
- The last character found in biblical narratives is the *supporting cast*. These helper figures may be individuals or groups functioning to support the main characters and the plot. When supporting cast members are mentioned in the story by the narrator, they are usually being used to signal an important point. As such, readers ought to take special note of their presence and purpose (e.g., the elders in Ex 17:1–7; the scribes observing Jesus' healing of the paralytic in Mark 2:1–12).

Why is character analysis important? Analyzing the characters found in biblical narratives is important because through them we learn about ourselves and we learn about God.

- The characters function in teaching us about ourselves. The narrator's use of characters is the primary way in which readers—past and present—identify with the main truths being taught through the story. The main truths of the story are often linked to the changes that the characters go through as the plot develops from problem to solution. Though more of these plot dynamics will be discussed in the next section, what the characters think, say, and do—whether good or bad—are often what the narrator intends for readers to learn about themselves. The characters often act as mirrors to our own intentions, convictions, and actions. Thus, as preachers, many of our applications to our contemporary hearers can be found by examining the characters in the narrative. How they respond faithfully or rebelliously (or even apathetically) to God's redemptive initiatives will be the primary ways to connect with our hearers.

• The characters also serve the function of teaching us about some aspect of God in the context of the history of redemption structured by covenant promises. God desires that all of his people, past, present, and future, grow in their love for and faith in him. Examining the characters in biblical narratives helps us interpret what the stories ultimately reveal about our covenant unfaithfulness and God's covenantal faithfulness. God has a plan to redeem and renew his covenant people. This need for rescue is why most bridges to Christ from OT narrative texts are found through the characters—the good, bad, and ugly aspects of the character (promise/fulfillment, type/antitype). Whether mediator, prophet, priest, or king, OT characters often anticipate Christ in their covenant symbolism.[4]

2. Plot: Related to the analysis of the people in biblical narrative, how does the *plot* work, and why is it important? From children's stories to movies, actions and incidents occur in a narrative that moves the story from beginning to end. What usually moves the story forward is some

---

4. For various OT symbols, see Edmund P. Clowney, *Preaching Christ in All of Scripture* (Wheaton, Ill.: Crossway, 2003), 20–26. For more on how Christ fulfills the OT offices of prophets, priests, and kings, see Dennis E. Johnson, *Walking with Jesus through His Word: Christ-Centered Bible Study* (Phillipsburg, N.J.: P&R, 2015), chaps. 7–9.

form of conflict that is introduced, propelling the story toward a resolution. Discovering the main problem as well as the solution to that conflict will provide the key truths that the human author wants to share with his readers. Furthermore, this discovery of the human author's main truths provides a link to the significance of these truths that the Divine Author wants to use to transform his people today through the gospel. (We'll see how this works later when we discuss the strategy of preaching narratives.) Aristotle gives the simplest description of plot dynamics by stating that a plot has a beginning, middle, and an end.[5] Using this as our outline, I will highlight some key components of plot dynamics that will help you interpret and preach OT narrative texts.

- Beginning: Most biblical narratives usually begin with shalom, or a sense of peace and well-being. There is a state of equilibrium and wholeness, an absence of conflict and distress. The action of the narrative begins when we sense that the relative peace is not what it appears to be. During this section, the narrative may provide further information through actions and dialogue that prepare us for the entrance of the conflict.
- Middle: The middle part of the narrative begins with the entrance of the conflict. A problem emerges or is generated that involves the main character in remedying the disequilibrium and distress. Further complications ensue until the conflict reaches its most intense state at the climax of the story. Usually in biblical narratives, conflicts occur where sin and sin's effects have infiltrated not only the hearts and lives of all the characters but also their environment. This is important because here is where the FCF of the passage is usually found.[6] Since narratives work more implicitly and indirectly, the primary spiritual problem that needs remedy needs to be discovered by examining the plot and how it resolves. Often narratives are complex, with multiple characters and multiple issues. Finding the narrative's primary

5. Aristotle, *The Poetics*, trans. W. H. Fyfe (Boston: Harvard University Press, 1973), 31.
6. Bryan Chapell, *Christ-Centered Preaching: Redeeming the Expository Sermon*, 2nd ed. (Grand Rapids: Baker, 2005), 48–55.

problem and the primary solution is key for interpretation and communication.

- End: The end of the narrative involves the resolution of the conflict and the restoration of some measure of shalom. In biblical narratives, the CFC is usually found in the solution to the primary problem. That is, the gospel of God's grace in Jesus is usually related to how the solution remedies the spiritual problem that the conflict either explicitly or implicitly reveals. Keep in mind, however, that this does not always mean the good guy wins. That is, the resolution of the problem could be due to a negative process, leading to a negative outcome. Take, for example, the story of the two sons in Luke 15. Often called the parable of the prodigal son, this story ends without any resolution regarding the older brother's distress and lack of peace over the father's forgiveness of the younger brother's sins. Here the direct narrator, Jesus, along with the author, Luke, are both signaling to the immediate hearers, the Pharisees, as well as to future readers, a warning about the pride that leads to a hardened heart of unbelief.

3. Places: In addition to the people and plot, another important feature of biblical narratives to be analyzed is the *places* that are described and used in the plot. Narrators do not often include descriptions of the physical surroundings and the geographic setting, so when such details are present, they are important. The mention of specific places and landmarks presupposes an understanding between the narrator and the reader. Israelite readers of the OT would have known, for example, the distances between cities and features of the land. Thus, when a narrator includes these features in his narrative, he is signaling emphasis and importance. Furthermore, changes in the setting and scenery also signal a change in the plot's movements. You need to ask, why the change and what is its significance? An example is found in the first chapter of Jonah. The changes in scene corresponding to the spatial movement in the first few verses are a physical symbol of Jonah's disobedience. As Jonah goes to Tarshish, then to Joppa, onto the boat, and into the belly of the boat, he is going in the

direct opposite direction of Nineveh, where he was commanded to go. All of this signals to the reader the significance of Jonah's sin.

4. Particulars: In addition to analyzing the people, plot, and places found in biblical narratives, observing other important *particulars* will provide clues to the meaning and significance of narrative texts. The human author often makes particular stylistic decisions in narratives that inform the meaning of the text.[7] Examining the following three narrative particulars may be helpful to the interpreter and preacher: omission, repetition, and dialogue.

- Omission: A particular feature often found in narrative texts is the omission of details. Biblical narratives omit the kinds of details that modern novels will usually dwell on, such as external physical descriptions and internal psychological motivations. Though most biblical narratives are written from the perspective of a third-person narrator who is often omniscient and omnipresent in the telling of the story, the narrator will rarely reveal explicit data that aid the reader in understanding the character's thoughts and motives. When the narrator shows restraint, the interpreter should respect his omissions, prioritizing what is emphasized but also trying to fill in the "gaps" the narrator purposely left. However, when the narrator goes out of his way to reveal certain details, the reader must pay attention and discern why the narrator did so. Often in these cases the narrator will intervene in the story to make a side comment (e.g., character expansions, cultural explanations, theological interpretation, etc.). These are exceptions to the storytelling norms of biblical narration and must be noticed.[8]
- Repetition: Another particular of biblical narrative that deserves analysis is the use of repetition. As is often the case in other biblical genres, repetition in narrative texts signals importance. One

---

7. Adele Berlin has a stimulating discussion on how particular literary techniques, such as omission and repetition, found in biblical narrative are similar to artistic techniques found in painting and music (*Poetics and Interpretation*, 135–39).
8. Longman, *Literary Approaches*, 85–86, 96–97.

particular type of repetition used by biblical authors is what is
called *leitwort*.[9] This word refers to the technique used by biblical
authors to signal the importance of a word or idea without having
to articulate it explicitly. This emphasis is accomplished by repeating a key word or phrase in strategic locations of the narrative.[10]

One example of this particular feature of biblical narrative is also
found in the opening five verses of Jonah. There the Hebrew word
translated "went down" is used several times: though told to go
to Nineveh, Jonah "went down" to Joppa, where he found a ship,
then "went down" onto the ship to flee from God, where he ultimately "went down" to the lower decks to sleep. Discerning the use
of this word reveals the narrator's intention. He wants the reader to
see the downward trajectory of Jonah's sinful disobedience.

- Dialogue: The use of dialogue by the narrators of biblical stories
is another particular literary feature that helps us discover the
meaning and significance of the text. As was stated before, narrative texts do not reveal much data regarding the inner world
of the characters. When the narrator wants to reveal some of the
motives of the characters, the actions of the plot provide some
clues. What is utilized more frequently in narratives to give us
a glimpse into the psychological and ideological perspectives
of the characters is the use of dialogue.[11] Usually the dialogue
between two characters is set in contrast to one another to reveal
details about their unique personalities. Take, for example, the
dialogue between Esau and Jacob in Genesis 25 and how the
contrast reveals their temperaments.[12] Thus, the use of dialogue

---

9. Robert Alter lists five different types of repetition used by biblical authors of narrative
texts: *leitwort*, theme, motif, sequence of actions, and type-scene (*The Art of Biblical
Narrative* [New York: Basic, 1981], 95–113).
10. Tremper Longman provides another example with the Hebrew use of "house" (*bayit*) in
the narrative found in 2 Sam 7, where God establishes a covenant with David. The word
is used several times: in reference to the temple (house) David desires to build, the palace
(house) that he has just completed, and the dynasty (house) that the Lord will provide
instead (*Literary Approaches*, 96).
11. For more information regarding the use of dialogue in narratives, see Alter, *Art of Biblical
Narrative*, 63–87; and Berlin, *Poetics and Interpretation*, 64–72.
12. Alter, *Art of Biblical Narrative*, 72.

serves to reveal the characters' inner attitudes and convictions. This is critical in determining the author's intentions.

In conclusion, when faced with the task of preaching from OT narrative texts, one needs to pay careful attention to the unique literary features of biblical narratives: people, plot, places, and particulars. Ultimately, all of these features should be examined during the interpretation process to help us as readers of the Bible and listeners of sermons to ask several important questions, such as: What is the author trying to communicate through the use of this story? What is significant about the characters and the plot? What are the truths trying to communicate to me in order to change me? God sovereignly uses the unique literary skills and artistry of the human authors to craft biblical narrative not merely for aesthetic admiration but ultimately for spiritual transformation.

Thus, biblical narratives are not only literary presentation but also historical explanation and theological communication. Authors are ultimately explaining redemptive stories that are grounded and accomplished in the concrete events of real persons within real history. These redemptive stories are then communicated purposely within the theological context of God's covenantal relationship with his people. God uses the faithful and accurate preaching of OT narrative texts, as he does all other genres of the Bible, for the covenantal purpose of conforming them to the image of Christ. What are some strategies that will help you preach Christ from this genre?

Strategies for Preaching Christ from OT Narrative Texts

In this section, I will present a three-step strategy for preaching Christ from OT narrative texts. These three steps correspond to Edmund Clowney's helpful biblical-theological model for the interpretation of Christ-centered sermons, his hermeneutical rectangle for typology. Keep in mind that these three moves should not be equated with the three points often found in a sermon outline. These are the steps for interpretation, leading to communication. Furthermore, these are dynamic steps of interpretation that can and should circle back around one another during the process, influencing and enhancing previously held ideas.[13] Unlike an escalator that only moves in one direction, you can and should move back and forth between these steps to refine your understanding.

Figure 4.1. Clowney's Hermeneutical Rectangle[14]

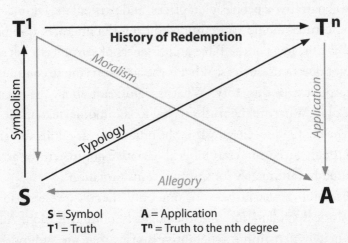

$$T^1$$ **History of Redemption** $$T^n$$

Symbolism

Moralism

Typology

Application

Allegory

S   A

S = Symbol   **A** = Application
T^1 = Truth   **T^n** = Truth to the nth degree

Clowney's hermeneutical trajectory involves the move from text to significance through the history of revelation and redemption. As a character or event is described in the OT, it has meaning for the original readers or hearers through symbolism, here signified as T to the first power (T^1). This meaning is discovered through the linguistic, literary, and life-setting analysis of the text's truths according to the original human author. The truth or concept then finds ultimate fulfillment in Christ through the history of revelation, here signified as T to the nth power (T^n). The history of revelation is essentially a history of redemption, culminating in the person and work of Jesus Christ. This symbolism

---

13. For a summary of the way history, literature, and theology all work together in the interpretive process, see Andreas J. Köstenberger and Richard Duane Patterson, *Invitation to Biblical Interpretation: Exploring the Hermerneutical Triad of History, Literature and Theology* (Grand Rapids: Kregel: 2011), 23–27.

14. This illustration is found in Edmund P. Clowney, *Preaching Christ in All of Scripture* (Wheaton, Ill.: Crossway, 2003), 32, figure 1. Used by permission of Crossway, a publishing ministry of Good News Publishers, Wheaton, IL 60187, www.crossway.org. See also Edmund P. Clowney, "Interpreting the Biblical Models of the Church: A Hermeneutical Deepening of Ecclesiology," in *Biblical Interpretation and the Church: The Problem of Contextualization*, ed. D. A. Carson (Nashville: Nelson, 1984), 83–95. See also Gordon P. Hugenberger, "Introductory Notes on Typology," in *Right Doctrine from the Wrong Texts?* ed. G. K. Beale, 339–41.

finding fulfillment in Christ, through analogy and escalation of meaning, is called *typology*. Significance for us then becomes possible in the third move, as the original concept moves from its original meaning, to its fulfillment in Christ, and finally to its meaning to contemporary hearers. The strategy outlined below follows this interpretive trajectory.

Note that when one makes the interpretive move from symbol to significance, bypassing the original meaning (T^1), the result is allegory, where arbitrary ideas are drawn from various details of the text without doing justice to the author's literary intent or theological purpose. Another problem emerges when one makes the interpretive move from original symbol and original meaning (T^1) to significance but bypasses the symbol's meaning through the history of revelation and redemption (T^n). This interpretive move results in moralism. Here, principles of good behavior are taught from the text without the need for Christ and the gospel. Both allegory and moralism are faulty interpretive methods, ultimately leading to a false gospel. Now let's look at these interpretive moves more specifically as it applies to OT narrative texts.

Layer One: Discovering the original purpose for the original audience through linguistic, literary, and life-setting analysis.[15]

- Pray for comprehension and transformation.
- Read the passage several times in its context.
- Formulate a preliminary sermon proposition statement in a consequential format.
- Linguistic Analysis:
  - Translate your passage from the Hebrew, using dictionaries and other helps.
  - Identify the syntax and structure of the passage.
- Literary Analysis:
  - Examine the text in light of the chapter, the book, and the rest of the Bible.
  - Analyze the genre: people, plot, places, and particulars. Consult commentaries.

---

15. These steps are described in detail in chapter 2.

- Life-Setting Analysis:
  - Investigate the historical and cultural context, using commentaries and other helps.
  - Determine the occasion and purpose.
- Discover the fallen-condition focus (FCF):
  - What is the primary problem of the plot? Does it cohere with the solution?
  - What spiritual concerns are connected to this problem?
  - What concerns do my hearers share with these original hearers?
- Reformulate your sermon proposition. Ask, What is the redemptive act of God in this narrative? How do characters in the narrative respond to this? How should they (and we) respond?[16]

Layer Two: Discerning how this passage points to Christ.

- Compare the covenant themes in this passage with those found in passages before and after it.
- Discern your Christ-focused connection (CFC), usually found in the resolution to the problem of the plot.
  - Type fulfillment: A person or action of the narrative is a symbol. Through analogy and escalation, there is fulfillment in Christ.[17]
  - Law fulfillment: An ethical principle in the narrative that cannot be satisfied forces the reader to find fulfillment in and through Christ.
- Relate the CFC to the gospel.
  - Christ as the penalty payer?
  - Christ as the probation preserver?
  - Christ as the power provider?
  - Christ as the passion producer?
- Reformulate your sermon proposition. Revise, asking, How is God's redemptive act seen in light of the gospel? How should we respond?

---

16. Adapted from D. Doriani, *Putting the Truth to Work: The Theory and Practice of Biblical Application* (Phillipsburg, N.J.: P&R, 2001), 181.
17. Typology was discussed in chapter 3.

Layer Three: Discovering how the gospel should transform my hearers and me.

- How does the problem of the narrative connect with my hearers and me? Review the characters and their response to the aspect of the gospel being revealed in this passage. Where do hearers find themselves in the story?
- How does the solution of the narrative connect with Christ and the gospel?
- In light of the text and the gospel, how should my hearers and I respond? Where do hearers find themselves in the story?
- So what? Now what?
- Do these answers correspond with my sermon proposition? If not, revise.

Preaching Christ from OT Poetry/Psalms

The second major genre found in the OT is poetry. What may surprise you is how much of the Bible is poetry. In addition to the 150 psalms found in the middle of our Bibles, poetry is found within many other genres, including narratives. The so-called Wisdom Literature (Job, Proverbs, Song of Songs, Ecclesiastes) and the major and minor prophets are primarily poetry. All this poetry combined constitutes about one-third of the Bible.

What is poetry and how is it different from prose? Scholars agree that the differences between these two genres are not that extreme. Some literary features such as parallelism and repetition would immediately be associated with poetry. These are, however, also found in prose. What is helpful, then, is to distinguish poetry as a genre that contains a larger degree of certain literary devices such as terseness, parallelism, and imagery.[18] Let's first examine these three general features of poetry and then discuss features particular to the book of Psalms. We'll conclude by offering some strategies for preaching Christ from the Psalms.

---

18. I am indebted to Tremper Longman for these categories (*Literary Approaches*, 119–34).

Features of OT Poetry

1. Terseness: This feature highlights the brevity and succinctness of poetry. Compared to prose, poetry tends to be short and to the point—something that a reader can ascertain visually. Terseness is often seen in the biblical poet's use of two devices: ellipsis and omission. An ellipsis occurs when a parallel word found in the first line of a poem is missing in the second line. This word, usually a verb, is thus presupposed by the poet and must be supplied by the reader. Related to this is the omission of conjunctions and particles commonly found in prose, such as *and, but, or, then, when, because,* and so on. These omissions are purposeful in forcing the reader to discern the poet's meaning. Terseness through ellipsis and omission is common in biblical poetry.

2. Parallelism: This poetic feature is probably the most familiar to readers of the Bible. Through parallelism, or the use of various types of repetition and correspondence between lines, biblical poets emphasize ideas and signify meaning. Parallelism can occur through the grammar and through semantics, or the meaning of the words. Semantic parallelism occurs when the poet uses similar but slightly different words between two lines, signaling to the reader to meditate on the comparison and contrast of thought. The second line usually carries forward the same thought of the first line but in a different way.[19] That difference is the clue to the emphasis the poet is trying to make. Another pattern of parallelism found in Hebrew poetry is symmetrical parallelism, often called *chiasm*. In this poetic device, the first ideas of a poem are presented linearly (e.g., point A, B, and C). Then the parallelism occurs in inverse order (e.g., C^1, B^1, and A^1). This way of writing poetry creates meaning with beauty.

3. Imagery: Longman defines a literary image as "a sensation evoked in the mind of the reader by the language of the text."[20] In poetry, these images are accomplished through figurative language, that is, going beyond the literal surface meaning. The most common device in biblical

---

19. Mark D. Futato, *Interpreting the Psalms: An Exegetical Handbook* (Grand Rapids: Kregel: 2007), 37–41.
20. Longman, *Literary Approaches*, 129.

poetry is the use of metaphor, which is "an image based on similarity within difference."[21] This principle of similarity can also be seen in the use of personification, allegory, and symbol. Two other common devices used in the biblical poetry are metonymy (substitution of one word for another) and synecdoche (a part representing the whole). Whatever device is used, the reader must carefully discern the poet's intent by examining the level of similarity between the ideas presented, knowing there will be a purposeful element of ambiguity and distance.[22]

Features of the Book of Psalms

Having looked at some general features of the poetry found in the Bible, let's examine some of the unique components associated with the Psalms to help you interpret and preach from them.[23]

1. Historical and Literary Considerations: While "psalm" can be defined simply as a "song," there are many elements that make the Psalms unique. Historically the Psalms have served the Israelites as their primary songbook, expressing their life in God through poetry and prayers. It is the most quoted OT book in the NT, with over 350 explicit and implicit references. In the interpretation of psalms, care must be taken to examine the poetry within its historical (if provided), literary, and redemptive contexts.

2. Purpose and Theme: As with many books, the theme and purpose of the Psalms can be found in its opening pages.[24] Psalm 1 tells us the purpose of the entire book: to instruct in happiness and holiness. Psalm 2 tells us the theme: The Lord Reigns. Like other Wisdom Literature in the Bible, the Psalms provide us with clues to how followers of God relate their faith in their daily lives. It expresses the joys and the sorrows, the pain and the pleasures, of life before the eyes of God. Full of beauty and truth, the poetry of the Psalms continues to comfort many of God's people and challenge them to holiness.

---

21. Ibid., 130.
22. Mark Futato offers tips on analyzing poetic images (*Interpreting the Psalms*, 41–49).
23. Futato provides a listing of helpful resources for the reading and interpreting of psalms in ibid., 132–37.
24. Ibid., 57–95.

DISCERNING CHRIST IN THE TEXT

3. Structure: The book of Psalms is divided into five books. Each of the five has an overarching theme that influences the meaning and significance of a particular psalm.[25] Psalms 1 and 2 serve as introductions to the entire book, while Psalms 145–150 function as a doxological conclusion. The themes of each book, however, also repeat throughout other books. Futato summarizes the Psalms by saying, "God desires that all peoples on earth take refuge in him and in so doing experience blessing from him, to the end that they, along with the whole cosmic order, might give glory to him."[26] Here are the themes to each of the five books.

- Psalms 3–41: Reign of the King
- Psalms 42–72: Refuge in the King
- Psalms 73–89: Blessing for the Nations
- Psalms 90–106: Passion of the King
- Psalms 107–144: Glory to the King

4. Categories: The 150 psalms can also be categorized thematically into several major types.[27] Knowing the thematic focus of the psalm will help in your interpretation.

- Hymns of praise: These psalms focus on praising God as Creator and Redeemer (e.g., Pss 29, 47, 105). They are usually structured in three parts: invitation to praise, reasons for praise, and confidence in praise.[28]
- Laments: The focus of these psalms is on honest expression when life is full of distress, discouragement, and disorientation (e.g., Pss 22, 30, 88). Though strong emotions such as sadness, fear, and even anger abound, these psalms end on a positive note of faith and praise.
- Thanksgiving: These psalms are related to hymns of praise and laments. As one is restored from lament, thanksgiving is offered

---

25. Ibid., 95–116.
26. Ibid., 116.
27. The first six categories are taken from Futato, *Interpreting the Psalms*, 146–73. The first three are the most common in Scripture.
28. Ibid., 146.

(e.g., Pss 30, 40, 144). They are full of joy and gratitude for rescue, redemption, and release.

- Confidence: The psalms in this category reveal the assurance of faith that pilgrims have who often live their lives between lament and thanksgiving (e.g., Pss 23, 27, 121).
- Royal: These songs focus on the theme of God's kingship (e.g., Pss 93, 97, 99).
- Wisdom: These psalms offer practical advice on how to live wisely before the face of God, especially by following his words (e.g., Pss 1, 37, 49).
- Didactic: These psalms are designed to teach (e.g., Ps 119).
- Liturgies: These psalms were probably used in worship settings of some sort (e.g., Pss 120–134).

5. Poetic Style: Many of the same poetic devices found in other biblical poetry are found in the Psalms (terseness, parallelism, and imagery). Throughout the Psalms, ideas will be compressed and expressions will be terse. As such, the reader is called to "fill in" the blanks. Parallelism is the most obvious device used, where the second line furthers the thought of the first line in some way (e.g., Ps 6:1). Many kinds of figurative language are also used to touch the mind, the heart, and the life.

Strategies for Preaching Christ from the Psalms

Layer One: Discovering the original purpose for the original audience through linguistic, literary, and life-setting analysis.

- Pray for comprehension and transformation.
- Read the psalm several times, looking at clues to the main point (topics, patterns, images, mood, etc.).
- Formulate a preliminary sermon proposition statement in a consequential format.
- Linguistic Analysis:
  - Translate your passage from the Hebrew, using dictionaries and other helps.
  - Identify the syntax and structure of the passage, especially the significance of its terseness, parallelism, and imagery.

- Literary Analysis:
  - Examine the psalm in light of these contexts: the surrounding psalms, the five "books" of the Psalms, and shared concepts from the rest of the Bible.
  - Analyze the genre: Determine the category of this psalm and its significance to the overall meaning. Consult commentaries and other resources.
- Life-Setting Analysis:
  - Investigate, if known, the historical and cultural context. Consult commentaries as needed.
  - Determine the occasion and purpose.
- Discover the fallen-condition focus (FCF):
  - What is the primary problem, implicit or explicit, of the plot? Does it cohere with the solution?
  - What spiritual concerns are connected to this problem?
  - What concerns do my hearers share with these original hearers?
- Reformulate your sermon proposition.

Layer Two: Discerning how this passage points to Christ.

- Discern your Christ-focused connection (CFC) by examining the following.
  - The experience of the psalmist: The connection to Christ can sometimes be seen in the psalmist himself. On the one hand, the psalmist's experiences of sin and sin's effects can connect to our sin and our need for a savior. In this case, the psalm highlights the need for Christ and his benefits. On the other, the psalmist may function as a type of Christ, revealing an aspect of who he is and what he's done for us.
  - The category of the psalm: The connection to Christ can also be found by examining the primary problem of the psalm (and its solution in Christ) in light of the psalm's category.[29] For example, most hymns praise God for being

---

29. Futato states, "It is helpful to read that psalm both as being spoken *by* Christ and as speaking *about* Christ" (ibid., 174). He also develops how Christ can be seen in each of the categories (175–81). For example, laments, thanksgivings, and wisdom align with

Creator and Redeemer. These themes find fulfillment in Christ as our Re-creator and Redeemer through his person and work. In laments, we see Christ as one who has experienced all of life's trials and tribulations for us. Without sin, he nonetheless suffered and died for sin so we would have the promise of an eternity without trial or tribulation. Thus, the psalm's category will reveal some aspect of Christ's person and work or our need for his person and work.

- Relate the CFC to the gospel.
  - Christ as the penalty payer?
  - Christ as the probation preserver?
  - Christ as the power provider?
  - Christ as the passion producer?
- Reformulate your sermon proposition, focusing the indicative on Christ and the gospel.

Layer Three: Discovering how the gospel should transform my hearers and me.

- How does the problem of the psalm connect with my hearers and me?
- How does the solution of the psalm connect with Christ and the gospel?
- In light of the text and the gospel, how should my hearers and I respond?
- So what? Now what?
- Do these answers correspond with my sermon proposition? If not, revise.

the "by Christ" perspective as we address Jesus as Lord of the covenant. Hymns and royal psalms align better with the "about Christ" perspective as we address Jesus as Servant of the covenant.

SAMPLE SERMON: OLD TESTAMENT NARRATIVE TEXT

The following sample is an early sermon I prepared when I was first learning about Christ-centered interpretation and preaching. Though we can't here discuss the linguistic analysis of the Hebrew text, let's examine the literary features of the narrative and attempt some preliminary conclusions regarding the meaning and purpose of the text.

Before reading the sermon, read the Scripture text below, noticing the characteristic pattern of a Hebrew narrative to discover the original author's intention: initial peace, entrance of conflict, escalation, and complications involved in resolving the conflict, climax of conflict, resolution, and finally, peace again.

Text: Exodus 17:1–7:

¹ All the congregation of the people of Israel moved on from the wilderness of Sin by stages, according to the commandment of the LORD, and camped at Rephidim, but there was no water for the people to drink. ² Therefore the people quarreled with Moses and said, "Give us water to drink." And Moses said to them, "Why do you quarrel with me? Why do you test the LORD?" ³ But the people thirsted there for water, and the people grumbled against Moses and said, "Why did you bring us up out of Egypt, to kill us and our children and our livestock with thirst?" ⁴ So Moses cried to the LORD, "What shall I do with this people? They are almost ready to stone me." ⁵ And the LORD said to

Moses, "Pass on before the people, taking with you some of the elders of Israel, and take in your hand the staff with which you struck the Nile, and go. ^{6} Behold, I will stand before you there on the rock at Horeb, and you shall strike the rock, and water shall come out of it, and the people will drink." And Moses did so, in the sight of the elders of Israel. ^{7} And he called the name of the place Massah and Meribah, because of the quarreling of the people of Israel, and because they tested the LORD by saying, "Is the LORD among us or not?"

What did you notice regarding the plot and the people involved? The primary "problem" of this story is the issue of the Israelites dying of thirst during their wilderness wanderings. The "solution" to this problem occurs when the rock is struck and water is provided for the Israelites. This provision of God encourages the Israelites to maintain their faith and trust in their faithful God who rescues them in time of need. You can already begin to see wonderful ingredients of a sermon here, as we make the "turn" to application, calling on people today to trust God during their "desert" experiences because he is the one who faithfully provides.

At this point, we need to ask: If this were the sermon proposition, would it be any different from what a rabbi in a Jewish synagogue might preach to his congregation? How do we find Christ and the gospel in this text? Once we do that, how do we then apply it to God's people today?

Read through the sermon, noticing not only how some of the linguistic, literary, and life-setting features add more meaning and texture to the sermon but also how discerning the Divine Author's intention in Christ transforms the sermon from a mere moral tale to a transforming gospel proclamation of grace.

"Rock of Ages"
© Julius J. Kim [30]

INTRODUCTION

"Rock of Ages cleft for me, let me hide myself in Thee."[31]

It's funny how specific songs conjure up particular emotions in me. One such song is the hymn "Rock of Ages." Whenever I sing it, at church or at home, my thoughts fly back to my youth, sitting with my grandmother, listening to her sing this hymn as I eagerly ate the after-school snack she had just prepared for me. Later in life, as she lay dying from cancer, we would sing this hymn together, finding strength and assurance from our God the Rock—especially during seasons of life that were anything but stable.

This hymn, however, always confused me. The first lines of the hymn allude back to the images found in Exodus 33. There is the great Moses up on Sinai, asking God to show him his glory. Knowing that Moses could not stand his overwhelming glory, God places Moses in a cleft in the rock, turns him around, and then shields him by his hand as the full *shekinah* glory of God passed by. God thus reveals himself to Moses in this awesome way, promising his powerful and protective presence to his people. So naturally I would expect the next lines of the hymn to extol God for his powerful prescence in our lives. But how do the next lines go?

---

30. This sermon was originally published in Dennis E. Johnson, ed., *Heralds of the King: Christ-Centered Sermons in the Tradition of Edmund P. Clowney* (Wheaton, Ill.: Crossway, 2009), 87–99. Used by permission of Crossway, a publishing ministry of Good News Publishers, Wheaton, IL 60187, www.crossway.org.
31. Augustus Toplady, "Rock of Ages."

"Let the water and the blood, from Thy wounded side which flowed,
Be of sin the double cure; cleanse me from its guilt and power."

Why suddenly the imagery of the cross? Is Augustus Toplady seeing something in Exodus 33 that I'm not seeing? How does being in the cleft of the rock lead to the cross? This first verse of this hymn always perplexed me until I read another passage in the book of Exodus—chapter 17, verses 1–7. For in Exodus 17 we come face-to-face with another Rock, the "Rock of Ages." We read in Psalm 95, verses 6–11:

"Oh come, let us worship and bow down; let us kneel before the LORD, our Maker! For He is our God, and we are the people of his pasture, and the sheep of his hand. Today, if you hear His voice, do not harden your hearts, as at Meribah, as on the day at Massah in the wilderness, when your fathers put me to the test and put me to the proof, though they had seen my work. For forty years I loathed that generation and said, 'They are a people who go astray in their heart and they have not known my ways.' Therefore I swore in my wrath, 'They shall not enter my rest.'"

As the psalmist here describes this important event in the history of the Israelites, he warns his readers not to follow in the hard-heartedness of their forefathers who grumbled their way throughout the wilderness wanderings. The psalmist goes out of his way to mention the names Massah, which means "trial," and Meribah, which means "strife." For this is no ordinary drama in the history of Moses and the people of Israel. He wants his reader to remember back in the Torah to Exodus 17, where the Israelites decided to take God ... to court.

And as you will soon see, a legal drama will unfold here in the desert courtroom of Massah and Meribah. In this story, you will see three major legal elements unfold: a charge will be presented; a verdict will be rendered; and a sentence will be executed.

THE CHARGE

Verse 2 sets the scene in this desert courtroom: "Therefore the people quarreled with Moses and said, 'Give us water to drink.' And Moses said to them, 'Why do you quarrel with me? Why do you test the LORD?'" The plaintiffs — the people of Israel — enter the courtroom. Then comes the defendant — Moses, the covenant mediator for God. How can I say this? The people actually bring a legal charge against Moses. The word used translated "quarrel" (Hebrew *rib*) has the connotation of litigation or contention. It is used elsewhere in Scripture in legal contexts with the meaning "to bring suit." In the Prophets, for example, it is used to express the lawsuit that God brought against Israel because they broke his covenant.

Who exactly is being charged? The charge is brought against the covenant mediator Moses *and* God himself. Moses replies "Why do you *contend* with me?" and "Why do you *test* the LORD?" God, via Moses, is being accused of abandoning Israel to die of thirst in the desert. So you must picture it in your minds: Here they are in the hot and arid Sinai peninsula. The scorching sun bakes as it penetrates through the thin cloths wrapped around their heads. Hot winds blow sand into the dry cracks on their faces, searing every portion of their skin. And in this parched land we call the Sinai, weary bodies that have been traveling for weeks become easily dehydrated. So the people cry out for water: "Give us water to drink!" And behind this plea is a charge. They bring an accusation with them. This is no ordinary complaint.

What exactly is the charge? In legal language, this is a breach of contract, otherwise known as treason. In this case, a failure to uphold a promise: the promise that God would be their God and they would be his people. Given to their great-great-grandfather Abraham, this promise stipulated that God would deliver them from bondage and multiply them as the sands on the seashore. "But now look ... we're about to die! Are you among us or not?" Furthermore, in verse 4 we read that Moses fears stoning, which was one of the sentences for treason, betrayal, disloyalty.

So instead of leaving the future up to chance, they decide to take matters into their own hands. They cry out, "You've broken your promise ... I'm not sure if I can trust you, we're taking you to court. We want out of this relationship. We want to control our own future. We don't need you anymore. We want a divorce."

But lest we become too harsh with the Israelites, let's stop and think about it. If we're honest with ourselves, I'm sure you've been in situations when you felt like nothing was going right, when it seemed that God had indeed abandoned you. Recently in my own life I struggled with the same emotions that plagued the Israelites. Holding my grief-stricken wife after a miscarriage, unable to utter a single word, I began to question in my heart, "Where are *you*, Lord? Why give us a baby, only to take it away after just eleven weeks? Are you among us or not?" These are real and honest feelings.

The charge has been recorded. The arguments have been given. What's next?

THE VERDICT

Moses is told by the Lord in verse 5: "Pass on before the people, taking with you some of the elders of Israel and take in your hand the staff with which you struck the Nile, and go."

Two things are significant about this.

First, as Moses walks ahead of the people, everyone knows that the verdict is "Guilty." Guilty as charged. How do we know that? Because Moses goes up with his staff. The people recognize the severity of the matter, for they see their leader Moses walking before them with the staff. This was no ordinary walking stick. This was the staff that was used to strike the Nile, turning it into blood. When Moses struck the Nile, it was a strike of judgment. The Nile River turned to blood in judgment of Egypt's gods and Egypt's disobedience. So now we see Moses going up, not as a criminal but as a judge. The staff will be used once again to bring justice. This staff was distinctive, for it symbolized God's direct power and judgment.

But another important element demonstrates the serious legal context of the setting. With whom does Moses go ahead of the people? In verse 5 we read that Moses is told by God to take along some of the elders of Israel. Why are they necessary? Again, because of the legal context of this situation, they must formally serve as a jury who will help deliberate this case. The air was probably thick with anticipation. Can you imagine what the Israelites were feeling? "There goes Moses, and he's carrying that ... that staff! And there go the elders too." The tension must have been palpable. It must have felt like that awkward, uncomfortable feeling you get when you know something bad is going to happen.

But who exactly is the guilty party? Is it Moses? After all, they grumbled against Moses. Is it God? They did put the Lord to the test. But has Moses, or in this case God, been unfaithful?

The Israelites had just recently witnessed one of the most incredible events in the history of their people—an event they would pass down from generation to generation. As they were fleeing Pharoah and his soldiers, the Lord miraculously opened up the Red Sea and allowed them to pass through the sea untouched! And as the last Israelite stepped up on the opposite shore, the Lord engulfed the Egyptians with a mighty roar of the waves. There they stood—*hearing* the cries of the soldiers, *seeing* the dead wash up on the shore, *tasting* the victory of the Lord. *Tangibly* the Lord had shown them his great love and protection. There's more. This is not the first time they have been thirsty. The Lord had already healed the bitter water in Exodus 15. Furthermore, he had provided manna and quail in chapter 16.

Time and time again the Lord has been there for them, yet at the first sign of trouble, they doubt. At the first sign of trouble, they sow their seeds of doubt to reap complaint and rejection. Yes, the desert is a hot and arid place; it's a place where a person can easily dry up, not just on the outside but also on the inside. Jeremiah was so right when he said that the heart is deceitful above all things. Who can know it? Our hearts are so prone to wander, to turn away at the first sign of trouble.

It is at this point that the irony of this courtroom drama emerges. As Ed Clowney wrote so poignantly regarding this passage: "Israel had just been shown God's care in the provision of manna for their hunger, yet they did not trust him to give water for their thirst. They failed to see that they, not God, were on trial at Rephidim."[32] Indeed, they are the guilty party, who at the first sign of trouble turned their back on God and betrayed the relationship.

The charge, treason. The verdict, guilty. What's next? The sentencing. The punishment for treason is death! But what about God's people? What about the promise that he would

---

32. Clowney, *Unfolding Mystery*, 122.

DISCERNING CHRIST IN THE TEXT

multiply their descendants? What about the promise that the Messiah would come from them? If he wipes out the Israelites, what then? Did God have another plan? Did he have another nation as "plan B"? Justice must be served.

THE SENTENCING

Here at the Rock of Massah and Meribah is the triumph of God's grace. Moses is commanded by the Lord to raise the rod of judgment in verse 6: " 'Behold, I will stand before you there on the rock at Horeb, and you shall strike the rock, and water shall come out of it, and the people will drink'. And Moses did so, in the sight of the elders of Israel." God tells his servant to strike the rock with the staff of judgment. But two seemingly insignificant words appear before this command. Two simple prepositions that make all the difference in not only understanding this passage but also finding comfort in God's grace. God says that he will stand there "before" Moses and that he will stand "on" the rock — "before" and "on." These two prepositions are significant.

First, God declares that he will stand "before" Moses. This is an astonishing statement. Throughout Scripture, especially in legal settings, it is man as the guilty offender who must stand "before" God. It is the guilty criminal who stands "before" the righteous judge. Deuteronomy 19:17 says: "then both parties to the dispute shall appear before the LORD, before the priests and the judges who are in office in those days." In this amazing trial, God says he will stand "before" them, taking the place of the accused, going "before" them as the criminal, waiting on the judgment block.

Second, what does it mean that God will place himself "on" the rock? While the Hebrew word used here (*'al*) can mean "before" or "beside," in light of the context, it is better translated "on" or "upon." Here God stands "on" the rock, symbolically identifying himself with it. And while we sing our songs in church extolling God as our Rock, our sure foundation, a bedrock that never moves, God is called "Rock" elsewhere in Scripture with different connotations.

> Deuteronomy 32:15b: "They abandoned the God who
> made them / and rejected the Rock their Savior" (NIV).
> Deuteronomy 32:18: "You deserted the Rock, who fathered
> you; you forgot the God who gave you birth" (NIV).
> Psalm 78:35: "They remembered that God was their Rock,
> that God Most High was their Redeemer" (NIV).
> Psalm 95:1: "Come, let us sing for joy to the LORD; let us
> shout aloud to the Rock of our salvation" (NIV).

A common theme that emerges from these verses shows "Rock" as having salvific connotations. Yes, we can praise God as a sure foundation that never moves in times of trouble. But here, the Rock has connotations of a Creator, a Savior, a Redeemer. What is God saying to his fickle and faithless people?

In the midst of their doubt, despair, and defiance, Israel would no longer trust that God was in control of their lives. At the first sign of trouble, they turned their backs on God, only to reap judgment for their rebellion and rejection. But in this amazing trial, God is declaring through the use of these simple prepositions that he will take their judgment. Though entirely innocent, he will sacrifice himself and be their substitute. For God's promises to continue, he himself must receive the charge, verdict, and punishment.

So Moses lifts the rod of judgment and strikes the rock on which God stands and with which he is symbollically identified. What is the result? As a result of the striking of the rock, water flows out. Not just any water, but life-sustaining water. Water that not only satisfies the mouth but enlivens the soul. For the rock at Massah is not just any old rock; it is the Rock of Ages. For in the fullness of time, Paul would write about the Israelites that they "all drank the same spiritual drink. For they drank from the spiritual Rock that followed them, and the Rock was Christ" (1 Cor 10:4).

So here the rock at Massah and Meribah is a type of Christ— a preview of the full drama that will reveal God himself coming in Jesus for frail and fragile, faithless and defiant people like you and me, who sometimes day after day, week after week, struggle with making sense of it all when bad things happen. And when bad things happen, God calls us to remember this rock, the Rock of Ages, who was struck for us so that we might drink fully from the great river of life that flows from his throne (Rev 22:1–2).

When Jesus died on the cross and the sword was thrust into his side, what poured out? Blood and water (John 19:34). It's no coincidence that there are all these references to water. You see, this is God's message for you, for you who thirst, who go through parched lives, who find yourself often in desert situations—to look to the cross. For when we look to the cross, we see a Savior who loved us so much, that he received the rod of judgment for our rebellion and rejection. We see our Lord, who though innocent, sacrificed himself in our place.

CONCLUSION

This is our God. God loved us so much that he did not spare his own Son, but gave him up for us all, so that we might never thirst again. Is the Lord among us? He not only is among us; he has become like us in the glory of the incarnation to endure the punishment of the cross as the wages of our sins: the sin of our hardened hearts, the sin of our independence, the sin of our rejection. What kind of love is this? What kind of grace is this? What kind of provision is this?

In a world that threatens to turn our eyes away from the Rock who created us and redeemed us, let us throw off everything that hinders and turn our eyes to the author and finisher of our faith. Let us "turn our eyes to Jesus and look full at this wonderful face. For the things of this world will grow strangely dim in the light of his glory and grace."[33] Amen.

---

33. Helen H. Lemmel, "Turn Your Eyes upon Jesus" (1922).

CHAPTER 5

PREACHING CHRIST FROM THE NEW TESTAMENT

It would seem counterintuitive to have a chapter on preaching Christ from the NT. After all, isn't Christ found all over the NT? How difficult can it be to connect the truths of the text about Christ and then apply it to our hearers? Surely it isn't difficult to preach the gospel from the Gospels, is it?

Surprisingly, the NT is often preached in ways that are not true, good, or beautiful. Take for example, sermons from passages that present Jesus as a model of compassion and mercy. Indeed, the Gospels are replete with stories that extol Jesus' sensitivity and sympathy to many with physical, emotional, and psychological needs. Clearly the "moral" of those stories is to emulate Jesus as we demonstrate Christlike kindness and love.

But is that all? Is the main point of these NT stories Jesus' exemplary love and mercy? Is this what the writers of the Gospels had in mind when they collected and recorded all the stories and sayings of Jesus? Certainly, emulating Jesus' love and compassion to those around us is a commendable way to behave and a beautiful thing to behold. It is not, however, completely true to both the human author's original intention and the Divine Author's gospel intention. Let me explain.

The human authors of the NT, like those of the OT, wrote with a central idea and specific purpose in mind. As such, everything they wrote needs to be interpreted in light of their original intent, considering the features that accompany their historical context and literary and redemptive purposes. Sound familiar? It should be. It's the same methodology that we used for our OT texts. The focus of this chapter is to outline the features found in the NT gospels and ethical/law passages and offer some strategies for how to preach Christ from them.[1]

Preaching Christ from the Gospels

Like OT narratives, the Gospels primarily contain stories and discourse—in this case, stories about Jesus and sayings of Jesus. As such, some of the essential literary features found in OT narratives are also present in the Gospels. Examining the people, plot, places, and particulars (see chapter 4) are important for the interpretation and communication of gospel passages. The Gospels are about Jesus, the protagonist and central character. Furthermore, each gospel is essentially one large narrative that climaxes with the death and resurrection of Jesus for the problem of sin. Each preaching passage must be seen and interpreted in light of this gospel plot dynamic created by both the human and divine authors.

In addition to these characteristics of the Gospels, there are some distinct features that preachers must consider when interpreting and preaching from these texts: gospel genre, purpose and occasion, and subgenres found in the Gospels. Let's examine these in turn.

Features of the Gospels: Gospel Genre

What is gospel genre? This may seem like a simple question, but in fact it's quite complicated. This is because the Gospels are more complex

---

1. Again, we are limited to these two primary genres. See the bibliography for further resources regarding other NT genres, such as apocalyptic literature. For example, see the following works for help with preaching Christ from the book of Revelation: Graeme Goldsworthy, *Preaching the Whole Bible as Christian Scripture: The Application of Biblical Theology to Expository Preaching* (Grand Rapids: Eerdmans, 2000), 212–21; Dennis E. Johnson, *Him We Proclaim: Preaching Christ from All the Scriptures* (Phillipsburg, N.J.: P&R, 2007), 382–95.

than they appear; after all, Jesus didn't write a gospel, and there are four of them.[2] Though the gospels of Matthew, Mark, Luke, and John may be considered the easiest sections of the Bible to read and understand, they actually contain a wide variety of literary forms and conventions that make them difficult to classify and interpret.[3]

Take, for example, the fact that the Gospels are essentially two types of literature: historical narrative (stories) and teaching discourse (instruction) — the works and words of Jesus. Seems simple enough. What complicates matters is that these stories of Jesus contain within them unique subgenres, such as parables. Furthermore, the instructions of Jesus can be further categorized into subgenres such as legal pronouncements and apocalyptic discourses.

Where can we turn to for help? Part of understanding the form and function of gospel genre is found in the OT. Gospel genre has roots in the OT, specifically the book of Exodus, which can be called "The Gospel according to Moses."[4] We will discover that one is a precursor to the other once we examine their thematic focus and literary structure.

In terms of thematic focus, the Pentateuch (the five books of Moses) primarily contains historical narrative and divine law. In fact, according to Meredith Kline, this combination of history and law was a regular feature of ancient Near Eastern treaty genre during the time of Moses. Similarly, the Gospels contain the same themes of historical stories and the authoritative sayings of Jesus. Second, in terms of literary structure, genre parallels exist between Exodus and the Gospels, especially when viewed through the context of the covenant between God and his people. Both recount the birth and public career of a covenant mediator: Moses (Ex 1–18) and Jesus. Both narratives place prominence on

---

2. Gordon D. Fee and Douglas Stuart, *How to Read the Bible for All Its Worth* (Grand Rapids: Zondervan, 1982), 103.
3. The book of Acts will have many similar features as these gospels, as it is the second volume to the gospel of Luke. For an excellent resource on Acts, see Dennis E. Johnson, *The Message of Acts in the History of Redemption* (Phillipsburg, N.J.: P&R, 1997). For our purposes, we will focus on these first four books in the NT.
4. I am indebted to Meredith G. Kline for this section: "The Old Testament Origins of the Gospel Genre," *WTJ Westminster Theological Journal* 38 (1975/76): 1–27. It is also found as an appendix in his book *The Structure of Biblical Authority*, 2nd ed. (Grand Rapids: Eerdmans, 1972), 172–203.

the inauguration of the covenant: at Sinai (Ex 19–40) and at Calvary. Thus, the OT book of Exodus and the NT gospels are a fulfillment form of covenantal history. Kline summarizes: "A document of the gospel genre is one that has as its literary center of gravity an account of the inauguration of a divine covenant, set within a record of the covenant mediator's career and of the law of the community promulgated by the mediator."[5] Christ is a new Moses, leading God's people in a new exodus, with new covenant stipulations.

So with this background context in mind, what is gospel genre? First, gospel genre is an *announcement*. This first characteristic is related to the way "gospel" was used in the NT. "Gospel" means to proclaim or to announce. As such, it has a public character.[6] Thus, the gospel does not just supply information but is a clarion call for some form of response. It is an announcement with massive implications. Why?

Because second, gospel genre is an *announcement of good news*, that salvation is found in Jesus Christ alone. This second characteristic is linked to the meaning of the word itself. As was described in chapter 3, the noun *euangelion* in the Gospels and Acts involves a proclaimed announcement that something good has transpired that has transformative repercussions. It is rooted in the redemption and deliverance that is promised in Isaiah 52, which has significance for the here and now. It is the good news that Jesus has come to bring forgiveness and new life. It is the written form of the heralded good news about Jesus, also known as the *kerygma*.[7]

---

5. Meredith G. Kline, *The Structure of Biblical Authority*, 2nd ed. (Grand Rapids: Eerdmans, 1972), 181. Interestingly, Martin Hengel (*Acts and the History of Earliest Christianity* [Philadelphia: Fortress, 1980]) makes a similar point with respect to the genre of Acts. Its closest parallels/antecedents are not Hellenistic historiography or Hellenistic romance, but OT prophetic and covenantal history.
6. See chapter 3. See also Greidanus, *Modern Preacher*, 266–67.
7. *Kērygma* is the Greek word meaning "proclamation, announcement, or preaching." With the publication of C. H. Dodd's book *The Apostolic Preaching and Its Developments* (London: Hodder & Stoughton, 1936), the word has taken on a technical meaning in NT scholarship. In his book, Dodd attempted to distill the heart and soul of apostolic preaching found primarily in the book of Acts. He argued that the heart of apostolic preaching included the following six components: (1) the age of fulfillment foretold by the prophets has dawned; (2) this is because of Jesus Christ's birth, life, ministry, death, and resurrection; (3) because of his resurrection, Jesus is the exalted head of new Israel; (4) the Holy Spirit in the church is the sign of Christ's present power and glory; (5) the

The third characteristic is linked to the movement of OT history and prophecy, namely, that the Gospels are the continuation of progressive redemptive history. Thus, it is an *announcement of good news set within God's history*. The gospel event, which is the saving event accomplished through Christ's life, death, and resurrection, undergoes development within the gospel narratives.[8] Thus, there is a history to the unfolding of the message and the events in the Gospels. What this means, for example, is that even as the gospel is stated at the beginning of Jesus' ministry in the gospel of Mark, it is framed in words that do not tell the whole story (Mark 1:14–15). We need to consider where there are continuities between the narratives of the Gospels and ourselves and where there are discontinuities. There exists not only a time and culture gap but also a theological or redemptive-historical gap. Remember, when we read everything Jesus says up to his death, it is said in anticipation of his death and resurrection. Instead of simply assuming that the teachings of Jesus stand for all time as normative instruction to the church, we have to exercise great care in our interpretation of past narratives and how we apply it to ourselves in the present.

Remember, genre analysis is important. Classifying the genre of the text enables us to clarify the meaning of the text.[9] If the Gospels share similar features as those in stories found in the OT, specifically Exodus, we need to approach the Gospels with similar expectations, not only as literary presentation but also as historical explanation and theological communication. The gospel writers are explaining the stories of Jesus for the purposes of sharing the good news of salvation that can be found only in him. The Gospels, then, are about the gospel, Jesus himself, who secured redemption in the real history of his life, death, and resurrection. Thus, as the OT narratives were communicated within the theological context of God's covenantal relationship with his people, so

---

messianic age will reach consummation in Christ's return; and (6) a call to repentance includes the offer of forgiveness, the Holy Spirit, and salvation. See also Robert Guelich, "The Gospel Genre," in *The Gospel and the Gospels*, ed. Peter Stuhlmacher (Grand Rapids: Eerdmans, 1991), 173–208.
8. Adapted from Goldsworthy, *Preaching the Whole Bible*, 223ff.
9. See chapter 2.

too the Gospels are given so that all may come into a real relationship with the Lord and Servant of the covenant, Jesus Christ.

Features of the Gospels: Purpose

That there are four gospels, three of which are very similar (the Synoptic Gospels of Matthew, Mark, and Luke), reveals another aspect of their features that is important for interpretation and communication: purpose. In God's mysterious providence, four authoritative presentations about the significance of Jesus' life and teaching have been recorded and handed down to us. These gospels were written to communicate the transformative story of Jesus with very unique purposes. Each gospel writer was writing not only to record their inspired version of Jesus' life, death, and resurrection but also to pass along this message to specific communities of faith. They provide for us two truths: the historical yet relevant good news about Jesus, and the hermeneutical model for us to model for our hearers today. Let me explain.

Studying the purposes for which the evangelists wrote will help us in discovering the truth, goodness, and beauty of their writings—the truth of the historical events, the goodness of what those events signify, and the beauty of their literary art. The authors of the Gospels provide clues to their purpose, not only for their entire gospel but also for certain passages. Discovering this authorial intent for both the parts as well as the whole of the gospel can be very helpful in determining the content's meaning and significance. While all the Gospels share similar themes focusing on the person of Jesus Christ and the kingdom of God, which he brings through his life, death, and resurrection, each of the Gospels has unique ways of revealing that purpose. Let's examine the three different ways the gospel writers reveal their purposes: through their text, their literary structure, and the occasion that prompted their writing.

1. Text: Purpose statements for both the whole gospel as well as for specific passages can be found explicitly within the *text* itself. Two of the evangelists explicitly state their purposes for writing their gospels. Luke states at the beginning of his gospel that his goal is to confirm the faith of those who believe in Jesus.

Inasmuch as many have undertaken to compile a narrative of the things that have been accomplished among us, just as those who from the beginning were eyewitnesses and ministers of the word have delivered them to us, it seemed good to me also, having followed all things closely for some time past, to write an orderly account for you, most excellent Theophilus, that you may have certainty concerning the things you have been taught. (Luke 1:1–4)

John's purpose in his gospel is to draw people to faith in Jesus Christ.

Now Jesus did many other signs in the presence of the disciples, which are not written in this book; but these are written so that you may believe that Jesus is the Christ, the Son of God, and that by believing you may have life in his name. (John 20:30–31)

In both of these examples, the gospel writers reveal their overall purpose in writing—to establish and promote faith in Jesus Christ. These broad purpose statements then provide the context for interpreting specific texts.

Purposes of specific passages can also be discovered from the text. Like the authors of OT narrative, gospel writers will sometimes interject their own commentary on the narrative. As this is not a common feature found in narratives, readers must take notice. In Luke 18:1, for example, Luke states the purpose of the parable of Jesus he is about to describe: "And he told them a parable to the effect that they ought always to pray and not lose heart." Furthermore, the gospel author will reveal his purpose by recording specific statements. For example, in Mark 2:10, Jesus states unequivocally the purpose of the miracle he is about to perform on the paralyzed man on the mat: "But that you may know that the Son of Man has authority on earth to forgive sins." Thus, there are often clues within the text itself that will help you determine the meaning and significance of the passage.

2. Literary structure: The purposes of the Gospels as a whole as well as for specific texts can be inferred through literary structure. Take, for example, Mark's gospel.[10] Between the introduction (1:1–15) and

---

10. For the literary structure of the other gospels, see D. A. Carson, Douglas J. Moo, and Leon Morris, *Introduction to the Old Testament,* 2nd ed. (Grand Rapids: Zondervan, 2005).

conclusion (16:20), the gospel of Mark is binary in structure. That is, the two main parts of his gospel essentially answer two questions, "Who is this Jesus?" (1:16–8:26) and "What did Jesus come to do?" (8:30–15:47). The hinge that connects these two questions is the passage that describes Peter's confession that Jesus is the Christ (8:27–30). Thus, Mark's literary structure provides clues to his overall purpose in writing his gospel: revealing who Jesus is and what he came to do so others will confess him as the chosen one, the Messiah-King, the Christ, who will save us from our sin. Knowing this overarching literary structure of the entire book helps frame all the specific passages within the gospel.

The purposes of the author can also be determined by the way he structures groups of stories together. For example, in Mark 2:1–3:6 we find a series of stories all sharing a similar theme of opposition to Jesus. In these four narratives, we find that the opposition to Jesus intensifies as we move from story to story. Furthermore, in Mark 4:35–5:43, we find another grouping of stories all sharing a common topic: the miracles of Jesus. As you examine these narratives, you quickly can see the intensification of Jesus' sovereignty over all things, from a stormy sea to the "storm" of death. Thus, this literary structure of grouping stories together provides us with clues to the author's intent.

3. Occasion: Another feature that will help you determine the purpose of the gospel, in part or in whole, is the occasion for writing. In addition to your linguistic and literary analyses of the text, you also must examine the life-setting contexts of the text. As with OT narratives, the Gospels were written with specific historical, ethnic, religious, and cultural contexts in mind—not only for those participating in the events themselves but also for the original recipients of the Gospels. When the inspired authors put together their gospels, they recorded what they heard and saw in light of those to whom they were writing. Matthew, for example, wrote as a Jew for Jews. Luke, the Gentile doctor, wrote for Gentiles.

You need to keep track of these contexts in light of two primary audiences: those who are participants and those who are recipients. One group listened to Jesus speak and witnessed many of his deeds prior to his death and resurrection. The other group is hearing stories and reading about Jesus within the context of the implications of Jesus' death, resurrection, exaltation, and blessing of the Holy Spirit. Though they are not too far removed in time, space, and history, these two audiences nonetheless have unique cultural and redemptive historical features. As such, it is important to distinguish the participants in the Gospels from the recipients of the Gospels when it comes to their redemptive-historical time frame. This analysis will aid in your discovery not only of the FCF and the CFC for previous audiences but also for your hearers today.

Features of the Gospels: Gospel Subgenres

Several unique features exist in some of the subgenres found in the Gospels. Knowing these features will help you in your interpretation and communication of those texts.[11]

- Birth narratives (Matt 1–2; Luke 1–2): Several themes are central to understanding this subgenre: (1) These narratives focus on Jesus as the *fulfillment* of OT prophetic promise. (2) They also reveal the scandal and wonder of the *virgin birth*. (3) These sections foreshadow the *suffering* that awaits Jesus. (4) The birth narratives also foreshadow Jesus' mission including Gentiles. These traits provide contextual clues to the interpretation of passages found in this subgenre.

- Miracle narratives: Many of the miracle stories in the Gospels share two characteristic traits. They are stories that *authenticate* the identity of the king (John 5:36; 10:38; Acts 2:22) and *illustrate* the nature of his kingdom (John 6:26–27, 30–33; Acts 3:7–8, 21). Thus, Jesus' authority and power are on display to reveal different aspects of his reign and rule as King over his kingdom. You must ask, how does this miracle story reveal him as King? What does this story teach us about his kingdom?

---

11. For insight into preaching Christ-centered sermons from gospel narratives, parables, doctrinal discourse, ethical application, Wisdom Literature, and prophetic-apocalyptic visions, see Johnson, *Him We Proclaim*, 331–95.

- Controversy narratives: The stories in this subgenre, in which Jesus finds himself in quarrels with the religious leaders of his day, share several attributes (Mark 2:1 – 3:6). They address the question of Jesus' *authority* as King, the *constituency* of his kingdom, and the *standards* of the kingdom. They answer these questions: Who is the King? Who belongs to his kingdom? How do kingdom dwellers live? These attributes and questions provide clues to the meaning and significance of the text.

- Parables: This subgenre and OT Wisdom Literature function similarly in that they use common life experiences and objects to teach spiritual truths. When put on the lips of Jesus, however, these memorable illustrations reveal specific truths about himself as an uncommon King of the promised kingdom of God. This feature of the unexpected nature of Jesus as King over his kingdom shapes the interpretation of many parables. This is because many parables function in the context of the paradigmatic parable found in Mark 4:1 – 9 (also Matt 13:1 – 9 and Luke 8:4 – 8). Here we find the story of the sower that spreads seed into multiple soils. This parable reveals how different hearts (soils) respond to the Word (seed) of God proclaimed. More importantly, it describes the surprising way in which Jesus brings his kingdom in two unexpected stages. Though the Jews expected a Messiah of political and religious power (as a reaper), Jesus came in apparent weakness (as a sower). This is the pattern of the kingdom that Jesus brings: suffering precedes glory.[12] These themes help us interpret and preach the parables.

- Passion narratives: Found at the end of each gospel, the narratives in this subgenre describe the suffering and death of Jesus. They possess certain themes that provide the context for their interpretation. First, all of the Gospels are structured to climax with the stories surrounding Jesus' suffering and death. Someone

---

12. See Herman Ridderbos, *The Coming of the Kingdom* (Phillipsburg, N.J.: P&R, 1962), 129–34. See also Craig L. Blomberg, *Interpreting the Parables* (Downers Grove, Ill.: InterVarsity, 1990).

once said, "All Gospels are passion narratives with long introductions." In terms of literary structure and significance for interpretation, that statement is helpful. Second, clues pointing forward to the passion narratives are found early in each gospel. From Jesus' words to his deeds, these earlier passages provide insights into the nature and effect of his suffering and death for us.

Strategies for Preaching Christ from the Gospels

Layer One: Discovering the original purpose for the original audience through linguistic, literary, and life-setting analysis.[13]

- Pray for comprehension and transformation.
- Read the passage several times in its context.
- Formulate a preliminary sermon proposition in a consequential format.
- Linguistic Analysis:
  - Translate your passage from the Greek, using dictionaries and other helps.
  - Identify the syntax and structure of the passage.
  - Compare and contrast parallel passages found in the other gospels.
- Literary Analysis:
  - Examine the text in light of the chapter, the entire gospel (especially as it climaxes in the death and resurrection of Jesus), and the rest of the Bible.
  - Analyze the narrative genre: people, plot, places, and particulars.[14]
  - Anaylze the gospel genre: How does this passage announce the gospel?
- Life-Setting Analysis:
  - Investigate the historical and cultural context, using commentaries and other helps.

---

13. These steps are described in detail in chapter 2.
14. See chapter 4.

- ◆ Determine the purpose through clues in the text, structure, or occasion.
- ■ Discover the fallen-condition focus (FCF):
  - ◆ What is the primary problem of the plot? Does it cohere with the solution?
  - ◆ What spiritual concerns are connected to this problem?
  - ◆ What concerns do my hearers share with the original hearers?
- ■ Reformulate your sermon proposition. Ask, What is the redemptive act of God in this narrative? How do characters in the narrative respond to this? How should they (and we) respond?

Layer Two: Discerning how this passage points to Christ.

- ■ Compare the covenant themes in this passage with those found in passages before and after it.
- ■ Discern your Christ-focused connection (CFC), usually found in the resolution to the problem of the plot.
  - ◆ Type fulfillment: A person or action in the narrative is a symbol. Through analogy and escalation, there is fulfillment in Christ.[15]
  - ◆ Law fulfillment: An ethical principle in the narrative that cannot be satisfied forces the reader to find fulfillment in and through Christ.
- ■ Relate the CFC to the gospel: You need to assess the relation between the event or narrative and the gospel's climax, the cross and resurrection. How does this event connect to the good news of Christ's atonement and resurrection? Does the solution of the problem in this narrative highlight Christ as penalty payer, probation preserver, power provider, and/or passion producer?
- ■ Reformulate your sermon proposition. Revise, asking, How is God's redemptive act seen in light of the gospel?

---

15. Typology is discussed in chapter 3.

Layer Three: Discovering how the gospel should transform my hearers and me.

- How does the problem of the narrative connect with my hearers and me? Review the characters and their response to the aspect of the gospel being revealed in the passage. Where do hearers find themselves in the story?
- How does the solution of the narrative connect with Christ and the gospel?
- In light of the text and the gospel, how should my hearers and I respond? Where do hearers find themselves in the story?
- So what? Now what?
- Do these answers correspond with my sermon proposition? If not, revise.

Preaching Christ from Ethical/Law Passages

At first glance, the task of preaching from the ethical passages of Scripture may appear straightforward. After all, reminding our church members to not lie, cheat, or steal, for example, is what many people believe is the primary role of the preacher. We can certainly agree that moral uprightness is a positive benefit for both individuals as well as for society at large. Preachers can and should use all the laws and rules found in the Bible to help promote personal and relational harmony. But is that all? Is the preaching of ethical/law texts this simple?

Preaching this genre actually presents many challenges. It is difficult to apply ancient standards to modern situations. Furthermore, preachers need to be aware of the potential danger of interpreting and preaching ethical texts in such a way so as to promote legalism on the one hand or license on the other. Law texts can be preached in such a way as to produce in people a belief that their being made right with God (justification) is based on their obedience. What the Bible teaches, however, is that their standing before God (justification) as well as their growing in holiness (sanctification) is all based on God's grace and not on their obedience. In fact, Scripture and our own experiences teach us that perfect, personal, and perpetual obedience to God's laws is impossible. Thus, law passages have the potential to be preached legalistically, undermining the Bible's unified message that the Christian life is based on the work of Gods' grace alone, through the work of Christ alone, received by faith alone.

Another potential problem that emerges from preaching law texts is that it may be seen as providing a warrant for licentious behavior. The logic goes like this: since Christ fulfilled all the laws in his perfect covenant-keeping life and sacrificial covenant-curse-bearing death, ethical precepts no longer apply to those who have been united to him. Also known as antinomianism, this tendency views the laws of God as being no longer applicable due to the finished work of Christ. What this position misses, however, is that while we are justified by faith alone through Christ alone, that faith is never alone. True faith in Christ, while resting completely on the vicarious obedience and suffering of Christ, also involves growing in holiness, with the law of God as our guide as the Holy Spirit transforms us day by day into Christ's image.

Features of Ethical/Law Passages

In light of these challenges, what are some features of ethical/law texts that we need to be aware of so we can interpret and preach them accurately and faithfully?[16] The features described below and the strategies that follow are generally applicable to texts found in both the OT and the NT.

Texts in this biblical genre are characterized by the "ethical standards God has for his people."[17] These laws that can be found in both Testaments are commands given by God himself or through his messengers. Thus, they can be the covenant demands of God to Adam in

---

16. See the following helpful works for more on interpreting and preaching texts in this genre: Edmund P. Clowney, *How Jesus Transforms the Ten Commandments*, ed. R. Clowney Jones (Phillipsburg, N.J.: P&R, 2007); Goldsworthy, *Preaching the Whole Bible*, 152–66; Daniel M. Doriani, *Putting the Truth to Work: The Theory and Practice of Biblical Application* (Phillipsburg, N.J.: P&R, 2001), 240–304; Johnson, *Him We Proclaim*, 293–303, 360–67.
17. Dan McCartney and Charles Clayton. *Let the Reader Understand: A Guide to Interpreting and Applying the Bible* (Wheaton, Ill.: Victor, 1994), 213.

the garden, for example, as well as the moral exhortations the apostle Paul gives to the church in Corinth. Since every ethical precept comes from God, the righteous law-giver, biblical writers often categorize all the commands of God under the singular title "law of God."

1. Law: Principles, Rules, and Instructions

Dan Doriani helpfully reminds us that biblical laws provide both general *principles* as well as specific *rules* that govern morality.[18] Principles are broad commands given by God for all humanity, such as the Ten Commandments. Rules are those instructions that seem to be tied to specific cultural contexts, such as the case laws of Israel found in Deuteronomy. Knowing these distinctions will often help the preacher determine the appropriate applicability of the law for his hearers.

The challenge is to determine how laws functioned in their original context and how to apply that to modern hearers, who often live in a very different world. Determining whether the law should be applied identically, analogically, or typologically is a complex task. Moral principles are usually applied identically since the principles transcend time and culture. Case laws, however, are by their nature less transferable since they are applications of general principles in a specific historical and cultural context. These laws are best applied analogically through a determination of the transferable principle underlying the law. Typological interpretation usually deals with those OT laws that pointed forward to their fulfillment through some aspect of Christ's person and work. Thus, one of the most important steps of interpretation is to ask what the law meant, whether principle or rule, to the original hearers and how it ought to be applied to modern hearers.

2. Law: Moral, Civil, and Ceremonial

In the OT, the Hebrew word for law is *torah*, which means *instruction*. These instructions were given in the context of a relationship — a covenant relationship between a holy God and his people. In this relationship, the covenant Lord provides ethical standards that covenant

---

18. Doriani, *Putting the Truth to Work*, 240–41.

servants must obey. Thus, biblical laws reveal the righteousness of God's holy character as well as the qualifications necessary for his servants to be in right relationship with him and with others. The laws that governed the covenant relationship between God and Israel are often categorized under three headings: moral, civil, and ceremonial. Recognizing the category of a biblical law is helpful in the interpretive process.

- *Moral laws* are the eternal standards that God has revealed to his creatures. These laws are binding for all time and for all places. They are usually found in summary form in both Testaments: the Ten Commandments in the OT and the two great commandments of loving God and loving neighbor given by Jesus in the NT. All moral laws are essentially commands to love God or love others.
- *Civil laws* are the judicial and administrative laws God established for the nation of Israel. Unlike moral laws, these laws are no longer binding on an individual Christian or any corporate nation since they were given specifically to the nation of Israel during a specific historical era. Nonetheless, the underlying principles of equity and justice that many of these civil laws express can still provide wise insights for living righteously.
- *Ceremonial laws* regulated the worship and identity of the Israelites. These laws included specific regulations for the priesthood, sacrifices, tabernacle, clothing, and food. As such, they revealed the sacrificial system for Israelite worship, especially for the atonement of their sins, but also the status of being a holy people separated from other nations. The NT reveals that all of these ceremonial laws were shadows and types of Christ (Heb 10:1), prefiguring his person and work. Because of the once-for-all finished work of Christ on the cross for sin, these laws no longer apply to the NT Christian and church.

Thus, biblical laws are the principles, rules, and laws that governed the moral, civil, and religious life of the Israelites in their covenant relationship to God. Seen within the context of this relationship, biblical laws are not just a list of ethical precepts that must be followed but are ultimately part of the way God executes the history of redemption, culminating in the person and work of Christ.

3. Law: The Three "Uses"

In addition to knowing what *categories* of laws exist in the Bible, knowing how they *function* is vital for interpretation. In the history of the church, scholars have shown how the law primarily functioned in the Bible. Though they are listed in various ways, they are often called the "three uses" of the law of God.[19]

- The first use of the law is called the *pedagogical* use. Here the law reveals the holy character and standards of God and our inability to keep the law (Rom 7:7; Gal 3:10–12). Thus, the law functions to drive sinners to Christ, who through his perfect life and sacrificial death saves us from the penalty for not keeping the law.
- The second use of the law is its *civil* purpose. The law in this case functions to curb sin and restrain evil in our world through the threat of judgment and punishment. The Bible teaches that the law of God has been written on all hearts, both believers' and unbelievers', working in the conscience of all to do what is right before God and preventing unrighteousness in society (1 Tim 1:8–10).
- The third use of the law is its *normative* function. Here the law is a guide helping believers grow in their holiness. Grateful for the grace of God that has provided forgiveness of their sins and new life in Christ, believers respond by using the law as a guide for loving obedience. The law reveals what is both pleasing and displeasing to God, prompting believers to obey the law through the power of Christ.

---

19. See the following on the three uses of the law: John Calvin, *Institutes of the Christian Religion*, 2.7.6–13; Louis Berkhof, *Systematic Theology* (1958; revised ed., Grand Rapids: Eerdmans, 1996), 614–15; Michael S. Horton, *The Christian Faith: A Systematic Theology for Pilgrims on the Way* (Grand Rapids: Zondervan, 2011), 674, 678–80.

4. Law: Within Redemptive History

Another helpful category to know when interpreting the law of God is to see how these ethical precepts functioned in their redemptive-historical context. Scriptures teach that man was originally created in the image of God. This image included true knowledge, holiness, and righteousness (Gen 3:10).[20] Adam and Eve knew the law of God, loved the law of God, and obeyed the law of God. Unfortunately, Adam and Eve did not stay in this blessed state. In their rebellion against God's reign and rule, they sinned against God. As a result of their sin, every aspect of man—his mind, heart, and will—became corrupt (Rom 3:10; Gen 6:5; Matt 15:19).[21]

This corruption, the Bible teaches us, affected all mankind since Adam represented all of humanity (Rom 5:12; 3:23).[22] And now all mankind is justly under the wrath and curse of the holy God, deserving death for their sin and inability to keep the law (Rom 6:23).[23] But in his great mercy, God sent his Son, Jesus, to perfectly obey the law of God in our stead. By dying on the cross, he also paid the penalty necessary for breaking the law in our minds, hearts, and lives. Since he was sinless, Jesus was raised from the dead. Through the Spirit, Christ provides believers with the power to know, love, and obey the law as they were originally created to do.

Seen through this redemptive-historical framework, the law of God is not just about changing behavior; it's about transforming the whole person as Christ comes to re-create us into his image of true knowledge, holiness, and righteousness. Now believers, though still sinful, have been transformed and view the law differently. Because of God's faithfulness to the covenant, believers obey his laws out of gratitude for the work of the covenant Lord and servant, Jesus Christ. Obedience is thus a product of the existing covenant relationship. When preaching from ethical/law texts, one of the key steps is to place the law within

---

20. Cf. WCF 4.2.
21. Cf. WCF 6.2.
22. Cf. WCF 6.3.
23. Cf. WCF 6.6.

this redemptive-historical framework. Or, in other words, how does this "imperative" (law) text connect to the "indicative" redemptive-historical context culminating in Christ?

Strategies for Preaching Christ from Ethical/Law Passages

Layer One: Discovering the original purpose for the original audience through linguistic, literary, and life-setting analysis.

- Pray for comprehension and transformation.
- Read the passage several times in its context.
- Formulate a preliminary sermon proposition in a consequential format.
- Linguistic Analysis:
  - Translate your passage from the original Hebrew or Greek, using dictionaries and other helps.
  - Identify the syntax and structure of the passage.
  - Compare and contrast parallel passages found in the other gospels.
- Literary Analysis:
  - Examine the passage in light of the chapter, the book, and the rest of the Bible.
  - Analyze the passage to determine the law/command to the original hearer.
    - Is it a general principle or a rule?
    - Is it in the category of moral, civil, or ceremonial law?
    - Is it primarily about loving God or neighbor?
- Life-Setting Analysis:
  - Investigate the historical and cultural context, using commentaries and other helps.
  - Determine the purpose by asking which "use" of the law is functioning.
    - First use: Is it pedagogical (driving me to Christ for salvation)?
    - Second use: Is it civil (upholding society through justice)?

- Third use: Is it <u>normative (guiding believers to be con-formed to the image of Christ)</u>?
■ Discover the fallen-condition focus (FCF):
  ◆ What is the "problem" of the law (i.e., the inability to keep it perfectly, personally, and perpetually)?
  ◆ How is it described in the context of the original hearer?
  ◆ How is this law transferable to the modern hearer (identical, analogical, typological)?
  ◆ How do we not keep this law?
■ Reformulate your sermon proposition. Ask, What is the redemptive act of God in this narrative? How do characters in the narrative respond to this? How should they (and we) respond?

Layer Two: Discerning how this passage points to Christ.

■ Compare the covenant themes in this passage with those found in passages before and after it.
■ Examine the law in its redemptive historical context.
  ◆ What does the law reveal about God and his holy character?
  ◆ What does the law reveal about me and my sinful character?
  ◆ What does the law reveal about my need for Christ?
■ Discern your Christ-focused connection (CFC):
  ◆ How does the law (imperative) point to Christ (indicative)?
  ◆ Which aspect of Christ does this law highlight (penalty payer, probation preserver, power provider, and/or passion producer)?
■ Relate the CFC to the gospel.
  ◆ Christ as the penalty payer?
  ◆ Christ as the probation preserver?
  ◆ Christ as the power provider?
  ◆ Christ as the passion producer?
■ Reformulate your sermon proposition, focusing the indicative on Christ and the gospel.

Layer Three: Discovering how the gospel should transform my hearers and me.

- How does the "problem" of the law connect with my hearers and me? Review the connection (identical, analogical, or typological).
- How does the "solution" to the law in the gospel transform the law from first use (driving us to Christ for salvation) to the third use (guiding the believer in Christlike character and behavior)?
- In light of the text and the gospel, how should my hearers and I reflect, rejoice, and respond to this law?
- So what? Now what?
- Do these answers correspond with my sermon proposition? If not, revise.

SAMPLE SERMON: NEW TESTAMENT ETHICAL/LAW PASSAGE

The following sermon is an example of how I would interpret and preach an ethical text. As I've mentioned in this chapter, the tendency for many preachers is to structure sermons that center on any one of the many moral commands found in Scripture in this way: (1) discover and explain the moral principle, and then (2) motivate and inspire hearers to obey it. This pattern could easily be duplicated with any or all of the Ten Commandments as well as the myriad of ethical standards extolled in the NT. The problem, of course, is that as marred and sinful humans, we can't perfectly, personally, and perpetually obey. Furthermore, this essential pattern sets up Christianity as yet another religion that demands moral allegiance in order to be accepted, loved, and valued by God. Surely there is another way.

As you read the Scripture text below, what is the primary ethical or moral command that is being expressed? Is it primarily about loving God or loving neighbor? How transferable is it for today's hearers? How does it hint at Christ's perfect person and redemptive work?

Text: Matthew 5:38–42:

38 "You have heard that it was said, 'An eye for an eye and a tooth for a tooth.' 39 But I say to you, Do not resist the one who is evil. But if anyone slaps you on the right cheek, turn to him the other also. 40 And if anyone would sue you and take your tunic, let him have your cloak

as well. [41] And if anyone forces you to go one mile, go with him two miles. [42] Give to the one who begs from you, and do not refuse the one who would borrow from you.

The general principle Jesus is teaching here is that we must love our enemies. Clearly, it is transferable to us today as we struggle with conflict with many around us—even those closest to us. Certainly none of us can obey this command of Jesus perfectly, personally, and perpetually. Is there any hope for those of us who want to obey Jesus' radical call to love our enemies? How does this text connect to Jesus himself? How does the gospel then transform us and our desire to love others?

Read through the sermon, taking special notice of how the life-setting context of the first century provides clarity and cogency to Jesus' words. Feel the tension that is elicited through the first part of the sermon as it becomes clear that none can love our enemies in the way Jesus commands. Indeed, all have sinned and fall short of the glory of God (Rom 3:23). Then notice how that tension is resolved via the gospel of Jesus Christ and how that becomes the key to unlocking not only the Divine Author's intention of the text, but also how the original author's intention reappears with new power and purpose for hearers today.

"Making the Invisible Visible: Kingdom Love"

© Julius J. Kim

INTRODUCTION

"Turn the other cheek. Go the extra mile. Love your enemy. Pray for those who persecute you."

For some people the phrases "turn the other cheek," "go the extra mile," and "love your enemy" are the essence, not just of Christianity, but of humanity. Men like Tolstoy and Henry David Thoreau had a profound effect on people like Mahatma Ghandi and Martin Luther King Jr., influencing them to espouse principles of nonviolence and pacifism. I'm sure you'd agree with me that responding to violence with pacifism is a good thing. But is this the *essence* of Christianity or the essence of humanity?

In our text, Jesus calls his disciples to make a radical choice: If you want to be my follower, don't retaliate but love your enemies. Jesus is calling us to radical kingdom living as we love our enemies by grace. Are we willing to follow him?

Here in the Sermon on the Mount, found in Matthew chapters 5–7, he begins his teaching with the Beatitudes, these statements of blessing: Blessed are those who are poor in spirit; blessed are those who are persecuted. By doing this, he introduces us to the characteristics and traits of those who are in the kingdom—this invisible kingdom that Jesus brings. He is saying, "Now those who belong to this kingdom, they live and act and think a certain way. Are you ready to follow me? Are you really ready to be a kingdom dweller — to live out these kingdom ethics, these kingdom rights and wrongs? Because before you think you understand what these phrases mean, let me explain to you exactly what I mean."

So Jesus launches into this discourse in these three chapters to explain to us the radical nature of kingdom living. Here specifically in our passage, he introduces us to the radical nature of making the invisible visible. Let me say that again: He introduces us to the radical nature of making the invisible kingdom visible, in our lives, as we love our enemies by grace. Three themes can help us understand and apply what Jesus is teaching us here: (1) confrontation, (2) expectation, and (3) transformation.

CONFRONTATION

Here in our passage, we find the fifth of six times where Jesus begins his teaching with a pattern that he began in Matthew 5:21. He starts by saying this, "You have heard that it was said …" then he quotes from the OT law. Then says, "But I tell you …" and introduces a seemingly opposite understanding of the law. Is he contradicting the OT? More specifically, is he contradicting what Moses taught the Israelites during the wilderness wanderings? He seemingly argues that the Mosaic law is invalid. He seems to be introducing a new and better way. Quoting from Deuteronomy 19:21, he states, "You have heard that it was said, 'Eye for eye, and tooth for tooth.' But I tell you, do not resist an evil person" (NIV). Then he quotes from Leviticus 19:18 in verse 43 when he states, "You have heard that it was said, 'Love your neighbor and hate your enemy'" (NIV).

But as we have seen thus far, Jesus is not arguing against the validity of the OT law. One of the simple reasons we know this is because Jesus says, "You have heard that it was … *said*" and not "You have heard that it was *written*." Furthermore, if you look carefully at Leviticus 19:18, it doesn't actually say, "hate your enemy." You see, he's not *contradicting* the OT law; he's *confronting* the teachers of the law. What is evident here is that Jesus was confronting the teachers of the law during his day who were distorting the intended meaning of the law based on their particular interpretations.

These teachers (most likely the Pharisees and scribes) were instructing their followers that exacting revenge and executing retaliation in certain cases not only were allowed but followed the proper interpretation of Mosaic law. After all, isn't that what Moses meant by "Show no pity: life for life, eye for eye, tooth for tooth, hand for hand, foot for foot" (Deut 19:21 NIV)? Known as the law of Talion, or the law of equity, this teaching in Deuteronomy articulated the principle that the punishment must fit the crime. Unfortunately, this law that was meant to limit and restrain retaliation was being misconstrued to permit vengeance and retribution to the nth degree. As such, in the hands of these Pharisees, this law of fair punishment was nurtured into a law of personal vengeance.

Clearly, this was to misunderstand the purpose of the law. Since this law was meant to restrain personal vindictiveness and retaliation, the real fulfillment of it would be found in a person who did not seek such revenge — whether that revenge came in the form of external physical retribution or, more importantly, internal spiritual hatred. And this is the connection between verses 38 – 42 and us. Jesus is not only confronting the Pharisees who misinterpreted the law, he is confronting us. Jesus confronts the heart of the matter; that is, he confronts the matter of the heart.

Like a skilled surgeon, he carefully cuts away and removes the external layers to get to the core of the disease — the disease of sin that causes us to hate, despise, and desire vengeance on those who mistreat us in any way. Whether it's the driver who cuts us off on the road or the offender who attacks our loved ones, how often our first response is one of hatred and revenge. If we're honest with ourselves, isn't this how we respond when we're provoked by the "enemies" all around us: a spouse, a child, a coworker, a neighbor? You know the feeling. And what the Pharisees, and sometimes we, as closet Pharisees, don't realize, is that our "enemies" are often those who are closest to us. Well, this is Jesus' confrontation: our hearts are so prone to the sin of hatred and retaliation because of idols such as anger, fear, entitlement, control, and comfort.

Someone who knew this temptation well was Ernest Gordon. Gordon was a British army officer captured at sea by the Japanese at the age of twenty-four. In his autobiography titled *Through the Valley of the Kwai*, Gordon tells an extraordinary story of sacrificial love that had the power to transform embittered hearts and lives.[24]

Gordon was sent to work on the Burma-Siam railway line that the Japanese were constructing through the dense Thai jungle for possible use in an invasion of India. Against international law, the Japanese forced even officers to work at manual labor, so each day Gordon would join a work detail of thousands of prisoners who hacked their way through the jungle and built up a track bed through low-lying swampland.

Naked except for loincloths, the men worked in 120-degree heat, their bodies stung by insects, their bare feet cut and bruised by sharp stones. Death was commonplace. If a prisoner appeared to be lagging, a Japanese guard would beat him to death, bayonet him, or decapitate him in full view of the other

---

24. Ernest Gordon, *Through the Valley of the Kwai* (New York: Harper, 1962).

prisoners. Many more men simply dropped dead from exhaustion, malnutrition, and disease. Under these severe conditions, with such inadequate care for prisoners, some 80,000 men ultimately died building the railway.

Under the heat and strain of captivity, many of these prisoners had degenerated to barbaric behavior — even to their fellow brother prisoners. Gordon writes,

> As starvation, exhaustion and disease took an ever-increasing toll, the atmosphere in which we lived became poisoned by selfishness, hate and fear. We were slipping rapidly down the slope of degradation. [Before], the patterns of army life had sustained us. [Before], we had still shown some consideration for each other [as fellow prisoners]. Now that was gone, swept away. Existence had become so miserable, the odds so heavy against us, that nothing mattered except to survive. We lived by the rule of the jungle — survival of the fittest. It was a case of "I look out for myself and to hell with everyone else."[25]

The band of brothers had become broken.

EXPECTATION

Jesus not only confronts the matter of our hearts that are prone to hate, he moves on in our text to express the expectations he has for those who want to follow the true meaning of the law. A second theme Jesus articulates in this passage is expectation. In verses 38–42, he calls on us to not retaliate when provoked but to give up our all. In verses 38–42 he gives four implicit commands to reveal the radical nature of his expectations. Now keep in mind that these are illustrations from Jesus' day that he uses to teach his expectations. So they need to be seen in light of that context and not as normative rules for living. Let's look at these four illustrations.

---

25. Ibid., 74–75.

First, turn the other cheek.
Jesus pictures a man being slapped on the right cheek. Two things are significant about this. First, such a blow was more grossly offensive to the mindset of the Jew than a violent crime. In their culture, it was an insult of massive proportions. Why? It was a strike with the back of the hand, something still regarded as degrading and insulting in the Near East. Second, it was an insult for which the only recourse was to take a man to court, as people might do today for libel or defamation of character. Did you know that the fine for such a blow and insult exceeded the average man's wages for an entire year?

So what in the world does Jesus mean here when he says, "When you've been grossly humiliated and insulted with a back-handed slap ... turn the other cheek." Surely he's not saying that his followers should deliberately put themselves in the way of further suffering and not pursue justice in the face of evil. No, Jesus is challenging them and us in this figurative way that to stand on our own rights and seek to have our dignity reaffirmed by retaliating—even in the face of a violent offense—is not the right response. His expectations are different: he wants us to love our enemies and turn the other cheek. I wonder what the disciples were thinking in their hearts as Jesus said these words. Matthew doesn't record for us what they may have said or what they may have been thinking. I wonder if it was something like what they said when they were called to forgive the sinner seven times: "Increase our faith!" (Luke 17:5).

Second, give away your cloak.
Here Jesus pictures a man in court being sued for his tunic. In the first-century legal context, the tunic, or what we would call our undershirt, would serve as a guarantee of payment if you needed to pay some sort of large fine.

To this Jesus adds, "Give away your cloak as well." What is he saying? The point of the saying makes sense when we remember that the outer coat of the Jew was considered virtually sacred. It was one of the most important possessions of a Jew. Often it was given to them as a special gift from their fathers. Remember the "amazing technicolor dream coat" that Joseph's brothers were jealous of? Further signifying the importance of this cloak, if it were lent out or given up, by Jewish law it had to be returned before nightfall, because for some it served as both clothing and bedding.

Again Jesus' point is that when his followers meet with opposition and persecution, they don't retaliate back with sin. Rather, those who follow Jesus are willing to give up the most precious thing they own—in this case their outer cloak. After all, love covers a multitude of sins. "Lord, increase our faith!"

Third, go the extra mile.
This phrase is understandable once again if we understand the historical context and background. The Roman army that occupied Palestine had the right to force any Jew to assist them and carry their armor for a mile—but not one step more. The Jews hated this practice more than anything else, because it publicly revealed the humiliation of being a subjugated people. We can easily imagine how the Romans must have abused this right.

Jesus says here, to the shock of many listening, that when you are "drafted" for service and have walked the thousand paces required by the Roman regulations, keep going. To the shock of everyone listening, Jesus tells them to carry the load one more mile! No soldier had the right to make someone do that. But Jesus says, do it voluntarily because maybe they may see that you belong to a different empire, with rules and regulations infinitely more wise and beautiful than all the laws of

Rome. Again, Jesus is not speaking literally. He is using this illustration to show the heart and life of a true disciple of Christ. These are the expectations when we follow him.

"Lord, increase our faith!"

Fourth, give to those who borrow or beg.
Giving to those who ask to borrow or giving to those who beg was not a legal duty for these early disciples. They were under no obligation to give. And yet Jesus is showing them that the same law that restrains evil acts is also meant to teach us to express a lifestyle of grace, which is the opposite of forbidden sin. That is, the same law that teaches us against the sins of commission indicts us of the sins of omission.

The true expression of the law of equity is found in the intentional yielding up of not only our rights but our very all—indeed, loving with our heart, soul, mind, and strength. Only when we show gracious love and sacrifice for our enemies will they see what the God-given meaning of the law really is. Perhaps then they will understand that our citizenship is in heaven and not in Palestine, Rome, Korea, or even America.

Turn the other cheek. Give up your cloak. Go the extra mile. Give to those who borrow or beg. These are Jesus' expectations. This is what he means by "Do not resist an evil person." This is the expression of kingdom love. In their hearts, the disciples must have cried out, "Jesus! Do you know what you're asking us to do? We can't do it!" Jesus knew exactly what he was asking. He knew the law of God and the demands of the law to be holy and perfect. He would say to them, "You're right. You can't do it. But I will. For you."

Shocking though it was to those first hearers, Jesus' teaching here in Matthew 5 would eventually produce men and women who would turn the world upside down for his kingdom. It included eleven ordinary guys who at first couldn't have understood what Jesus was talking about but ultimately discovered the key: the confrontation of sin and the expectation of the law could only be transformed by a sinless substitute who would pay the penalty for our sin of not loving our enemies but would also provide the power to truly love.

TRANSFORMATION

Having seen Christ's confrontation of our hearts that are so prone to hate, and Christ's expectation that we perfectly love our enemies, we turn to our last point: the confrontation of our sinful hearts, and the expectation to love our enemies, can only be accomplished through the penalty-paying and power-providing transformation of grace that only Christ can give. He becomes our penalty payer and our power provider. Why is this important? The only way we can ever confront our sin of not loving our enemies and receive the power to truly love our enemies is by putting our complete trust in Christ alone and receiving his grace. It's grace alone through faith alone in Christ alone!

The gospel writers Matthew and Luke demonstrate how the law against hatred and retaliation against our enemies found definitive and decisive transformation in the person and work of Jesus Christ. First, if we turn to Matthew chapter 27 and read from verse 27 on, an amazing correspondence develops between his teaching and our ability to follow it. Please turn there. Reading from Matthew 27:27–50 (NASB):

27 Then the soldiers of the governor took Jesus into the Praetorium and gathered the whole Roman cohort around Him. 28 They stripped Him and put a scarlet robe on Him. 29 And after twisting together a crown of thorns, they put it on His head, and a reed in His right hand; and they knelt

down before Him and mocked Him, saying, "Hail, King of the Jews!" [30] They spat on Him, and took the reed and began to beat Him on the head.

Turn the other cheek.

[31] After they had mocked Him, they took the scarlet robe off Him and put His own garments back on Him,

Give away your cloak.

and led Him away to crucify Him. [32] As they were coming out, they found a man of Cyrene named Simon, whom they pressed into service to bear His cross.

Go the extra mile.

[45] Now from the sixth hour darkness fell upon all the land until the ninth hour. [46] About the ninth hour Jesus cried out with a loud voice, saying, "ELI, ELI, LAMA SABACHTHANI?" that is, "MY GOD, MY GOD, WHY HAVE YOU FORSAKEN ME?"

[50] And Jesus cried out again with a loud voice, and yielded up His spirit.

Give to those who borrow or beg.

Is this coincidence? Or planned all along? The only way you can love your enemies is if you've been transformed by grace, from the inside out. You see, Christ did it all. He turned the other cheek, he gave up his cloak, he went the extra mile, he prayed for those who persecuted him, he did good to those who hated him, he blessed those who cursed him, and he, like his Father, was gracious to all. How? By giving up his life for sinners like you and me so that we would be united to him by faith. Christ is our penalty payer.

But he's also the power provider. Luke 24:44–49 states,

Amazing

Then he said to them, "These are my words that I spoke to you while I was still with you, that everything written about me in the Law of Moses and the Prophets and the Psalms must be fulfilled." Then he opened their minds to understand the Scriptures, and said to them, "Thus it is written, that the Christ should suffer and on the third day rise from the dead, and that repentance and forgiveness of sins should be proclaimed in his name to all nations, beginning from Jerusalem. You are witnesses of these things. And behold, I am sending the promise of my Father upon you. But stay in the city until you are clothed with power from on high."

The power that raised the sinless Jesus from the dead is the same power Jesus promises to those who put their trust in him. He promises the Holy Spirit, who can renew our hearts and change our lives so that we can begin to truly love others, even our enemies, because of the gospel of grace. The confrontation of our sinful hearts, and the expectation to love our enemies, can only be accomplished through the penalty-paying and power-providing transformation of grace that Christ offers and that we receive through repentance and faith. It is this grace that will transform your heart and your mind, your words and your deeds, so you can love your enemy as Christ loved you. Ernest Gordon experienced this miracle of grace by the River Kwai.

Through the strain of captivity, many of these prisoners had degenerated to barbarous behavior, but one afternoon a miracle happened that would forever change the camp.[26]

The Japanese guards carefully counted tools at the end of the day's work, and on that day, a guard shouted that a shovel was missing. He walked up and down the ranks, demanding to know who had stolen it. When no one confessed, he screamed,

26. Ibid., 104–5.

"All die! All die!" and raised his rifle to fire at the first man in the line. At that instant one prisoner stepped forward, stood at attention, and said calmly, "I did it."

The guard fell on him in a fury, kicking and beating the prisoner, who despite the blows still managed to stand at attention. Enraged, the guard lifted his weapon high in the air and brought the rifle butt down on the soldier's skull. The man sank in a heap to the ground and did not move. Although it was clear that he was dead, the guard continued kicking his motionless body, stopping only when exhausted. When the assault finally stopped, the other prisoners picked up their comrade's body and marched back to the camp. That evening, when the tools were counted again, the work crew discovered a mistake had been made: no shovel was missing.

One of the prisoners remembered the verse "Greater love has no man than this, that a man lay down his life for his friends."

Word spread like wildfire through the whole camp. An innocent man had been willing to die to save the others! The incident had a profound effect: the men — who for months had lived like animals trying desperately to survive — began to treat each other like brothers. With no prompting, prisoners began looking out for each other rather than themselves. Although to be caught meant death, prisoners undertook expeditions outside the camp to find food and medicine for their sick fellow prisoners. Thefts grew increasingly rare. Men started thinking less of themselves, finding ways to help others. Sacrificial love transforms.

CONCLUSION

As the newly "appointed" chaplain to his fellow prisoners, Ernest Gordon experienced firsthand the transforming power of sacrifice and grace.[27] One day as he and his fellow prisoners

27. Ibid., 220–21.

were being transferred by train, they noticed that a group of wounded Japanese soldiers were on the same train. No longer fit for action, they were packed into railway cars for Bangkok. They could see that their uniforms were encrusted with mud, blood, and excrement. Their wounds were sorely inflamed and full of pus, crawling with maggots; clearly they had been left in this predicament for weeks without any treatment. The prisoners were immediately moved by compassion for these men, so without hesitation, one of the prisoners gathered the prisoners' canteens of water and began to clean the wounds of a dying Japanese soldier. Other prisoners began to join in, offering food and water.

The Japanese guards tried to prevent them from helping these sick men, who were clearly no longer fit for action. Apparently whenever one of them died en route he was simply thrown off into the jungle. The prisoners finally understood why the Japanese guards were so cruel to them: they barely cared for their own. Gordon and his fellow soldiers ignored the guards and knelt by the side of the enemy to give them food and water, to clean and bind their wounds, to smile and say a kind word. Grateful cries of "Thank you!" were uttered. On being rebuked by another Allied officer, the simple yet powerful words of Jesus came to Gordon, "Love your enemies." Sacrificial love has transforming power.

Such was the transformative power of grace, that when liberation finally came, the prisoners treated their sadistic guards with kindness and not revenge, with love and not hate.

When the victorious Allies finally swept in, the survivors, looking like human skeletons, lined up in front of their captors. The liberating Allied soldiers were so infuriated by what they saw that they wanted to shoot the Japanese guards on the spot. Only the intervention of the victims prevented them. The captors were spared by their captives. "Let mercy take the place of bloodshed," said one of the exhausted but forgiving men. "Not an eye for an eye, a limb for a limb." They all insisted: "No more hatred. No more killing. Now what we need is forgiveness."[28]

Here is the power of grace, transforming ordinary people, like you and me, into extraordinary followers of Christ, with kingdom faith, hope, and love. Amen.

---

28. Adapted from ibid., 230.

PART 3

DESIGNING THE SERMON ACCORDING *to* TRUTH, GOODNESS, AND BEAUTY

CHAPTER 6

THE BLUEPRINTS OF
SERMON DESIGN — PART 1

I'm sure you've seen this drawing before. Do you know who drew it? Do you know its name? Drawn by Leonardo da Vinci around 1490, the *Vitruvian Man* is arguably one of his most recognizable works. It depicts a man in two different positions with his arms and legs spread apart within both a square and a circle. It is often called the *Canon of Proportions* due to the artist's profound understanding 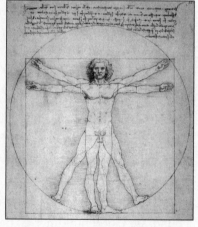 of proportion. The accompanying text outlines da Vinci's observations regarding the unique qualities of design found on the human body that correlates to patterns and proportions found in nature. Did you know, for example, that the length of the person's outspread arms is equal to his height?

What is even less well known is the source of da Vinci's drawing. This drawing is based on the artist's careful reading and study of the ancient Roman architect Vitruvius — thus the name of the drawing. In his book *De Architectura*, Vitruvius stated his belief that the study of the human body was a foundational source of ideal proportion for architecture.[1] His treatise on architecture, written in approximately 20–30 BC, was one of the first texts in history to connect principles of proportion found on the human body to that of buildings. One of the enduring statements he made regarding great design is still quoted by architects today: "The ideal building has three elements: it is sturdy, useful, and beautiful."[2] Or, in words that would have been common in Roman literature, good design has the elements of *truth, goodness,* and *beauty*.

Preaching is the Spirit-directed interpretation, explanation, proclamation, and application of the gospel of Jesus Christ, revealed in God's trustworthy Word, communicated to the church, so that the Father would save and sanctify his people. Preaching involves not only discovering and discerning the truth of the text but also designing and delivering the sermon. The goal of this chapter is to help you design a sermon according to the foundational principles of truth, goodness, and beauty. What do I mean by that?

Designing the Sermon with Truth, Goodness, and Beauty

Vitruvius argued that an architect should be motivated by three central themes: *firmitas* (strength, solidity, firmness), *utilitas* (purpose, functionality, utility), and *venustas* (beauty, delight, proportion). These are the foundational convictions prior to the actual blueprints being drawn up for a building. Good buildings all possess these fundamental characteristics: they are true to their nature, good for their occupants, and beautiful to all.

One finds similar themes in classical textbooks on rhetoric, from the foundational claims of the Sophists to the paradigmatic work

---

1. Several English translations of Vitruvius's book exist. The two most commonly available are: *Vitruvius: Ten Books on Architecture*, trans. Ingrid Rowland (Cambridge, U.K.: Cambridge University Press, 1999); and *Vitruvius: De Architectura*, trans. Frank Granger (Boston: Harvard University Press, 1931).
2. This quote is a modern translation of Henry Wotton's 1624 version (*The Elements of Architecture*) of the sentence found in *Vitruvius: De Architectura* (1.iii.2): "Well building hath three conditions: firmness, commodity, and delight."

of Aristotle.[3] For classical rhetoricians like Aristotle, Cicero, and Quintilian, the art and science of persuasion involved the whole person: intellect, emotion, and action — the head, the heart, and the hands. Aristotle argued that the speaker prepares and makes arguments that are sound in logic (*logos*, truth), ethical in character (*ethos*, goodness), and emotional in response (*pathos*, beauty).[4] One author highlights the importance of this unified approach:

> Perhaps the most valuable contribution of Aristotle — and one which needs to be kept at the forefront when examining his ongoing influence — is his sense of the rhetorical enterprise as a comprehensive unity. At every moment in the process of persuasion — from conceptualization through delivery — are present the necessary components of speaker or author, the audience or hearer, and the speech or discourse. Aristotle reminds us of the simultaneous presence of all these elements, and their ability to work together to bring about change and action.[5]

All truth, goodness, and beauty are found in God and flow from God, both in his Word and in his world. For these reasons, these three words provide a helpful paradigm for the design and delivery of sermons.

1. Truth: The preacher must design a sermon that is characterized by *truth*. Vitruvius and the ancient rhetoricians argued that buildings and speeches, respectively, needed to be characterized by a solidity and strength that is true to the nature and purpose of their respective subjects. Vitruvius writes, "The principle of *soundness* will be observed if the foundations have been laid out firmly, and if, whatever the building materials may be, they have been chosen with care but not with excessive frugality."[6] For Aristotle, virtuous action was based on right reason (*logos*), which was based on right explanations.[7] Similarly, preachers

---

3. For a helpful introduction to classical rhetorical theory and practice, see George A. Kennedy, *Classical Rhetoric and Its Christian and Secular Tradition from Ancient to Modern Times* (Chapel Hill: University of North Carolina Press, 1980). See also Brian Vickers, *In Defense of Rhetoric* (Oxford: Oxford University Press, 1988).
4. Aristotle, *Rhetoric*, 1355b25 – 26.
5. David Cunningham, ed., *To Teach, To Delight, and To Move: Theological Education in a Post-Christian World* (Eugene, Ore.: Cascade, 2004), 22 – 23.
6. Rowland, trans., *Vitruvius: Ten Books*, 26.
7. See Jessica Moss, "Right Reason in Plato and Aristotle: On the Meaning of *Logos*," *Phronesis* 59 (2014): 181 – 230.

must prepare and deliver sermons that share this characteristic—true to its nature and right for its purpose.

As mentioned before, the one preaching from God's Word is a steward and a herald, called on by his King to arrange and speak a message that is not his own. He is "entrusted with the gospel ... not to please man, but to please God who tests our hearts" (1 Thess 2:4). Thus, his first and foremost goal is to prepare his message so it is accurate and consistent with the message that was entrusted to him. In this case, the preacher faithfully represents the meaning and intentions of both the human and divine authors of the Holy Scriptures. Thus, in the design and delivery of his sermon, the preacher must communicate words that are true to the nature and purpose of who he is, or more accurately, *whose* he is. As a herald of the King, he must truthfully convey both the meaning and intentions of the King's words and heart.

2. Goodness: The preacher must design a sermon that is characterized by *goodness*. Vitruvius was convinced that buildings must be designed and built so that they ultimately benefit those who use it: "The principle of *utility* will be observed if the design allows faultless, unimpeded use through the disposition of the spaces and the allocation of each type of space is properly oriented, appropriate, and comfortable."[8] This was more than merely having a utilitarian function. While utility is an important functional quality in the design of buildings, Vitruvius argued that buildings ought to give positive benefits to its users. As the body of certain animals provide benefits for their survival, so too buildings must provide goodness for humans.[9]

Similarly, Aristotle believed that speakers must establish credibility and good will with their audiences. In his classic *The Art of Rhetoric*, Aristotle argued "For the orator to produce conviction three qualities are necessary ... good sense, virtue, and good will."[10] Ultimately, speakers are attempting to persuade their audience with ideas that meet the

8. Rowland, trans., *Vitruvius: Ten Books*, 26.
9. He compares the bodies of birds, fish, and land animals to derive this principle of design, that is, to design structures so that their users benefit and receive goodness (ibid., 27).
10. Aristotle, *The Art of Rhetoric*, trans. J. H. Freese (Boston: Harvard University Press, 1967), 171.

ethical test of being in the best interest of the hearer. What speakers say must benefit their hearers. Truth and goodness are qualities that work together, not only in architecture, but also in speech. Cicero argued, for example, that rhetorical study must coincide with moral training. Thus, wisdom and eloquence work together: "Wisdom without eloquence does too little for the good of states, but ... eloquence without wisdom is generally highly disadvantageous and never helpful."[11]

The apostle Paul would agree with this theme of demonstrating goodness in one's ministry and preaching. Throughout many of his letters in the NT, Paul describes his own ministry to the churches in tender words reminiscent of a parent to a child.[12] In doing so, he reveals one of his primary goals of ministry: revealing the grace of God in Jesus Christ so that those who hear and believe would be blessed. In stark yet tender words, he writes to the believers in the church in Philippi,

> For to me to live is Christ, and to die is gain. If I am to live in the flesh, that means fruitful labor for me. Yet which I shall choose I cannot tell. I am hard pressed between the two. My desire is to depart and be with Christ, for that is far better. But to remain in the flesh is more necessary on your account. Convinced of this, I know that I will remain and continue with you all, for your progress and joy in the faith, so that in me you may have ample cause to glory in Christ Jesus, because of my coming to you again (Phil 1:21–26).

Elsewhere he writes,

> Now I rejoice in my sufferings for your sake, and in my flesh I am filling up what is lacking in Christ's afflictions for the sake of his body, that is, the church, of which I became a minister according to the stewardship from God that was given to me for you, to make the word of God fully known.... Him [Christ] we proclaim, warning everyone and teaching everyone with all wisdom, that we may present everyone mature in Christ. For this I toil, struggling with all his energy that he powerfully works within me (Col 1:24–29).

---

11. Cicero, *De Inventione. De Optimo Genere Oratorum. Topica*, trans. H. M. Hubbell (Boston: Harvard University Press, 1968), 3.
12. See Acts 20:17–35; 1 Cor 4:14–21; 9:19–23; 2 Cor 2:4; 4:5; 6:3–13; Gal 4:18–20; Phil 1:7–8, 21–25; 4:1; 1 Thess 2:7–12.

Like Paul, preachers never forget what ultimately benefits their hearers: the gospel. As heralds of the King, they know that the good news of Jesus' life, death, and resurrection is life-transforming. So as they design and deliver their gospel-centered sermons, they present God's truths faithfully and God's goodness forcefully because they know it changes lives for the better.

(3) Beauty: In addition to truth and goodness, the preacher should design a sermon that is characterized by *beauty*. Vitruvius stated, "That of *attractiveness* will be upheld when the appearance of the work is pleasing and elegant, and the proportions of its elements have properly developed principles of symmetry."[13] While beauty and attractiveness can be subjective categories, Vitruvius attempted to provide categories that would help would-be architects design buildings that also moved people's souls. He believed that beauty could be learned through a study of nature, specifically, universal laws regarding proportion and symmetry. As a result he studied the human body as a model of proportional perfection coinciding with geometric forms found in nature. The "ideal" could be discovered, studied, and correlated for the purposes of designing buildings that shared principles of beauty.

We also see this theme in the history of rhetoric. Influenced by Cicero, Augustine said that preachers "should speak in such a way that he teaches, delights and moves."[14] He quotes Cicero by stating, "To teach is a necessity, to please is a sweetness, to persuade is a victory." Many teachers of rhetoric knew that stirring the emotions through beautiful language, logic, and style was a necessary component of effective speaking. The combination of truth and beauty will more likely move the listener to do what is right.

The NT writers were not only influenced by the OT understanding of God's beauty in worship. They were also influenced by the principle of ancient rhetoric of pursuing delight through words. They understood it was necessary to utilize certain devices for their words to reach their full potential with specific audiences.[15] Paul, for example, wrote, "I

---

13. Rowland, trans., *Vitruvius: Ten Books*, 26.
14. Augustine, *On Christian Doctrine* (New York: Macmillan, 1958), 27.
15. Kennedy, *Classical Rhetoric*, 120–32.

have become all things to all people, that by all means I might save some" (1 Cor 9:22). Paul wanted to see the audience experience the full power of the truth he proclaimed. To do so, he had to use methods contextualized to the needs of the audience. One is moved not only when minds are persuaded with the truth and goodness of the gospel but also when souls are stirred. This stirring occurs when beautiful content and communication are enjoined.

In sum, truth, goodness, and beauty are essential goals in sermon design and delivery. What does this look like practically?

The Blueprints of Design — Part 1

You've prayerfully meditated on your text in relation to your congregation. You've completed all the necessary analyses of the text (linguistics, literary, life-setting). You've asked God to help you understand and apply the truths of the text to your own heart and life. Now it's time to design a sermon that embodies truth, goodness, and beauty. Like an architect hired to design a dream home for a family, you start with this vision.

A sermon characterized by truth, goodness, and beauty will hopefully promote maximum attention, retention, integration, and transformation. What blueprint shall we use to design and structure our sermons? Though many design models exist, I recommend structuring your sermon using a broad framework of a story.[16] Storytelling is one of the oldest forms of communication known to man. Often simple yet poignant, stories have a way of communicating ideas that are memorable and transformative. Stories move us, shape us, and change us.

Sermon Structure: Story Arc

From Aristotle's three-act structure of beginning, middle, and end to Gustav Freytag's five acts of exposition, rising action, climax, falling

---

16. Bryan Chapell offers helpful insights regarding the structure of the sermon as well as a sample sermon of his method (*Christ-Centered Preaching: Redeeming the Expository Sermon*, 2nd ed. [Grand Rapids: Baker Academic, 2005], 129–73, 376–86).

action, and dénouement, many have shown how the world's most memorable stories share certain structural elements.[17]

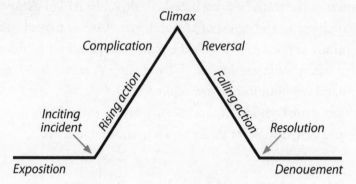

Figure 6.2. Gustav Freytag's Dramatic Arc

Great stories share this dramatic arc in which the hero figure in the story is introduced to a problem or issue, only to find the problem build to a moment of greatest tension, resulting in a resolution of the problem that often leaves the hero transformed from his original state. Readers experience the highs and lows the hero figure experiences, culminating in a new awareness. Rationally and emotionally, stories are powerful. Interestingly, researchers have shown that some of the world's most memorable speeches follow this story pattern.[18] And while speeches and sermons are not stories, they can be designed utilizing this basic framework. How can sermons be designed to look and feel like stories?

In preaching, hearers play the role of the hero figure, not the preacher. It is the hearers that must be taken on a journey from beginning, middle, and end. Specifically, hearers are the heroes that must be taken from their original location to a greater destination because of the transformation that hopefully occurs as the herald proclaims the King's words. Let me explain.

Our task as preachers is to help hearers see and feel themselves in

17. Aristotle, *The Poetics*, trans. W. H. Fyfe (Boston: Harvard University Press, 1973); Gustav Freytag, *Technique of the Drama: An Exposition of Dramatic Composition and Art*, 6th ed., trans. E. J. MacEwan (New York: B. Blom, 1968).
18. See Nancy Duarte, "The Secret Structure of Great Talks," TEDxEast (Nov. 11, 2010); http://www.ted.com/talks/nancy_duarte_the_secret_structure_of_great_talks.

the drama being presented in the stories of the Bible. As they relate to the characters and their struggles, they are able to know and feel the truth, goodness, and beauty of the gospel as it's being portrayed in that particular text. I recommend that preachers structure their sermons following the flow of the narrative itself: beginning problem, middle action rising to climax, and end resolution and call to action. The sermon's exposition and application through its main points would be structured around the primary problem (FCF), God's solution (CFC), and a call of response. This is the basic story arc structure that preachers can use for any passage of Scripture, regardless of genre.

Preachers are heralds, who in representing their King proclaim a message with such clarity and integrity that those who hear will hopefully be transformed by its truth, goodness, and beauty. Preaching, then, is proclaiming God's desire to take hearers from where they are to where God wants them to be through the gospel. Utilizing the dramatic story arc as the framework for sermon structure is one way to accomplish this. Though the details of this will be discussed later, a general framework can be laid out. Let's use Aristotle's categories of the beginning, middle, and end to outline the sermon structure.

1. At the *beginning* of the sermon, the preacher introduces his hearers to what God's Word says about two things: their "current location" (beginning of the story arc) and God's "desired destination" (end of the story arc). Every passage of Scripture that you preach will say something about their current spiritual state that is in need of change. Further, every passage of Scripture will say something about what will transform them, changing them so they are not the same as they were at the beginning of the sermon. Ultimately, it is the gospel of Jesus Christ that will transform them. Following the pattern set out by Jesus himself, the paradigm is one of suffering then glory, preaching the Word of God so as to reveal the transformative power in the gospel. When the gospel proclaimed is received by faith, hearers will be moved from where they are to where they should be, because of what God has done for them in Jesus Christ. For preachers, this theme presents what God has done in Christ and his desired response.

2. After introducing hearers to where they are and where they should be, the *middle*, or the body of the sermon, is characterized by the presentation and resolution of various complications that the hearers will face along the way. Using Freytag's diagram, the middle of the sermon is composed of main points that in themselves have some element of exposition, rising action, climax, falling action, and dénouement. Perhaps Freytag's diagram would be helpful here:[19]

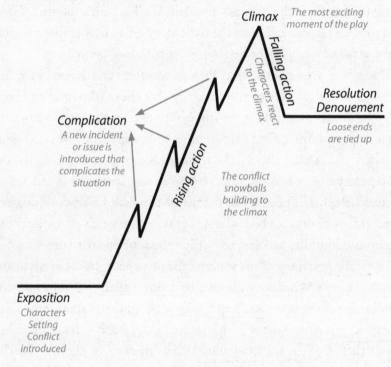

Figure 6.3. Gustav Freytag's Pyramid

The multiple up-and-down movements, or complications, form the body of the sermon with penultimate climaxes of their own, all building up to the ultimate climax of the sermon.

3. The *end* of the sermon structured in this way is characterized by falling action, leading to the dénouement. This is when the hearer is able to see how the truths of the text has led the hearer from their

19. http://coursecontent.learn21.org/ENG3x-HS-U10/a/unit03/en3_3.b.11.html; accessed Jan. 22, 2015.

original location to God's desired destination. In this new position, they are called on to respond to God in new faith and commitment because of a new awareness and understanding of the gospel. The conclusion to the sermon informs and inspires, often with dramatic language and passionate delivery. Thus, the sermon's arc, much like a story's arc, has transformative direction, moving the hero-hearer from *what is* to *what could be*.[20]

Sermon Structure: The First Three Components

Now let's walk through the first three components of sermon design.

1. Sermon Proposition
2. Main Points
3. Subpoints

The next chapter will cover the remaining elements for sermon design (transitions, applications, illustrations, introductions, conclusions, and composition). Note that these steps are laid out according to the order you should follow in designing your sermon. These are the basic blueprints that serve as a guide that will helpfully hone your own unique process. Over time you will develop your own steps based on your unique gifts and skills, the makeup of the congregation, and the time that you have in that given week to prepare your sermon.

Design Element 1: The Sermon Proposition (the Central Idea and Purpose Statement)

The first step in designing your sermon is to formulate the sermon proposition based on your preaching passage. Why is this so important? This one-sentence sermon idea will control and direct the entire sermon. It contains both the central idea of the text and the specific purpose of the sermon, linking the indicative and the imperative, the truths and the applications, the *what* and the *so what*. All other constituent parts of the sermon work together in and through this sermon proposition. This one sentence will provide the unity your sermon needs as you move your

---

20. Language from Duarte, "Secret Structure."

sermon toward your planned outcome. The sermon proposition sets up and summarizes what you hope to preach and why it is so important for your hearers.

At this point, it's important to keep in mind the difference between the one-sentence sermon proposition and the exegetical thesis of your passage. As mentioned before, part of your goal is to discover what the passage teaches in light of your linguistic, literary, and life-setting analysis. Through this interpretive process and study, you come to certain conclusions regarding what the human author was communicating to his audience through his writing. The summary of that conclusion is your exegetical thesis. After that step, you interpret the human author's intention for the passage through the lens of the Divine Author as you discern where the person and work of Jesus Christ is found in that text. In doing so, you reformulate your exegetical thesis to reveal the gospel heart and soul of the text, that is, the Christ-centered good news. Now you're ready to move onto the sermon proposition that will guide your sermon design and delivery.

The sermon proposition consists of two key parts: (a) the central idea, namely, the primary Christ-centered good news that the unique preaching text presents, and (b) the specific purpose, or the gospel response required of the hearers as a result of this text. The first half describes the *gospel indicative* of the text, the primary good news about God in Christ through the Spirit. This is a statement of truth that describes *what* God has done. The second half declares the *gospel imperative*, that is, how hearers of this sermon should respond in light of the good news about God in Christ through the Spirit. This is a statement of command that declares *how* we should respond. Thus, the sermon proposition proclaims what this passage is uniquely teaching about the gospel and why it matters.

Unlike an exegetical thesis of a given text, which only describes the "What is this text about?" question, the sermon proposition goes one step further, adding the "How should I respond?" question. How do you come up with it? In formulating your sermon proposition, make sure it is covenantal, Christ-focused, cogent, and consequential.

Covenantal: The two-part indicative/imperative nature of the sermon proposition is related to the unique relationship God has with his people. The Bible teaches that God in history relates to his people by way of covenants.[21] Simply defined, a covenant is a contractual agreement between two or more parties that stipulate how each party will relate to each other. In the Bible, this idea is not only what governs the relationship between God and mankind but also what structures the entire biblical story line.

Whether corporate Israel in the OT or individual Christians in the NT, God's people throughout the ages have been in a relationship with God that can be summarized by this statement of God: "I will be your God; you will be my people."[22] In this formal alliance, God initiates and establishes a binding and unchangeable contractual agreement with mankind.

Throughout the Bible, one sees this pattern of God's divine actions that precede mankind's obligatory response. Thus, the sermon proposition is patterned after this covenantal pattern: Because of God's divine actions, then we must respond appropriately.

Christ-Focused: As argued previously in chapter 3, the entire biblical story line comes to a covenantal climax in the redemptive work of Jesus Christ for his sinful people. Thus, our sermons must find their primary focus on this gospel message, and the necessary response to that truth. Whether your sermon is from the OT or the NT, gospel sermons have Christ as its focus. Thus, in the formulation of the sermon proposition, especially in the indicative half, what aspect of Christ's person and/or work connects with the text? Or, what is the CFC that will ultimately connect hearers to the truths of the text? Is the focus of the text and

---

21. For more on the nature and function of biblical covenants, see the following: Meredith G. Kline, *Kingdom Prologue: Genesis Foundations for a Covenantal Worldview* (Eugene, Ore.: Wipf & Stock, 2006); O. Palmer Robertson, *The Christ of the Covenants* (Phillipsburg, N.J.: P&R, 1981); Michael S. Horton, *God of Promise: Introducing Covenant Theology* (Grand Rapids: Baker, 2006); Michael Brown and Zach Keele, *Sacred Bond: Covenant Theology Explored* (Grandville, Mich.: Reformed Fellowship, 2012). Some key verses related to biblical covenants: Gen 3:15; 12:1–3; 15:6; 17:7; Ex 17:14; 34:10, 27; Deut 4:13; 2 Sam 7:8–16; Jer 31:31–36; Hos 6:7; Gal 3:7, 16, 26; Heb 11:8–16.
22. Ex 6:7; 19:5–6; Lev 26:12; Jer 7:23; 11:4; 30:22; 31:33; 32:38; Ezek 11:20; Joel 2:27; Zech 13:9; 2 Cor 6:16; Heb 11:16; Rev 21:7.

sermon on Christ as penalty payer, probation preserver, power provider, passion producer, or a combination of these?[23]

Bryan Chapell helpfully reminds us that Christ-centered sermons are full of grace. He rightly says, "Christ-centered preaching is not merely an interpretive method; it is an exegetical obligation with necessary implications for the saving and sanctifying messages we preach."[24] He then outlines four categories of grace-saturated Christ-centered sermons: "grace despite our sin; grace canceling the guilt of sin; grace defeating the power of sin; and grace compelling holiness."[25] These categories are instructive for preachers seeking to find the Christ-centered redemptive themes of the text.

Cogent: The sermon proposition should also be logical and clear as it moves from indicative to imperative. It needs to reveal the connection between how the imperative flows naturally out of the indicative. As you formulate the proposition, it should meet the test of being convincing, compelling, and comprehensible for the average listener. Formulating a cogent sermon proposition forces you to think through your unique audience's circumstances, needs, and issues. Does my proposition do justice to both what the text is teaching and what my audience needs? Is it simple enough to be communicated and understood within the time allotted for preaching?

Consequential: When deriving the sermon proposition, Bryan Chapell's advice is helpful.[26] He argues that using a consequential format identifies more clearly the balance needed between the indicative status of what Christ has done in the gospel and the imperative response required. The proposition, of course, must find its warrant in the preaching passage. Chapell suggests using this format to create it: The first word is "Because." An indicative statement of Christ's person and/or work, based on the exegesis of the text, follows. The second half begins with "then," followed by the imperatival response required by the truths of the text.

---

23. See chapter 3 for these categories.
24. Chapell, *Christ-Centered Preaching*, 311.
25. Ibid., 312.
26. See ibid., 143–47.

Design Element 2: Main Points

After formulating your sermon proposition, you need to determine how to flesh out that goal through the main movements of your sermon. While much has been written regarding the benefits and liabilities of having discrete points in a sermon, I'm of the opinion that having clear points in the sermon helps the listener with their attention, retention, and integration, which hopefully leads to transformation. In formulating the main points of your outline, make sure they are textual, truthful, transferable, and traveling.

Textual: It should be obvious to the listener that your main points are derived from the preaching text. This does not mean that you need to find words or phrases from the text itself for your main points (though that can be helpful). It does mean that there should be a clear coherence between the wording of your main points and the truths you are expounding from the text. As I stated in chapter 2, there are two main ways to formulate your outline with your main points, *textually* or *topically.* That is, should the main points follow the main ideas as they are presented in the text, or should they be topical points derived from various locations of the text? While both methods have strengths and weaknesses, the first step is to consider the genre of the text.

Outlines formulated from narrative and doctrinal/ethical texts often work better if the main points follow the flow of the text. With poetry and prophetic/apocalyptic literature, due to the unique characteristics of those genres, a more topical reconstructive outline of main points seems to help both the preacher and the listener grasp the main ideas that don't always follow a linear pattern. Generally, my advice to novice preachers is to try to follow the flow of text as it was given. Several benefits result from this: (a) following the flow of the text through its main movements (not a verse-by-verse outline per se) allows us to "hear" the text as it was first given, (b) it models for your congregation submission to the text and the author's intentions, and (c) it makes it easier for your audience to track with your sermon along with the biblical text before them.

Truthful: Make sure the ideas for your main points emerge naturally from the text and are consistent with the truths presented in relevant co-texts and context. In expository preaching, one of your goals is to derive and explain truth from the text of Scripture as it is presented. Using again the imagery of a herald, your job is to represent the message of the King, not to create your own ideas. The King has spoken and has given you what he wants his subjects to hear. Make sure the main ideas of your sermon find their source and meaning from the text at hand. Your listener should be able to find the connection between your main points and the truths revealed in the text. Furthermore, truthfulness involves making sure that your main points are related to the main movements of the text. As was described in a previous chapter, you want your points to be the main concerns of the passage. While secondary and tertiary ideas in the text can find a place in your sermon, your main points should be proportionately related to the main ideas of the text.

Transferable: Try to formulate your main points so that they are relevant to your hearers. You want your main ideas to connect with your hearers. Thus, you must find ways to communicate truth so that it is accessible to their minds (cognitive understanding), hearts (emotive feelings), and lives (volitional living). This does not mean that each main point has to be three sentences long. What this means is that regardless of how you word your main points, be it a word or a sentence, you want to ensure that you are thinking about connecting the indicative and imperative. For example, if the goal of the first point of your sermon from the David and Bathsheba narrative is to articulate David's sin, you will want to make sure that you accurately and personally connect David's sin with our sin. Thus, the main point may be titled "David's Sin," with the idea that you will conclude that section by connecting David's sin and our own sinful hearts and lives. Or perhaps that point could be titled "The Reality of Our Sin" to show that there's a connection between what both the human and divine authors were communicating to us.

Traveling: Remember that the points of a sermon are not merely isolated pearls strung next to each other on a string. That is, they are not merely individual, semi-related topics found in an informative lecture. They are stepping-stones to a destination; rungs on a ladder, or successively staged booster rockets intended to work in concert, each working in order to deliver a payload. Thus, you want your main points to travel to a specific destination, that is, the specific goal found in your sermon proposition. Your main points are a logical pathway for you to get across your central idea and achieve your specific purpose. Your sermon will surely have elements of instruction in the truth, but it also embraces persuasion, motivation, exhortation, and application.

What are some tips to make sure your points are textual, truthful, transferable, and traveling?

- Structure your main points so that they do justice to both the FCF and the CFC.
- Try a problem-solution or a problem-result-solution pattern.
- Formulate your main points in complete sentences at first.
- Shorten your main points into succinct phrases or words.
- Make your main points more memorable through rhetorical devices (parallelism; alliteration of sounds, ideas, themes; anaphora; chiasm; ellipses; questions).
- Ask yourself, Do the main points come from main truths of the text? Do they transfer to the listener's life and experience? Do they travel toward the goal of the sermon proposition?

Design Element 3: Subpoints

At this stage of sermon preparation, you are "filling in" your sermon outline with the information you have unearthed from your discovering and discerning stages. What are some principles to help you decide what to include and how to include it?

Selective: Choose data that support the main idea, which in turn supports your sermon proposition. Much data from your research may be interesting, but if it doesn't support the main point, leave it out; you can always use it at a later time. After reviewing your sermon proposition and your main points, ask yourself this question regarding the data you've collected: Is this information *crucial, optional,* or *nonessential*? This process is not as simple as it sounds. Prioritizing content into these three categories is a vital step in honing your sermon's focus.

This principle of selectivity and subordination includes the use of important data such as other Scripture passages and quotes from other resources (commentaries, journal articles, biographies, etc.). Some verses outside of your preaching text will be essential to the development of your argument. Other verses, though true, may not be significant in getting to your planned outcome. As for quotes from other works, make sure they are concise in length, concrete in insight, and clear in style. Some quotes that may "sound" good to your eyes when you read them for the first time often end up flat when heard through the ears. Selectivity is an exacting yet essential principle of sermon design.

Simple: Adopt simplicity over complexity. Overloading your audience with information that is irrelevant will undermine your sermon. Eliminate details that are not supportive and not clear. Use language that is universal; that is, it appeals and is accessible to all types of peoples, in all times and in all places. Your goal is maximum comprehension through clarity. Remember though that simplicity differs from being a simpleton. Don't allow your desire to be simple override the hard work needed to distill complicated ideas into clear but also creative words and sentences that will stir your hearers.

Specific: Express yourself with words and sentences that are distinct and focused on the main point. When you are specific in your statements, hearers do not have to fill in the gaps. Say what you mean, and of course, mean what you say. This requires you to be precise in your language, removing any ambiguity or mystery that may hinder your hearers' comprehension. While giving room for the creative yet strategic use of poetic (which is often implicit and figurative) language in your sermon, err on the side of being explicit and straightforward.

Succinct: Aim for brevity both in the presentation of ideas and the length of sentences. While being succinct will often be influenced by the message you want to get across, editing ruthlessly will always benefit both speaker and hearer. Your hearer will not have the benefit of seeing your words on a page or screen. Rather, they are processing what you say through their working memory, which is limited. Be concise in style and substance.

Significant: Confirm relevance to your hearers throughout the sermon. One of the most important steps in your sermon preparation process is determining how to make what you say significant to your hearer. From the introduction to every major section of your sermon, you need to reveal the relevance of the information being shared. Admittedly, this is not only difficult but also quite subjective. What is significant to one hearer may be irrelevant to the next. Nonetheless, good preachers must connect truth to experience. Many young preachers fall prey to the temptation of spending the entire sermon explaining all the information gathered from research without showing how that information has bearing on listeners' souls, lives, and futures, for example. So as you are creating and reviewing the content of your sermon, especially in your subpoints, stop and ask, "So what?" If up to that point in the sermon you have not answered that question to the satisfaction of your hearers, then you need to adjust your content and insert implications and applications (more on this later).

Sympathetic: Reveal your care and kindness throughout the sermon. It may be obvious, but being a sympathetic preacher is important. Much of your sensitivity and care will be shown in your delivery, but having sympathetic content is just as important. As you think about your explanation and application of Scripture, find ways to reveal the heart of a pastor. For a pastor is one who laughs and cries with his sheep. You are a shepherd first, preacher second. Preaching should be viewed as one of the main tasks of the shepherd, not something that defines you. Shepherding the flock entrusted to you involves knowing, feeding, leading, and protecting your sheep.[27] Good preaching involves revealing compassion, warmth, tenderness, and understanding in both your words and your deeds.

---

27. See Timothy Z. Witmer, *The Shepherd Leader: Achieving Effective Shepherding in Your Church* (Phillipsburg, N.J.: P&R, 2010).

Sensitive: Anticipate and answer the potential questions and objections that may arise in your hearers' minds and hearts as you preach. Good preachers make wise assumptions about what their hearers will be thinking and feeling at different moments in the sermon. Put yourself in the shoes of your hearers, asking yourself, What would I be thinking at this point in the sermon? Will the hearer be hospitable or hostile, agreeable or averse? With both believers who are members of your church and unbelievers who are visiting for the first time, be sensitive to factors that will color their reception of your sermon (e.g., age, background, culture, education, gender, etc.). In light of certain assumptions you can make about your audience's conviction and disposition to your topic or to you, respond with sensitivity. Predict interior questions and objections, propose answers to questions and objections in order to persuade and convict.

Symmetrical: Attempt to create balance in the length of your main points and subpoints. If you must have one point longer than the rest, it is wise to have more information earlier in the sermon when your hearers have more attention. Remember that proportion and symmetry are categories that promote beauty. Balance the amount of time given to each of your subpoints.

Sticky: Create language that is memorable and compelling to the whole person. When you engage only the intellect (cognitive), the possible retention of that material decreases. Research in neuroscience has shown, however, that if you create content that engages the intellect, emotions (affective), and will (volition), the likelihood of attention and retention by the hearer increases. Thus, your "sticky" content will not only be understood but also remembered, with lasting impact.

Surprising: Find ways to say things that are unexpected and unique. Utilize poetic devices such as allegory and metaphor. Deliver your words with a certain rhythm and cadence that turns prose into poetry. At key moments in the sermon, especially pastoral moments when your preaching is essentially counseling, using poetic words with expressive delivery can provide emotionally climactic moments for both speaker and hearer. Furthermore, this kind of surprise heightens attention because the brain is called to focus on this novel and passionate content or delivery.

Conclusion

From Aristotle to Augustine, Plato to Paul, many of history's greatest thinkers were also great speakers. They not only captivated the mind but also stirred the soul. As heralds of the King, we have the awe-inspiring privilege to continue this legacy of presenting words of truth, goodness, and beauty so that God would save and sanctify his people through it. Having looked at the first three design elements for achieving maximum attention, retention, integration, and transformation, the next chapter outlines the remaining six components.

- Design Element #1 — Sermon Proposition (Central Idea + Purpose Statement)
  - Exegetical Thesis + CFL = Sermon Proposition
  - Sermon Proposition + Specific Purpose = Sermon Proposition Central Idea
    (Idicative + Imperative) = Sermon Proposition

- Design Element #2 — Main Points
  - Textual • Transferable
  - Truthful • Traveling

- Design Element #3 — Subpoints
  - Selective • Significant • Sticky
  - Simple • Sympathetic • Surprising
  - Specific • Sensitive
  - Succinct • Symmetrical

CHAPTER 7

THE BLUEPRINTS OF SERMON DESIGN — PART 2

In the previous chapter, we covered the first three components in the design process: developing your sermon proposition, your main points, and your subpoints. In this chapter, we will continue in the process of sermon design according to the values of truth, goodness, and beauty.

Sermon Structure: The Final Six Components

Now we will complete the blueprints of sermon design by looking at the final six components of sermon design.

4. Transitions
5. Applications
6. Illustrations
7. Introductions
8. Conclusions
9. Composition

Design Element 4: Transitions

After having formulated your sermon proposition and main points, especially noting how your main points travel toward the goal, it's important to clarify and articulate your transitions. Though you haven't fleshed out all the content of the main points yet, it's important to think about how to connect the whole sermon through your transitions. You'll come back after all the content of the sermon is added to refine your transitions, but it's vital at this stage to ensure that the direction of the sermon as it moves from point to point is clear.

Like the seemingly insignificant ligaments in the human body that connect your bones and muscles, transitions are what hold the whole sermon together so that the sermon displays unity and beauty. This is arguably one of the most important steps in your sermon preparation and design, for this is where you will either see unity, symmetry, and proportion or you will not, forcing you to recalibrate and reformulate your main points.

Furthermore, listeners are already at a disadvantage when they are listening to your sermon. They have short attention spans and are likely to tune out if they get lost or are uninterested. They need your help to maintain attention and interest. Preaching is like taking your listeners on a journey with many sights to see and remember. Good transitions function to help them know where they are going, where they've been, and how much longer the journey will last. All of this increases the chances that your listeners will stay interested. What do you need to know about transitions, and what kinds of transitions should you use?

As their name implies, transitions help connect one idea to another. You want your ideas, be they main points or subpoints, to connect together *logically* and *linearly*.

To ensure that your argument is logical, you can ask some questions. Is my presentation, more specifically, the development of main points, valid or invalid? What am I trying to prove? Do I prove it? Is the argument rational and complete? Your sermon will be composed of many propositional statements that will hopefully follow logically from others. These statements include reasons, grounds, or evidence to accept your conclusions. As your hearers follow your reasoning, inferences will be made regarding the relationships between your propositions and their truth value. It's important to ask during the sermon-preparation process, Does this make sense to my audience? Remember, the logic of your audience is more important than your own logic. If it makes sense to you but doesn't make sense to them, it's useless. You must communicate knowing that their logic always wins.[1] Transitions between your main points, connected conceptually to your sermon proposition, need to make sense.

You also want to ensure that your main points (and subpoints) connect linearly.[2] Ask yourself, Does my presentation flow naturally and continuously between the sender and receiver? Is my intended meaning the received meaning? Am I taking into account the latent or obvious feedback from my audience? Part of your job is to anticipate the kinds of questions and objections your listeners will have as you present the main movements of your sermon as articulated by your main points and transitions. In fact, using questions to frame your transition from one major idea to the next is very helpful in not only connecting your concepts but also propelling your listeners to the next idea. This helps you connect with your audience since they sense you are engaging their

---

1. For further reading in logic and fallacies, from an evangelical Reformed point of view, see Vern S. Poythress, *Logic: A God-Centered Approach to the Foundation of Western Thought* (Wheaton, Ill.: Crossway, 2013). Another helpful introductory textbook is Ernest Lepore, *Meaning and Argument*, 2nd rev. ed. (Hoboken: Wiley-Blackwell, 2012). For a more comprehensive book, consider Patrick Hurley, *A Concise Introduction to Logic*, 12th ed. (Boston: Cengage Learning, 2014); or Irving Copi, *Introduction to Logic*, 13th ed. (Upper Saddle River, N.J.: Prentice Hall, 2008). A book that helped me understand common fallacies, especially in historical writing, is David Fischer, *Historians' Fallacies* (New York: Harper, 1970). See also D. A. Carson, *Exegetical Fallacies* (Grand Rapids: Baker, 1996).
2. With the use of this term, I am not implying that preaching is a purely one-way mode of communication vis-à-vis the Shannon-Weaver model of the linear communication process (Claude Shannon and Warren Weaver, *A Mathematical Theory of Communication* [Chicago: University of Illinois Press, 1949]; see also David Berlo, *The Process of Communication: An Introduction to Theory and Practice* [New York: Holt, Rinehart, & Winston, 1960]). While most audiences do not speak back to the preacher (some traditions notwithstanding), the communication that occurs between the preacher and congregation is two-way; that is, it is more like the transactional model of communication introduced by Dean Barlund ("A Transactional Model of Communication," in *Foundations of Communication Theory*, ed. K. K. Sereno and C. D. Mortensen [New York: Harper, 1970]). This model recognizes that communication between the two parties is simultaneously occurring and the listener is not just passive. Though words are not spoken, listeners are communicating through their body language, facial expressions, etc. Furthermore, in this model, the context of the speaking situation and the culture of the listeners are also taken into account since they also impact the communication process. As such the preacher must take into account the nonverbal messages being communicated conceptually or physically by his audience.

own thought processes. When this is done well, preachers will often hear their listeners admit after the sermon, "How did you know what I was thinking?"

There are several kinds of transitions that you can use in your sermons and presentations. Whichever you use, make sure they do three things, especially the transitions between your main points: *connect* to the previous idea; *propel* you to the next idea; and *relate* to the sermon proposition. Let me highlight the four types that are most common.

Internal preview: As the name implies, these transitions preview the information that is to follow. Using this technique, the preacher provides a preview for listeners of the main points of the sermon during the introduction. They can also be used elsewhere in the sermon to preview an extended list. For example, if there are many subpoints or a long list of data coming up in the sermon, an internal preview can help the listener track the points.

Internal summary: Often used in the conclusion of the sermon, this type of transition summarizes information that was previously stated. It can also be utilized in other places of the sermon where extended listing has taken place, rehearsing for the listeners the salient points that they should remember.

Signposts: Like signs on a road that orient travelers to where they are or how much farther they need to go, these types of transitions are simple verbal phrases and statements that give listeners a clear sense of location and comfort. They can be stock phrases that signal to your hearers that you are transitioning to a new idea ("Let's move on," "Turning to our next …") or repeating key ideas ("Recapping," "Let me say it again"). They can be simple words or phrases, like cardinal numbers (1, 2, 3) or ordinal numbers (first, second, third).

Connectives: These types of transitions conceptually link the previous point or idea to the next point or idea. These work well between the main points of a sermon. There are several different ways they can be used: *complementary* transitions add one idea on to another ("also," "and," "next," "in addition to"); *causal* transitions establish a cause-and-effect relationship between two ideas ("consequently," "resulting in," "because"); *contrasting* transitions show how two ideas are different ("but," "although," "on the other hand"); and *chronological* transitions show how one idea proceeds or follows another in time ("next," "further," "then").

Design Element 5: Applications

Preaching is a combination of explanation, proclamation, and application. Preachers bear the privilege and responsibility of explaining the truths of the text and proclaiming Christ in the text. In addition to this, they must also apply all of these insights to the minds, hearts, and lives of their hearers. While maintaining attention and increasing retention are important goals of every sermon, the preacher is ultimately seeking the transformation of all who hear God's Word proclaimed. And while this life-changing process is ultimately a Spirit-driven activity, the Bible teaches us that the Word of God preached is a means of receiving God's grace.

God's grace changes us. God's grace is dispensed through means, specifically, the faithful preaching of the Word, the administration of the sacraments, and prayer.[3] Thus, one of the primary ways God nourishes his people with grace is through preaching. He uses the words of the preacher as an instrument for the transformation of believers. Throughout the NT, examples abound where the apostles concluded their preaching of Scripture with a call to faith and repentance. They applied the implications of who Jesus was and the salvation he offered through his sinless life and sacrificial death. They called their hearers to turn away from their sin in remorse and to put their complete trust in Christ alone for salvation. Furthermore, the apostles admonished believers with the implications of this gospel — in their homes,

---

3. "The outward and ordinary means whereby Christ communicateth to us the benefits of redemption are, his ordinances, especially the Word, sacraments, and prayer; all which are made effectual to the elect for salvation. The Spirit of God maketh the reading, but especially the preaching, of the Word, an effectual means of convincing and converting sinners, and of building them up in holiness and comfort, through faith, unto salvation" (WSC, Q&A 88–89). "The grace of faith, whereby the elect are enabled to believe to the saving of their souls, is the work of the Spirit of Christ in their hearts, and is ordinarily wrought by the ministry of the Word: by which also, and by the administration of the sacraments, and prayer, it is increased and strengthened" (WCF 14.1).

churches, workplaces. They applied God's truths via the gospel to their hearers. We must also apply the truth to the hearers.

How do we apply God's truths to our hearers, especially when the Bible doesn't cover all the issues we will face personally or pastorally? As I've stated before, preaching is both an art and a science, as is application. Humility and diligence is therefore needed to connect God's truths to your unique hearers—humility because you know it's the work of the Holy Spirit in changing people's minds, hearts, and lives; diligence because the Bible was not originally written for twenty-first-century North Americans. The Holy Scriptures are composed of multiple languages, diverse authors describing distant people, cultures, and lands, in various genres.[4] Yet in spite of all this, there is a unified message and a focused goal because of the Divine Author and his intentions to redeem a people for his own from multiple tribes, languages, peoples, and nations (Rev 5:9; 7:9; 14:6).

What follows are some general *principles* to guide you in any preaching setting. I cannot foresee the unique circumstances and people that you will face as a shepherd of a flock of God. As you go about your daily and weekly calling to pastor your people, you will undoubtedly face particular issues and problems, whether you are visiting someone in the cancer ward or counseling a couple whose marriage is falling apart. Through humble prayer and reliance on the Holy Spirit, you will need to discern how to apply God's truths to these unique issues and problems.[5] Keep these principles in mind as you develop applications from the preaching text: make sure they are present in the text, perceptible to the mind, penetrating to the heart, and practical to life.

Present in the text: Applications should cohere with what the text is either directly or indirectly communicating. It should be obvious to your hearers that the applications are present in the text as it has

---

4. Dan Doriani helpfully reveals how all genres of Scripture contain application (*Getting the Message: A Plan for Interpreting and Applying the Bible* [Phillipsburg, N.J.: P&R, 1996], 141–42).
5. Exercise wisdom in how much you share from the pulpit regarding personal counseling cases and issues within the church. In addition to legal ramifications, you want to honor the pastor-counselee privilege, in which conversations are kept confidential.

been explained and proclaimed in the sermon. They should appear to flow naturally from the preaching text and surrounding context. While many applications are possible from the text, prioritize what's emphasized in the text (i.e., the author's intentions). What are the main concerns and problems the human author is addressing for his original hearers? What applications does the author state directly or indirectly? If the applications of the text are culturally distant, what are the main principles behind them? How are these general concerns and problems present in the lives of my listeners today? How can I apply while being faithful to sound principles of interpretation? Based on the Divine Author's intention, how do these applications flow out of the gospel?

Perceptible to the mind: Make sure that the applications are comprehensible to your hearers' minds. Do the applications make sense to their reasoning? What *facts* are you trying to establish, change, or reinforce through the gospel?

Penetrating to the heart: Make sure that the applications are compelling to your hearers' hearts. Do the applications affect their convictions? What *values* are you trying to establish, change, or reinforce through the gospel? What idols of the heart is this text addressing? What idols of the heart does the gospel address?

Practical to life: Make sure that the applications are concrete with your hearers' lives. Do the applications practically impact their lives? What *actions* or *speech* are you trying to establish, change, or reinforce through the gospel?

In addition to these principles, here are some final tips regarding application.

- Embed at least one meaningful application for each main point of the sermon. While not an absolute, listeners need to see the relationship between the truths of the text and their own lives.
- Signal to your hearers that an application is forthcoming. Let them know through your language and delivery that something important is about to be said. In many ways, the applications in your sermon can be seen as emotional high points within

your main points. As music uses intensification (crescendo) to build up to a climax, so too build up your language and vocal dynamics to signal emphasis to your hearers as you approach the applications in your sermon.

- Be explicit in showing the relationship between the indicative and imperative. Applications are inherently in the imperative voice. Without proper grounding in the gospel that drives our gratitude-motivated responses, your applications can easily be received as merely moral advice. Connected to the reality of who Jesus is and our union with him by the Holy Spirit, our head, heart, and hand responses are part of our growth in grace.

- Remember, application is more personal. It requires a delivery that is more heightened than your normal conversational tone and style. Depending on the emotional weight of the application, it's important to convey the appropriate emotion in both your verbal and nonverbal communication. More will be said on this in the following chapters.

- Don't be afraid to state the obvious applications that are either directly stated in the text or implied by the text. You may think it's clear, but listeners are not in the same vantage point as you are. You've spent much more time thinking and meditating on the text and its implications. If not told explicitly, hearers will not get your point on their own, or more often than not, will refuse to hear the point.

Design Element 6: Illustrations

In addition to applications, illustrations are another tool to help us connect the truths of the text to the lives of our hearers. Illustrations are brief stories that help our hearers identify experientially with key points we are trying to make in our sermons. They differ from figures of speech, allusions, or examples because of the use of sensory details and emotional descriptions.[6] Let me offer some reasons for using illustrations and some

---

6. See Bryan Chapell, *Using Illustrations to Preach with Power* (Wheaton, Ill.: Crossway, 2001), 20–21.

strategies to help you use them effectively. For much of what follows, I am indebted to Bryan Chapell's excellent chapter on illustrations.[7]

Reasons for Using Illustrations

Before we begin, it may be helpful to present some potential pitfalls with the use of illustrations. First, some preachers may believe that illustrations are only helpful to keep people awake. Unfortunately, this places illustrations in the category of pure entertainment, serving no other purpose for the sermon except to distract. As heralds of the King, we are not called to detract from the King's message or squander the people's time with words that only detract. Second, some argue that illustrations are necessary because it keeps the message simple. While clarity and simplicity are praiseworthy goals in preaching, this excuse is usually given to warrant shallow sermons without much content. Again, as heralds sent with a life-transforming message, we must be diligent to faithfully and completely communicate God's message for his people.

If these are the pitfalls, what are some reasons for using illustrations? In addition to the six reasons Chapell gives, here are a few more reasons.[8]

- To supplement and complement the propositions we are declaring.
- To make abstract truths of the Bible more concrete and thus comprehensible.
- To help our hearers retain attention and increase retention.
- To make truth more meaningful by connecting the mind, heart, and will.

This last point is important. Illustrations help connect our own life experiences to the truths of Scripture that are meant to transform

---

7. Bryan Chapell, *Christ-Centered Preaching: Redeeming the Expository Sermon*, 2nd ed. (Grand Rapids: Baker Academic, 2005), 174–207.
8. Chapell gives six reasons why we must illustrate: (1) the crisis in preaching: preaching is considered irrelevant; (2) currents of culture: people in this visual age need more than just words; (3) footsteps of giants: past preachers used illustrations; (4) path to perception: postmodernism has changed the way people perceive reality; (5) guidance of Scripture: the Bible teaches we were created as holistic beings; and (6) way of the master: Jesus engaged in illustrating (ibid., 179–90).

us from our heads to our hearts to our hands. Chapell rightly states, "Illustrations persuade, stimulate involvement, touch the heart, stir the will, and result in decisions. *Thus, the primary purpose of illustrations is not to clarify but to motivate.*"[9] ✰

Strategies for Using Illustrations[10]

Be Connected: Make sure you connect the main idea of the illustration to the main point of the proposition. If possible, repeat key words or ideas to ensure a conceptual connection.

Be Clear: Make sure you are explicit with the insight following the illustration. Hearers often are incapable of drawing obvious conclusions or implications out of the presented illustration. You must draw clear conclusions for them. Shepherd your people by drawing out the implication, insight, application, and conclusion.

Be Concrete: Make sure the illustration is relevant to your hearers' real-world experiences. Make sure it connects with their whole person: mind, heart, and will.

Be Concise: Make sure you are succinct in the telling of your story. Since illustrations are stories, make sure you set the scene, introduce a problem or tension, come to a climax, and resolve the tension.

Be Colorful: Make sure your illustrations are vivid, utilizing all the senses so that hearers feel as if they are experiencing the story. Try to sense the emotional tone and mood of the story and re-create it through your words. Be careful not to include too many extraneous details. Be selective with your words to get the main idea and emotion across.

Be Careful: In this last category, I list several cautionary items regarding illustrations. The biblical point must take priority over the illustration. Make sure there's proportion; don't use too many illustrations.[11] And make sure you are accurate, honest, appropriate, sensitive, humble, and diligent.[12]

---

9. Ibid., 186; emphasis his.
10. See also Chapell's helpful reminders to use illustrations prudently and pastorally (ibid., 200–204).
11. Chapell recommends one illustration per main point (ibid., 201).
12. Chapell provides some helpful clues to find, store, and retrieve illustrations (ibid., 204–6).

The more I preach and the more I hear and evaluate sermons every week, I'm convinced that illustration is a vital component of sermons that are compelling to the hearers. Not only is it one of the easiest ways for a preacher to connect truth in the hearers' minds to their hearts and lives, but it also provides moments of cognitive rest when the content being presented is "heavy" in their experience. That is, many preachers often overload their messages with propositional content without any breaks. I find myself asking the preacher, "So what?" An apt illustration, inserted at the end of a three- to four-minute section of explanation or exposition, often provides listeners with the rational and emotional shift that helps consolidate the points being made. It's surprising how many times I've said to myself when evaluating a sermon, "He needs an illustration right now."

Design Element 7: Introductions

At this stage in the sermon-building process, you basically have all the components of your sermon. Now it's time to consider how to introduce your sermon. Let's look at four components that are the building blocks for effective introductions.[13]

Interest: Good introductions begin by building the interest of your hearers in the vital truths to be presented. Preachers should not assume that their hearers have the same conviction regarding this preaching moment. Many come to church with various and competing emotions, often not excited about you or the sermon. Though there are many ways to accomplish the building of interest, the key is to involve them with something impactful.

Inspiration: Related to building interest, good introductions provide inspiration in your hearers' minds and hearts. They need to be told why meeting with God in this moment is so significant. Tell them why they should listen. Tell them how God wants to transform them. As you inspire them, you will not only establish relevance in their lives, prompting more attention, but you will also establish good will by showing the selfless care and concern you have for their well-being. Here is where you may want to reveal the FCF of the text.[14]

---

13. For some helpful types of introductions, see ibid., 246–49.
14. See chapter 2 for a discussion of Bryan Chapell's understanding of the FCF.

Intention: Good introductions also set forth the main intention of the sermon. Revealing the carefully crafted sermon proposition in the introduction statement accomplishes this. In addition to building interest and showing relevance, introductions help hearers understand the main purpose of the sermon through the consequential format of the proposition. This format ensures you are connecting your overall goal to the text of Scripture you are preaching from that day. Repeat the sermon proposition if necessary to ensure comprehension.

Index: The last element of a good introduction is to index, or preview, your main points. Reveal the map of the journey you will be leading your listeners on. Help pre-encode their brains with the main ideas that they need to pay attention to so that their brains will fire on the information for encoding. Some may argue that revealing the points up front undermines the possibility of mystery. I'm convinced that during the early years of one's preaching career, one should choose clarity over creativity.

Design Element 8: Conclusions

Though this topic is listed last in the order for sermon design, this may be one of the most important components. Not only does the conclusion bring the sermon proposition to its stated goal, but it also brings the sermon to its emotional close. Unfortunately, many young preachers neglect preparing the conclusion for various reasons. Perhaps they ran out of time since they focused on the main points. Or perhaps they think conclusions are unimportant in contrast to the rest of the sermon. Whatever the reason may be, conclusions require careful discernment and design. The following are some important features of good conclusions to keep in mind.

Closure: Good conclusions provide closure for the entire sermon. First, signal to your hearers that you are actually ending. Perhaps you can even use the same device you used in the introduction to provide a sense of unity. Do not introduce any new ideas. Make sure you close, keeping it succinct.

Coherence: Make sure you connect back to the sermon's main purpose in the sermon proposition. You should be able to show how the whole sermon coheres, primarily by revealing how your main points contributed in bringing your sermon to its natural end.

Conviction: Your conclusion also needs to end with conviction, moving your hearers through closing statements that motivate their will to respond to the main gospel applications you have articulated in the sermon. Let their last impression of you be one of heralding the King's heartfelt desire for his people to love, trust, and obey him more.

Design Element 9: Composition

As you compose your sermon, remember that there are three kinds of outlines you may use during the sermon-preparation and delivery process. First, you will have a *working outline*, which is the informal and initial outline that you used to structure the main points and main movements of your sermon. Much of the wording in this outline will be single words and phrases that help you in the construction phase of framing the entire sermon. Second, you will have a *formal outline*, or manuscript. This outline fills out the informal outline by expanding on the words and phrases, turning them into complete sentences so that anyone reading it can understand the flow of thought. Now you've added the floors, walls, and roof to the sermon so that it is complete. Third and last, there is the *speaking outline.* This is the outline you will use when you go into the pulpit to preach. As each preacher has unique strengths and weaknesses in terms of memory ability, this outline may look different from preacher to preacher. What's important is that you take only what is necessary so that eye contact is not undermined.

Let's now review the nine design elements for sermons that are full of truth, goodness, and beauty.

1. Formulate your *sermon proposition* in a consequential format ("Because ..., then ...").
2. Pattern the *main points* that will structure your entire sermon.
3. Develop the *subpoints* that will supplement your main points.
4. Build the *transitions*, paying close attention to the logic and flow.
5. Generate appropriate *applications*.
6. Include insightful *illustrations*.
7. Create your *introduction*.
8. Create your *conclusion*.
9. *Compose* the sermon.

At this point, I recommend that you write out your sermon exactly the way you would speak it, remembering to write for the ear, not for the eye. You will refine this initial manuscript, but it helps to write it out completely. As you go over the manuscript, edit ruthlessly, replacing complexity with clarity. A twenty-five-minute sermon is about 2,500 words (7 pages double spaced).[15] Once you believe the written manuscript is in its best shape, read it aloud. Is the language natural, simple, clear, and vivid? If not, rewrite. Keep fighting to get it right. Remember, words matter. Usually first drafts will be 20–30 percent too long. You will need to tighten, cut, clarify, and strip. This is actually the fun part.

After reading the sermon aloud again, go ahead and close with prayer as if you just finished the sermon and God's people are there before you. As you pray aloud in this setting, see if any of the ideas and words of the prayer might be helpful to incorporate into the application sections of the sermon. I often hear many wonderful exhortations and applications in the closing prayers of student preachers that they did not include in the body of their sermon. Early in your preaching ministry, this is a helpful exercise that will aid you in your preparation.

Now that you have your manuscript polished, prepare your preaching outline. I advise against taking a manuscript up to the pulpit, as it will often force you to read your sermon and not engage with your audience. Rather, focus on the core 25 percent of the sermon that you believe is most important for your hearers to know at the end of the sermon. You may want to try the following five-page model for your preaching outline.

- Page 1: The Scripture text, the prayer of illumination, and the introduction (all scripted word for word).
- Pages 2–4: An outline of each point, with certain sentences manuscripted (main points, key insights, transitions). The rest can be fragments in outline format.
- Page 5: Conclusion and closing prayer (scripted word for word).

---

15. See Chapell, *Christ-Centered Preaching*, 350–51.

PART 4

DELIVERING THE SERMON *for* ATTENTION, RETENTION, INTEGRATION, *and* TRANSFORMATION

CHAPTER 8

THE INFLUENCE OF NEUROSCIENCE ON THE DESIGN AND DELIVERY OF THE SERMON

This chapter begins with a simple premise: <u>the design and delivery</u> ☆ <u>of a sermon is just as important as the discovery and discernment</u> <u>of the biblical text.</u> Remember what Proverbs 25:11 states?

A word fitly spoken is like apples of gold in a setting of silver. (ESV)

The right word at the right time is like precious gold set in silver. (CEV)

Good content (right words) have great value (like precious gold) when they are designed and delivered (set in silver) for maximum impact. Great preachers seem to have effortless delivery. But behind that seemingly impromptu ability is great design. Conversely, valuable content is often squandered through disordered design and dreary delivery.

As a professor of preaching, and more importantly, as a preacher myself, I want to discover ways to preach more effectively with fidelity for God's glory and for the good of the church. To that end, one particular area of research that has aided me is the growing field of neurology, or neuroscience. What follows is a brief look at twelve interesting facts about how the *brain functions*, followed by *preaching implications* of these facts for sermon design and delivery. Many of these implications for sermon design and delivery will be expanded in the following chapters.

Before we begin, however, a few caveats are necessary. It should be obvious that this chapter cannot adequately provide all the necessary details related to the data on neuroscience. After all, there is an enormous amount of information related to neuroscience, and this chapter represents a very small and limited scope. I am merely providing simple explanations of the recent discoveries in brain science that have applicability for sermon design and delivery. Thus, I will not provide many footnotes and detailed scientific explanations. For those interested in further reading, please consult the bibliography.

To state the obvious, every brain is different. Every brain is wired differently due to the complex ways in which the brain grows and learns through experience. As such, this chapter can only provide broad generalizations regarding the way our brains function. The sheer enormity of the diversity within the brain added to the amount of actual brains in the world prohibits precise definitions and prescriptions.

Much of what you will read may seem like common sense. Perhaps you've read these ideas before, or more likely, your life experience has revealed some of the insights we will discuss. Either way, I think that the more we learn about how our God has fearfully and wonderfully made us, especially our brains, it will help us to be faithful stewards of all that we have. This chapter is an attempt to learn more from science so that as preachers we can return to God the glory that is due his name and bless his people with sermons that are like gold in settings of silver.

1. "Character Matters."
Brain Function
Brain research has demonstrated that the hearers' perception of the speaker directly correlates to their levels of attention and retention. If the speaker is considered credible and the speaking environment is considered safe, the levels of attention and retention in the hearers increase.

Conversely, if the hearers perceive the speaker to be arrogant, untrustworthy, or insincere, it will be a long thirty minutes for both parties. One study in a scientific journal revealed that the part of the brain involved in mediating emotions, the amygdala, influences the ability to pay attention and learn.[1] The perception of your character can enhance or diminish your effectiveness as a speaker. While even negative perceptions can command the attention of a hearer, speakers do well to demonstrate their integrity and authenticity in the sermon. Character does matter.

Many ancient rhetoricians agreed that credibility was vital in fostering the best possible listening atmosphere for persuasion. Influenced by Aristotle's concept and his belief in the importance of *ethos* (credibility) in the speaker, Quintillian stated,

> What really carries weight in deliberative speeches is the authority of the speaker. For he, who would have all men trust his judgment as to what is expedient and honorable, should both possess and be regarded as possessing genuine wisdom and excellence of character.[2]

Establish your credibility and build rapport with your hearers, especially at the beginning of the sermon.

Preaching Implications

- One of the simplest ways to demonstrate credibility is in your *dress*. Hearers will *see* you before they *hear* you. Thus, dress in such a way as to promote your credibility and integrity.[3]
- Further, your *demeanor* can also help or hurt your chances of being heard. Your facial expressions and body language will communicate to your hearers. You want to communicate credibility with authenticity. Now, for most pastors, the ongoing

---

1. James McGaugh, C. McIntyre, and A. Power, "Amygdala Modulation of Memory Consolidation: Interaction with Other Brain Systems," *Neurobiology of Learning and Memory* 78 (2002): 539–52.
2. *Institutio Oratorio of Quintillian*, vol. 1, trans. H. E. Butler (Boston: Harvard University Press, 1958), 485.
3. Appropriate dress will differ between cultures and times. Some pastors wear an ecclesiastical robe or gown to reveal the distinction between the minister and others, and some wear clothing similar to their church members. The key is to be intentional—building credibility with your unique audience so as to promote their willingness to hear you.

relationship you have with your congregation clearly influences the culture of trust you want to build not only for your sermon on Sunday but also for your general ministry. Nonetheless, you will be a more effective speaker if you build genuine rapport with your hearers every time you enter the pulpit to preach.

2. "Ready, Aim, Fire!"
Brain Function

The brain goes through a three-step process for maximum attention and retention to occur. Like a gun, it loads, aims, and fires. The brain loads information when the brain is alerted to take notice. The brain then aims by looking for more of the same information. The brain then fires when it acts on the information given. Designing your sermon with this three-step process in mind increases the chances that your hearers will listen and learn. Why is this important? One of your goals in preaching ought to be a high "return on investment." That is, for every word you preach, your goal is for maximum encoding to occur in the minds and hearts of your hearers.

Research also shows that our memories vary in strength. For maximum retention to occur, three variables need to be considered: the intensity of the initial firing of the brain, the number of repeated firings, and the relevance of the memory.[4] This is important because of the way the brain pays attention. Generally, the brain is attentive to the information it is given in two primary ways: "top-down" and "bottom-up." Top-down attention occurs when the brain voluntarily and intentionally chooses to pay attention to the stimuli (e.g., words and ideas). Bottom-up attention is the involuntary and unconscious way our brain responds to stimuli (e.g., sirens, babies crying, seeing a familiar face at the store). Normally, in life and in sermons brains are engaging in both, with competition and distractions occurring simultaneously. Thus, intentionality in design and delivery is crucial.

4. Timothy A. Berner, "Preaching with the Brain in Mind: Can Neuroscience Enhance Biblical Preaching?" (DMin project, Luther Seminary, 2008), 64.

Preaching Implications

- Preview your points to help pre-encode the brain and then repeat those ideas later in the sermon to encode them into the brain. This is especially effective in the introduction of the sermon and when your main points have many subpoints. Transitions are also a key area where effective encoding can take place as you repeat and preview ideas.
- Present your points in novel, unique, and repetitive ways to ensure encoding. Include surprises in your *content* (aphorisms, turns of phrases, poetic word choices, leitmotifs), *design* (narrative arc, parallelism in main points, unexpected transitions), and *communication* (rate, pitch, volume, movement, facial expressions) to increase attention and retention.
- Illustrate with focused imagery. Think about illustrations with this 3-step process: *load* the key insight you want to teach, help the brain *aim* by telling the concise illustration, then help the brain *fire* by explicitly stating the insight. Many of us will often remember a good illustration from a sermon but not remember the main points. This is because of the brain's ability to fire on information that is attached to a pre-encoded idea along with focused imagery. Furthermore, illustrations are also memorable because they are meaningful; they connect with hearers personally.
- Other skills that help in the encoding process are: tight organization, meaningfulness (more on this later), and focused imagery.[5]

3. "One at a Time, Please!"
Brain Function

The brain is a self-organizing, self-maximizing memory system that naturally creates patterns. The brain normally organizes information

---

5. See Joshua Foer, *Moonwalking with Einstein* (New York: Penguin, 2012), for the power of focused imagery for memory.

in a linear, serial pattern (one thing at a time). People process most effectively when they learn sequentially with a specific goal in mind.

The brain is like a conveyer belt: it handles information units one item at a time (contra multitasking brain function). If a lot happens at the front of the belt and gets clogged up, nothing moves forward. Or if there is not a clear end point, all the information becomes a random mess. Thus, even though you may have the best content in the world, randomness of ideas leads to confusion and disorientation at best, frustration and disengagement at worse. Why?

This is because most preachers are instinctively sender-oriented.[6] Whether we realize it or not, we tend to prepare and give sermons and speeches with information that interests us rather than with what our hearers actually need. Thus, our sermons are loaded with information that is often unrelated or irrelevant to our desired outcomes. We thus fire-hose whatever material we excavate from our texts without any awareness of whether or not it aids in building up to our homiletic goal. To use another metaphor, we often "show up and throw up" or we "spray and pray" that something sticks. More volume does not always equal more value. Often, the opposite is true.

Preaching Implications

- Be selective with your information. Be selective with your material in order to reach your homiletic destination along a logical and linear pathway. Don't aimlessly ramble. If you give information that is not aligned with your pre-encoded direction, encoding the right information to arrive at your intended location is made more difficult. Don't overload your sermon with irrelevant info. Ruthlessly edit, asking yourself whether or not the data that you have before you are crucial, optional, or nonessential.[7]

- Be simple with your ideas. Be simple and clear with your supporting material. Complex words, abstract ideas, and long

---

6. I am indebted to Tim Pollard for these insights. See the website www.oratium.com for more information on his training program on effective presentations.
7. See chapter 6 for more on the principle of selectivity.

sentences will tire your hearers (unlike reading). At best, their brains will need to shut you off to process and figure out what you just communicated, and they won't hear what you're saying next. Remember, the goal of being simple is different from being a simpleton. One is an adjective describing something that is clear and uncomplicated. The other is a noun describing a fool who, for example, does not heed the often-repeated advice to keep his sermons simple.

• Be succinct with your words. In your design and delivery, make sure you choose conciseness in light of audience capacity. Again, your goal is high return on investment. Most audience members will not be able to accommodate too much information that is processed through the ears. Be intentional and concise with your language.

4. "Head, Heart, and Hands."
Brain Function

The area of the brain that is primarily being activated while listening to a sermon is the prefrontal cortex. This part of the brain deals with such functions as abstract thinking, reasoning, and evaluating. Not only is it primarily involved in problem solving and maintaining attention, but it also inhibits emotional impulses.[8] It includes making choices between right and wrong as well as governing social cues, such as suppressing or exhibiting emotion. Thus, it connects the head, the heart, and the hands.

Brain research shows that when information is emotionally relevant to the hearer, the likelihood of attention, retention, and integration is increased. When people listen to sermons, they use their working memory to process what is said. Working memory, or short-term memory, involves several stages in the brain.[9] First, all sensory stimuli from the

8. John Medina, *Brain Rules: 12 Principles for Surviving and Thriving at Work, Home, and School* (Seattle: Pear Press, 2008), 40.
9. This section is adapted from Berner, "Preaching with the Brain in Mind," 69–70.

sermon (what is seen and heard) go to the thalamus, which relays signals to the cortex and the amygdala for further processing. While both of these parts of the brain play a role in attention, memory, and language processing, the amygdala plays a unique role in checking the newly arrived information for emotional relevance. It does this by comparing what it just received to long-term memories stored in the hippocampus, especially emotional ones. When the brain notices a pattern between the new and the old, it reacts. If it triggers negative emotions such as fear, the body receives signals to either fight or take flight.

When the amygdala connects the data to favorable emotional memories, however, the body can experience positive reactions. Thus, one of the brain's functions is to connect newly received data with older data tied to emotions in long-term memory. One of the fundamental emotional systems that the brain uses is this "seeking" process (reward and pleasure).[10] This may partially explain why some sermons are so memorable and transformative to us—because they were emotionally meaningful and relevant. Brains are "wired" emotionally to seek what is meaningful and relevant. We want to preach in ways that connect emotionally to our hearers.

It's important to remember that this process of working memory has some amazing capabilities but is also very limited. Scientists for years have learned that phone numbers should be limited to seven numbers, since working memory can only hold onto seven, plus or minus two, units of information. It's not all bad news though. The brain is also a very powerful organ. Take, for example, this string of letters. Reading through these letters just once, try to memorize as much as you can:

IBMFBICIAJFKLSDNOW

Now, without looking back at this page, how many letters can you recall? Six? Seven? Did you also notice something happening as you

---

10. The others include fear, rage, and panic (Jon Panksepp, *Affective Neuroscience: The Foundations of Human and Animal Emotions* [Oxford: Oxford University Press, 1998]; cited in Berner, "Preaching with the Brain in Mind," 71).

were looking at them? Now look at the same string of letters put into this pattern:

IBM FBI CIA JFK LSD NOW

What's the point? You want to maximize the capabilities of your audience's working memory. Maximizing storage and retrieval capabilities becomes a vital factor for preachers who desire to aid and not diminish their hearers' use of their working memory. One way to do that is to remember how working memory likes patterns. Another way is to remember that the emotional environment in which learning takes place affects the quality of learning.[11] For preachers, the emotional environment is often made up of the relationship they have with their congregants. If hearers feel safe and loved, the potential impact of the sermon increases. Thus, engaging both the rational part of the prefrontal cortex and the emotional part, the head and heart, will more likely influence the volitional part, the hands.

Preaching Implications

- State directly in the introduction why the sermon is relevant to the hearers. Why should they listen? Why does it matter? Connect the main idea of the sermon to their lives. Answer the "So what?" question that will be lurking in the minds of your hearers as you begin the sermon.[12]
- Apply each critical point/idea in the sermon. Don't wait until the end of the sermon to give "three applications." Rather, learn to apply the truth to hearers' lives for maximum impact on working memory. As one of my former colleagues used to teach our students, "Strike while the iron's hot." That is, after a period of exposition and explanation of the text and its truths, the preacher should connect the significance of the data to the experiences of the hearers.
- Use illustrative material (stories, anecdotes, etc.) to help connect

---

11. Medina, *Brain Rules*, 45–46.
12. This is covered in detail in the discussion of the sermon proposition in chapter 6.

truth to emotion, resulting in more attention and retention. The vivid and concrete elements of storytelling help forge relevance as memories and emotions are stirred in the listener. When an illustration is told following a particular explanation of a doctrine, for example, the brain is given another perspective of the data. Propositions stated in prose format are complemented by an illustration told in narrative genre. Multiple perspectives of the same truth, especially when emotions are triggered and relevance is experienced, yields heightened attention and retention. Also, make sure to answer the "So what?" question that hearers will be asking at the end of an illustration. Explicitly state the insight.

- Choose words, sentences, and ideas that help the listener connect truth in real, concrete, and vivid ways. This may be called "experiential truth" in that it *engages the head, the heart, and the hands*—reason, emotion, and volition. Connecting truth with an emotion creates more meaningfulness and relevance for the hearer, thereby increasing the potential for deeper memory storage and retrieval.
- Focus on common human experiences and heart issues (idols). This is because it is difficult to tailor truth explanations and truth experiences for each individual in your congregation.
- Find creative ways to repeat and pattern critical points, ideas, and themes throughout the sermon. Repetition that impacts the head, heart, and hands aids hearers to move information from working memory to long-term memory. This is especially important in the conclusion as you close with coherence and conviction. Repeat to remember.

5. "Don't Get Your Wires Crossed."
Brain Function
At birth, the brain of a baby has approximately 100 billion neurons. These neurons receive and give information to regulate many different

processes that take place in the human body. The interconnections in the brain are called synapses, and they continue forming as the child learns and experiences new things. Research into this network of neurons in our brains has revealed that every brain is wired differently and continues to grow and change over time.

The brain has three types of "wiring" built into it.[13] Experience *independent* wiring is composed of the circuits of neurons that control basic functions like breathing, the beating of your heart, and knowing where your foot is without looking at it. Experience *expectant* wiring are the circuits that are semiformed but unfinished at birth, waiting for experiences to "finish up" its development, for example, visual acuity and language acquisition. And experience *dependent* wiring refers to the neural networks that are flexible and grow only through external life experiences.

If every listener's brain is wired differently and every listener's brain grows differently through experiences, then preachers cannot approach all their listeners in the same "cookie-cutter" way. Rather, wise preachers should develop and increase their skills in theory of mind. That is, they need to build and develop their empathy for and sensitivity to their unique audiences. According to John Medina, theory of mind is defined as "the ability to understand the interior motivations of someone else and the ability to construct a predictable 'theory of how their mind works' based on that knowledge."[14] Whether one is a parent or preacher, the ability to predict the thinking of a child or hearer can tremendously influence their effectiveness in teaching them. Another way of talking about this is learning the art and science of audience analysis. Effective

---

13. Medina, *Brain Rules*, 60.
14. Ibid., 67. For more on the theory of mind, see D. Premack and A. Premack, *Original Intelligence: Unlocking the Mystery of Who We Are* (Boston: McGraw Hill, 2003), 1–28; M. Siegal and R. Varley, "Neural Systems Involved in the Theory of Mind," *National Review of Neuroscience* 3 (2002): 463–71; R. Peter Hobson, *The Cradle of Thought: Exploring the Origins of Thinking* (New York: Macmillan, 2002), 61–94; Roger Lewin, *Human Evolution: An Illustrated Introduction*, 4th ed. (Oxford: Blackwell Science, 1999), 192–94; Nicholas Humphrey, *The Inner Eye: Social Intelligence in Evolution* (Oxford: Oxford University Press, 2003); Mark H. Davis, "Measuring Individual Differences in Empathy: Evidence for a Multidimensional Approach," *Journal of Personal Social Psychology* 44 (1983): 113–26.

communication involves knowing your audience and effectively crafting your message to reach them. For preachers, this skill of empathy also
involves knowing and loving the "sheep" in their churches.

Preaching Implications

- Anticipate questions and objections from various groups in your
  audience. As you interpret your preaching passage, an important
  element of communicating the truths you discover is to foresee
  how your hearers will receive it. Will they readily believe and
  accept it, or will they be suspicious or even hostile? This pre-
  sumes, of course, that you know your audience and insofar as
  you can, deduce how they think.
- Answer the questions and objections that you believe are emerging
  in the hearts and minds of your audience as you go through your
  sermon. If you deduce that your audience will be thinking or
  feeling a certain way as a result of what you just stated, answer the
  nagging question or objection that is present. Often, stating the
  obvious question and answering it in the sermon will help your
  hearer connect rationally and emotionally to you and your message.
- Ask questions to persuade and propel. Another great way to
  connect to your hearers with empathy is to ask rhetorical questions that they may be thinking. Even if they're not thinking it,
  a well-timed relevant question will often propel your hearer to
  logical conclusions that they did not previously consider. These
  types of questions serve well as transitions in a sermon.
- Apply points to the whole person (head, heart, hands). Preachers
  will want to connect truths from Scripture holistically, that is,
  reveal how God's Word applies to the way they think, feel, and
  live. Grow in your ability to see the connections between God's
  truths and the lives of your people. This will demonstrate your
  sensitivity as you reveal relevance. This is especially vital in the
  parts of the sermon where you want to emotionally connect with
  your audience (e.g., the introduction, key pastoral moments, and
  the conclusion).

6. "Look into My Eyes."
Brain Function

Research has shown that the intensity of a stimulus influences how the brain pays attention. Said another way, the attention and retention of the brain is increased by the intensity of sound, light, smell, and so on.[15] In the context of preaching, intensity correlates to emotions. One researcher stated this principle this way: "Emotions drive attention, create meaning, and have their own memory pathways."[16] If the speaker shows heightened emotion, it is more likely that the hearer will receive and remember what is said. Simply put, brains are stimulated to pay attention and remember when strong emotions are present.

One of the reasons this is the case is the presence of mirror neurons in our brains. As the name implies, these neurons "mirror" what is being said, and more importantly, emoted. Hearers "feel" the same emotions the speaker is expressing. If you preach with passion and emotional intensity, it will not only draw the attention of your hearers but also increase the likelihood of retention, hopefully leading to integration and transformation. These neurons are sensitive, especially to eye contact and facial expressions. Thus, in addition to the work of the Holy Spirit, we are wired to mirror what we observe. Thus, the speaker's passion and conviction, especially as seen in his eyes and face, will impact reception and retention. Eye contact and facial expressions are more important than you may have realized.

Preaching Implications

- Spend about two or three seconds on each set of eyes — not much longer! Make sure you sweep the entire room, focusing on small groups of people. Don't stare too long at one person, especially when discussing sensitive topics. Be strategic and

---

15. This is why commercials are recorded louder than normal television programming.
16. Joseph LeDoux, *The Emotional Brain: The Mysterious Underpinnings of Emotional Life* (New York: Simon and Schuster: 1996), cited in Eric Jensen, *Teaching with the Brain in Mind*, 2nd ed. (Alexandria, Va.: Association for Supervision and Curriculum Development, 2005), 69.

intentional when you look down at your notes and when you look up at the audience.

- Signal to the audience degrees of emphasis through the intentional and strategic use of volume, pace, pitch, facial expressions, and body language. Good speakers signal the audience when to "lean in" and listen with extra care and "lean out" and take a cognitive break.[17] This means you've prioritized content and picked out what you'll emphasize in light of the limited amount of your hearers' lean-in/lean-out capacity.
- Show passion and emotion when appropriate and when it's helpful to the sermon. Display a balance of joy and gravity, warmth and seriousness. You want to reveal genuine and infectious enthusiasm. Most speakers are never nearly as expressive with facial expressions and gestures as they should be.

7. "Two Are Stronger Than One."
Brain Function

Sensory processes in the brain are wired to work together.[18] Here's an illustration to help you understand how the brain naturally integrates senses. Imagine you were shown a video with the person saying the word "ga." Minutes later, the same video was shown, but there was one change: the audio had been switched and the sound that came out was "ba." The mouth formed the word "ga," but the sound that came out was "ba." In this instance, the confused brain attempts to reconcile the dissonance and compromise. For most people watching the second video, the sound they actually hear is "da." This is the brain's way of integrating the senses.

For a more practical application, Richard Mayer demonstrated that students using multisensory environments always perform better than those in unisensory environments. His experiments involved subjects

---

17. I am indebted to Tim Pollard of *Oratium* for these ideas of strategically signaling the audience to "lean in" and "lean out" based on the goals of your presentation.
18. Medina, *Brain Rules*, 201–3.

receiving information via one sense (sight or sound) and other subjects who had the same information delivered with a combination of both sight and sound. The group with multisensory input always did better recalling the information than those with just one sensory input. In fact, their recall had better resolution and lasted longer. In another study, he demonstrated that those learning in multisensory environments had 50 to 75 percent more creative solutions on a problem-solving test.[19] As a result of his research, Mayer developed interesting "rules" for multimedia presentations.

- Multimedia principle: Students learn better from words and pictures than from words alone.
- Temporal contiguity principle: Students learn better when corresponding words and pictures are presented simultaneously rather than successively.
- Spatial contiguity principle: Students learn better when corresponding words and pictures are presented near to each other rather than far from each on the page or screen.
- Coherence principle: Students learn better when extraneous material is excluded rather than included.
- Modality principle: Students learn better from animation and narration than from animation and on-screen text.[20]

These examples reveal the brain's powerful integrative instincts. Two are indeed stronger than one. Thus, the learning ability of the brain, especially when dealing with working memory, is optimized if the environment for learning is multisensory. More cognitive input from various sensory channels increases the likelihood of recall because it increases the ability of the brain to integrate new information with previous information. Conversely, the more unisensory an environment is, the less likely effective attention and retention will occur. In the context of preaching, the difference would be listening to a sermon

---

19. Richard E. Mayer, "Multimedia Learning: Are We Asking the Right Questions?" *Educational Psychology* 32, no. 1 (1997): 1–19. See also Richard E. Mayer, *Multi-Media Learning* (Cambridge, U.K.: Cambridge University Press, 2001).
20. Summarized in Medina, *Brain Rules*, 210.

through your iPod (unisensory) versus experiencing a sermon live at a church (multisensory). Medina writes, "There is no question that multiple cues, dished up via different senses, enhance learning. They speed up responses, increase accuracy, improve stimulation detection, and enrich encoding at the moment of learning."[21]

Preaching Implications

- Ensure when you preach that your words and your actions are integrated for maximum impact on your audience. That is, make sure there is no dissonance between content and communication. Rather, complement and supplement your words and actions to achieve your sermonic and pastoral goals. Be aware of how your verbal communication factors (e.g., volume, pace, and pitch) integrate with what you are saying. Also be aware of how your non-verbal communication skills (eye contact, facial expressions, hand gestures, body movement) are working together with your content.

- Take advantage of the opening moments of the sermon. If your sermon at this critical cognitive moment is multisensory, overall retention will likely increase. As you initially state the life-transforming relevance of the sermon, reveal both your passion for these truths and your compassion for your hearers.

- Repeat key ideas of the sermon using multisensory cues. If you repeat information at timed intervals employing multiple senses, the memory consolidation of your hearers will increase.[22]

8. "Repeat, Then Repeat Again."
Brain Function

If our goal is for gospel integration to occur in the lives of our hearers, ideas need to move from working memory to long-term memory. For

---

21. Ibid., 214.

22. Medina summarizes an interesting experiment in which the reexposure of a scent helped memory recall increase from 86 percent to 97 percent (*Brain Rules*, 215). See also Björn Rasch et al., "Odor Cues During Slow-Wave Sleep Prompt Declarative Memory Consolidation," *Science* 315 (2007): 1426–29.

ideas to transfer from working to long-term memory, verbal rehearsal is necessary. Verbal rehearsal is the process through which strong memories that can last a lifetime are created. While long-term memory is still mysterious to neuroscientists, research has shown that verbal rehearsal, which is a "mechanism that uses auditory signals to code information into the working memory," is key to this transfer.[23] In other words, when the brain engages in the rethinking and reexperiencing of information that is patterned similarly, the transfer of data from working to long-term memory is more likely to occur. When information in working memory experiences a lot of verbal rehearsal (coupled with emotional intensity), the neural networks that are involved grow in strength to the point of becoming part of long-term memory.

Preaching Implications

- Be convinced that only the gospel of Jesus can change lives. The gospel saves and makes holy; it justifies and sanctifies. Thus, preachers must believe that preaching the gospel faithfully from every part of Scripture is the key to new life.
- Be consistent and persistent in preaching the gospel and its implications to life. Done patiently over time, this will help hearers integrate truths in their lives. Thus, preachers must practice the art and science of preaching the gospel week in and week out with clarity, cogency, compassion, and consistency.

9. "Wake Up!"
Brain Function

Researchers have shown that the prefrontal cortex tires very easily, especially when confronted with irrelevant, uninteresting, and uninspiring information that is delivered without variation. I'm sure many of us have experienced this ourselves! When tired, the brain will shut down on its own accord, whether you realize it to or not. The brain is only 2 percent of our body weight, but it uses 20 percent of our body's energy.

---

23. Berner, "Preaching with the Brain in Mind," 65.

Furthermore, the brain can only simultaneously activate 2 percent of its neurons at any one time because if it used more, the glucose supply in our bodies would be spent and we would faint.[24]

This is why people in church—perhaps even you—get so sleepy in the middle of a sermon: not because you didn't sleep well the night before but because your brain is on overload and needs to shut down and rest. Delivery includes both high-intensity and low-intensity variations. The key problem is not the level of intensity (high or low), but the continuation of one type of intensity, be it consistent high volume (think screamer) or monotonous slow pace (think mumbler).

Preaching Implications

- Insert cognitive breaks in the sermon for processing and rest. This can be done with delivery. If you have to use a difficult word or complex ideas (propositions), slow down, use intentional pauses to allow hearers to process and learn more effectively.
- Build into your sermon sections that allow the brain some downtime so it is not working too hard for too long. Insert low-intensity material (stories, illustrations, anecdotes) in strategic places to give the brain time to process and rest. These provide "lean out" moments for your audience to sit back and relax before you build up to a climax.
- Though this is not discussed much in preaching books, this brain function may have implications for what is done in the worship service after the sermon. Perhaps allowing time for your hearers to reflect quietly after the sermon may allow for more efficient processing and integration of the material. In fact, research has shown that times of rest when the brain is not actively engaging in new learning is crucial in forming long-term memories. This is the time when the brain has the freedom to organize and prioritize what it recently learned.

24. Ibid., 20.

10. "Quiet, Please."

Brain Function

The brain naturally inhibits and blocks out distractions, whether or not we are even aware of it. This has both positive and negative aspects. Think for example, of how we are able to block out background noise in a restaurant while talking with our spouse. But think how difficult it is to listen to the sermon at church while a baby is crying in the back of the room. Sometimes we don't even know the impact it can have. For example, researchers have shown that the reason you are physically tired after a plane ride is because of the brain's natural process of trying to block out the high volume (approximately 100 decibels, compared to the point when hearing loss can occur with sustained exposure: 90–95 decibels).

Unfortunately, many sermons are designed and delivered with too many things that distract the listener—be it perplexing content, convoluted organization, or awkward communication. In speech-communication theory, this is known as *interference*. Anything that interferes with the intended message of the speaker becomes the actual message that is received and accepted by the hearer.

Distractions are more detrimental to preaching effectively than preachers imagine or know. <u>Researchers have discovered that distractions essentially cause the brain to automatically multitask</u>. One definitive study revealed the problems that occur in the brain when it is forced to deal with competing stimuli.[25] When a person's attention is divided, the brain experiences decreased cognitive control and loss of ability to process information. It is hard to focus when the brain is fractured. Add to this the effect technology has had on people in our generation and their resulting lack of attention and retention spans. In his book *The Shallows*, Nicholas Carr has effectively argued that Internet use practically causes brain damage.[26] So you need to be aware of and respond to factors that may inhibit the encoding process.

---

25. Eyal Ophira, Clifford Nass, and Anthony D. Wagner, "Cognitive Control in Media Multitaskers," *PNAS: Proceedings of the National Academy of Sciences* 106/37 (August 24, 2009): 15583–87; http://www.pnas.org/content/106/37/15583.full (accessed January 23, 2015).
26. Nicholas Carr, *The Shallows: What the Internet Is Doing to Our Brains* (New York: W. W. Norton, 2011).

Preaching Implications

- Remove potential distractions in the sermon. This may include both content (jargon, abstract ideas, nonlinear logic, etc.) and delivery (bad pace, distracting mannerisms, annoying volume, etc.). Be aware of the distractions in the sermon that are competing with your hearers' ability to process, learn, and remember.
- Respond to potential and real distractions in the room. Good speakers intentionally and strategically prepare for anything that may distract—both external factors present in the room (e.g., temperature, lighting, noises) as well as internal factors present in the hearers (e.g., hostility, apathy, hunger).
- This implication is especially important in the introduction as you establish your credibility by putting them at ease and placing their interests before yours.

11. "Practice Makes Perfect."

Brain Function

The brain can use hundreds of neural pathways to move aural information to its desired destination.[27] This is one reason you as a preacher are able to remember some parts of your sermon but forget others. But neuroscience has revealed that practicing one's presentation creates thicker and stronger neural pathways for a particular subject or idea. Without practice, our brains often take random neural paths that are used to move information or use old ones that are not as efficient. With consistent practice, the possible pathways are reduced from 100 to 8–10 possible ones. This confirms something you've already experienced: practice makes perfect.

Also, practicing increases serotonin levels in the brain, which suppresses the part of the brain that produces fear and worry. Practice decreases anxiety while it increases precision, which increases clarity, which increases confidence, which increases conviction and

---

27. See David Weiner, *Reality Check: What Your Mind Knows, But Isn't Telling You* (Amherst, N.Y.: Prometheus, 2005), for more on how our brains operate in this way.

believability. And when speakers have a higher sense of control and personal certainty, the prefrontal function of the brain increases. Practicing boosts confidence and competency as well. Conversely, when the speaker feels tense and out of control, higher cognitive functions diminish.

Preaching Implications

- Do practice aloud, multiple times. Often, the sermons we write on our computer screens or on our notepads may look good, but once they are spoken aloud, they don't sound good. Verbalizing your finished sermon, or even sections of your sermon during preparation, is advantageous for clarity of logic, pronunciation of words, and knowing when it feels like you need to change the type of literary devices you are using.
- Do assess your first two minutes. Usually during the first two minutes of a sermon, preachers manifest their unique nervous tendencies. This can be verbal, such as loud or soft volume, or nonverbal, such as shifting their weight or playing with their hands. Early on in your preaching career, it's helpful to discover your nervous tendencies and tame them. Practice the introduction and conclusion multiple times.
- Don't practice in front of a mirror. This may cause you to be overly concerned with your facial expressions to the point that you diminish genuineness and authenticity. Rather, have someone videotape your sermons during a "live" setting. Review your videos, looking for areas of improvement for content, structure, and delivery. Take note of what you'd like to work on and try a few things (not all!) during your next sermon.
- Don't memorize the entire sermon. Focus on what I call the "core 25" — that is, the core 25 percent of the sermon that you want to make sure your hearers receive and retain. This will include the following: the sermon proposition, main points, applications, pastoral insights, transitions, introduction, and conclusion. Most of the subpoints and other content can be

reviewed as time permits, but focus on what you'd most like your hearers to remember.

12. "Know Pain, Know Gain."

Brain Function

Research has shown that exercise improves mental alertness and creativity. One of the reasons exercise is beneficial is because it regulates the release of three neurotransmitters that influence mental health positively: serotonin, dopamine, and norepinephrine.[28] Exercise also improves the ability to identify visual and oral stimuli. It also improves concentration and mental perseverance.[29]

Humans need three essential things to survive: food, water, and air.[30] The body can survive up to approximately thirty days without food and seven days without water. The brain, however, can only live up to five minutes without oxygen before the risk of serious damage occurs. Furthermore, as we stated earlier, the brain accounts for 20 percent of the body's energy usage. It requires a lot of food. Exercise increases and improves the access of blood and oxygen to the brain. As you exercise, new blood vessels are formed, creating better channels for food to come to the brain and waste to be removed. One specific area in the brain that benefits from exercise is the dentate gyrus region of the brain. Exercise increases blood volume to that area, which is the key area for memory formation.

Preaching Implications

- Exercise regularly, based on what researchers have recommended: about 20–30 minutes per day. If you're busy, perhaps you can be creative. Some people have installed treadmills in their offices so they can exercise while they work.
- Encourage the congregation to live healthy lives with good

---

28. Medina, *Brain Rules*, 17.
29. Ibid., 18.
30. This section is adapted from ibid., 20–22.

nutrition and exercise. We want to be faithful stewards of what God has given to us to use for his glory and the good of those around us.

Conclusion

This chapter began with a simple premise: The design and delivery of a sermon is just as important as the discovery and discernment of the biblical text. Now, does knowing and executing on all of these twelve implications guarantee the perfect outcome? Of course not. Many things remain out of your control, least of which is the ministry of the Holy Spirit as you faithfully proclaim God's Word. But many of these implications for sermon design and delivery you can control. Much of being able to preach well is a gift from God. Yet, even that gift needs to be nurtured with self-discipline and strategic decision-making. Hopefully this chapter will aide you in that effort.

CHAPTER 9

DELIVERY: NONVERBAL COMMUNICATION

Part of the process of preaching the whole counsel of God involves communicating the truth, goodness, and beauty of the Word of God and the gospel to your hearers. While much can be said about the delivery of sermons, I will be focusing on how to communicate in ways that hopefully maximize the attention, retention, integration, and transformation of your hearers. Such ambitious plans must always be tempered by the fact that preachers are but mere messengers of God, serving the King in ways that bring honor to him and his revealed Word, the Scriptures. Further, preachers must remember that true transformation of hearts and lives will occur only through the work of the Holy Spirit. So again, we pray. We pray that God will use all that we have for his purposes, that we will communicate in ways that clearly and compellingly present God's Word. Faithful heralds must therefore think wisely about and execute intentionally their delivery, both in verbal and nonverbal communication.

Words are not the only way we communicate during a sermon. This chapter focuses on nonverbal communication. As the name implies, this refers to all the wordless cues that are sent and received between preachers and their hearers. Research has shown that nonverbal communication, such as facial expressions, gestures, and body language, accounts for two-thirds of all communication.[1] Most of us don't even think about the many nonverbal cues we use and receive in everyday conversation. *How* one speaks is just as or even more important than *what* one speaks. Think, for example, of how babies first learn how to communicate with their parents. They are able to understand their parent's pleasure or displeasure based solely on facial expressions. As they grow and learn how to communicate verbally, their perception of nonverbal cues fades more into the subconscious.

Many preachers however, remain unaware of the many nonverbal messages they communicate through their eyes, face, hands, and body. In fact, young preachers often focus so much on the accuracy and fidelity of their interpretation of the Scriptures (which is appropriate and admirable) that when they communicate they don't realize that their body language may be distorting the intended message. The goal is for all of our nonverbal communication to complement and reinforce our verbal content. This becomes especially important in the opening minutes of a sermon. Much of the preacher's trustworthiness and credibility is determined by the audience even before the first words are spoken. Whether you like it or not, audiences make judgments regarding your character based on how you dress, walk, look, and move.[2]

A few final words may be helpful regarding nonverbal communication and preaching. As you deliver your sermons, it's important to reveal to yourself and to your audience that you are there to glorify God for their good. It will calm you, give you confidence, and boost your credibility. Most audiences are generally rooting for you. They want you to succeed and feel comfortable. And besides, it's not about you anyway. You're representing the King as his herald. Do your best with the gifts and skills that he's given you and communicate his truth, goodness, and beauty. This perspective of self-forgetfulness will also help your

1. Teri Kwai Gamble and Michael W. Gamble, *Interpersonal Communication: Building Connections Together* (Thousand Oaks, Calif.: Sage, 2014), 152.
2. Some researchers argue that paralinguistic cues such as volume, pitch, rate, and inflection should be classified as nonverbal communication. For our purposes, we will categorize them as verbal cues and discuss them as such in chapter 10.

nonverbal communication. You will then be more likely to display the nonverbal cues with your eyes, face, and body that complement rather than contradict your verbal messages. Will you be nervous? Of course; you're human. But you can turn nervousness into excitement by remembering that through this event, lives can be transformed. Dead people can come to life. And you can be a part of that unimaginable privilege of God's transforming work. That's exciting!

Early on in their preaching ministry, inexperienced preachers may want to videotape their sermons to gauge whether or not their nonverbal cues are helpful or distracting, complementary or contradictory to the words being spoken. Though painful, this process can aid the preacher to become more self-aware and, hopefully, self-confident as he grows in this skill. Also, I've found that the preacher's spouse can be a very helpful evaluator of whether or not the nonverbal cues are natural, appropriate, and effective. I often recommend, however, that sermon evaluations given by the spouse take place a few days after Sunday. The drive home from church is not the best time to engage in this helpful yet often pride-challenging exercise.

It's important to note that nonverbal communication is not universal. Culture plays an important role in how one defines and understands nonverbal communication. Every culture interprets facial expressions and body language differently. A hand gesture that may be perfectly acceptable in one culture may be grossly offensive in another. While some research has shown the universality of some facial expressions (anger, disgust, fear, happiness, sadness, and surprise), many nonverbal cues convey various meanings.[3] This chapter is written with a Western context in mind, from which most of my students come. Readers should contextualize the following based on their own cultural setting and expectations.

Since nonverbal communication can contradict the verbal message, emphasize the points, regulate the conversation, complement the message, and substitute for spoken words, it behooves preachers to think

---

3. David Matsumoto, "Culture and Emotion," in *The Handbook of Culture and Psychology*, ed. David Matsumoto (New York: Oxford University Press, 2001), 171–94.

carefully and strategically about this important part of sermon delivery.[4] Remember to be engaging, inspiring, and shepherding in your nonverbal communication.

Engaging

Eye Contact: Good speakers are engaging with their eye contact, creating an intimate bond with their hearers that is genuine and intimate. There is scientific evidence that the observer experiences (neurologically) the same feelings of the performer. The same neurons that are being lit up in the speaker light up in the hearer. This is due to what have been called "mirror" neurons in the brain.[5] These neurons are sensitive, especially to eye contact and facial expressions. The point? We are wired to mirror what we observe, including a speaker's passion and conviction. So spend roughly two to three seconds on each person. That is the length of a sentence or a discrete unit of thought. Think about how you communicate one-on-one: you look into the eyes for extended periods of time. Since it's impossible to have lengthy eye contact with everyone in an audience, try to hold your eye contact with each individual for each unit of thought or sentence. Some preachers use the "four corners" technique when they start their sermon in order to connect immediately with the entire room.[6] For this technique, make eye contact with the people sitting in the four corners of the room: front row, far right; back row, far right; back row, far left; and front row, far left. You will be more engaging to those individuals as well as to the entire audience that is watching you.

Facial Expressions: Facial features are what we use to interpret the feelings and emotions of others. Faces communicate emotional feelings, such as passion and conviction but also boredom and confusion. Thus, the nonverbal cues being given by the preacher are just as important as the ones being given by the audience. How you communicate with your face is just as vital as how your hearers are responding with their faces. Are they interested or bored? Engaged or confused? As such,

---

4. See Gamble and Gamble, *Interpersonal Communication*, 153–54.
5. See chapter 8.
6. Marsha Hunter and B. K. Johnson, *The Articulate Advocate: New Techniques of Persuasion for Trial Attorneys* (Prescott: Crown King, 2009), 53.

preachers will want to make sure that they display with their face and expressions qualities such as passion and conviction along with warmth and joy as needed. Your face should complement and not contradict your verbal messages. Furthermore, preachers need to be aware of the kinds of nonverbal messages being given by the faces in the audience and respond appropriately if necessary.

Gestures: Gestures are body movements that the preacher makes consciously or unconsciously that convey messages. Used intentionally and appropriately, gestures can aid in the communication process, enhancing the understanding of the message, amplifying and emphasizing the words and ideas being stated, engaging the audience. Preachers need to be aware of the types of gestures they are using. Be careful of unconscious repeated gestures, distracting habits that may impede your message. But also take care not to use overly rehearsed, theatrical gestures, as they will not come across genuine. This is where videotaping can be helpful.

Body Control: Researchers have shown that we make judgments of people based on their body language. How we control our body, consciously or not, impacts the way people perceive how we may be feeling. We may appear to be nervous and defeated on the one hand, or confident and relaxed on the other. Movements such as nose scratches, hand over lips, chin stroking, and hair twirling can be perceived as signs of nervousness, tension, or apprehension.[7] Thus, if you have an erect but relaxed posture, use dynamic but natural gestures, and use sustained eye contact, you will be perceived as confident and secure, and thus, engaging. Furthermore, the way we control and use our body language not only sends messages to our hearers but also changes our body chemistry. One social psychologist has demonstrated that standing in a position of confidence, for example, increases the testosterone levels (dominance hormone) while decreasing cortisol levels (stress hormone) in our brains, correlating to our chances for success.[8] Stand tall, as if someone above you was pulling on your hair.

---

7. Gamble and Gamble, *Interpersonal Communication*, 164.
8. Amy Cuddy, "Your Body Language Shapes Who You Are," *TEDGlobal* (June 2012); http://www.ted.com/talks/amy_cuddy_your_body_language_shapes_who_you_are. See also Jennifer Tracy and David Matsumoto, "The Spontaneous Expression of Pride and Shame: Evidence for Biologically Innate Nonverbal Displays," *Proceedings of the National Academy of Sciences*, vol. 15, no. 33 (August 2008): 11655–60.

Hands are best placed in front of you on the podium, which relaxes the arm and shoulder muscles and provides the best location from which to display gestures. You want your feet about shoulder width apart with one foot slightly ahead of the other, which will decrease the likelihood of shifting your weight between legs. When engaging the audience with your eyes, make sure you move your body to face where you are looking rather than just panning your head from side to side.

Humor: While the use of humor can be advantageous to the overall perception and acceptance of a preacher, one should use humor wisely and appropriately. Sensitivity to the cultural norms of the audience is key to one's success. In fact, restraint is a helpful virtue in the use of humor from the pulpit. Use humor that is natural to you and acceptable to your audience. Usually, planned humor is always safer than spontaneous jokes.

Inspiring

Conviction: Good speakers inspire their audiences when they speak out of their own conviction. Sam Sinek has discovered that inspired leaders and organizations "think, act, and communicate from the inside out."[9] Inspiring speakers reveal *why* they do what they do and not just *what* they do. They speak out of their own heart convictions and beliefs, testifying to the transformation that has occurred in them. Using the company Apple as an example, Sinek reveals that conviction and belief in an idea ("We believe in changing the status quo and thinking differently") is far more inspiring than the product ("We make great computers that function well").[10] For preachers, your conviction in the truth, goodness, and beauty of God's Word and the gospel is what will help your delivery. You want your hearers to believe what you believe. Furthermore, when speakers or hearers have a higher perception of control and personal certainty (whether it is actual or not), the prefrontal

---

9. Sam Sinek, "How Great Leaders Inspire Action," *TEDxPuget Sound* (September 2009); http://www.ted.com/talks/simon_sinek_how_great_leaders_inspire_action?language=en.
10. See also James H. Gilmore and B. Joseph Pine, *Authenticity: What Consumers Really Want* (Boston: Harvard Business School Press, 2007).

function of the brain increases, which means more likelihood of attention and retention. Conversely, when we feel out of control, our higher cognitive functions diminish.[11]

Passion: Related to conviction is passion. Good speakers maintain a consistent, high-level of energy. This strengthens your audience's engagement with you as you reveal your own conviction through what you say and how you say it. Showing enthusiasm can be infectious. Remember, the audience will never be more excited about your content than you are. If you come across as uninterested, so will your audience. How does one show passion? First, keep in mind that revealing passion will differ among preachers and their contexts. Second, showing passion is not accomplished with just one type of nonverbal or verbal cue. Preachers need to wisely discover and discern the effective and appropriate ways to reveal passion in order to inspire.

Respect: An audience will disengage from speakers who insult or annoy them. So be careful with your tone, terms, and attire. In terms of tone, you want to come across as gracious, humble, and irenic (vs. condescending, arrogant, and polemic). As for terms, you want to use familiar and accessible vocabulary for your audience and be restrained in the use of rhetorical devices. And while your attire is part of your culture and context, you need to dress appropriately so as to not draw attention to yourself. Historically, this is one reason ministers from certain traditions decide to wear plain black robes not only to signify the authority of the minister's office but also to not create any distractions from the task at hand, heralding God's message to his people.

Shepherding

Empathy (vs. Sympathy): Sympathy is defined as the feeling of care and the understanding of other's suffering. Empathy, however, is the ability to experience the thoughts, emotions, and direct experiences of others.

---

11. See David Rock, *Your Brain at Work: Strategies for Overcoming Distraction, Regaining Focus, and Working Smarter All Day Long* (New York: HarperBusiness, 2009), for more on the importance of control and certainty.

Sympathy is recognition or acknowledgment. Empathy is "deeper" understanding because of a mutual experiencing of thought, feeling, or experience. Empathy, as a result, forms deeper connection and community. Preachers are shepherds first, pastorally caring deeply for the flock entrusted to their care. As such, shepherd-preachers must display and declare the kind of heart and speech that demonstrates pastoral empathy and love.

Joyful Gravity: Preachers should also display a balance of pastoral joy and seriousness in both their tone and terms. Many who come to church will be broken and confused by their sin and the effects of sin on their lives. Shepherd-preachers express a satisfaction that comes from knowing and experiencing God's grace as well as a solemnity from knowing and experiencing the trials of a sin-cursed world. As appropriate, preachers should display the type of joyful gravity that parents intuitively reveal to their children as they care for them through the various ups and downs of life.

Inhibition: Part of the shepherd-preacher's task is to be ruthless in resisting the temptation to speak unplanned words and ill-chosen remarks. Should we always "stick to the script" and not stray from our preaching outline? Priority and proportion is necessary. As a general rule, preachers should prioritize what they have prepared while still being open to giving proportionate time to ideas that may emerge during the sermon. Inexperienced preachers should avoid the temptation to speak "off the cuff" while still remaining sensitive to spiritual cues that may be from the Holy Spirit as well as nonverbal cues that may be coming from the audience. Further, you will want to be sensitive to time constraints since speaking extemporaneously may lengthen the overall length of the sermon. These decisions, again, require wisdom and are culturally and contextually conditioned.

Allow me to conclude by offering some practical advice on how some of this is executed in a given sermon, especially at the beginning stages.

- Before you step up to the pulpit, take a few deep belly-expanding breaths. Deep breathing reduces your heart rate and oxygenates the blood. This decreases the cortisol levels in your brain, reducing stress and anxiety while increasing confidence and control.

- As you begin your sermon, don't start talking right away. Stand straight, make eye contact with people and smile. This will help relax you and your audience.
- Place your hands directly on the podium in front of you. Don't hang them at your sides, which tenses your shoulder and neck muscles. Don't put them in your pockets, which may signify unintentional casualness that does not correlate to the task at hand (heralding the King's message).
- Start by speaking slowly. Most people tend to rush when they are nervous. Establish a good pace and rhythm, and if necessary, vary your intensity to signal emphasis.

DELIVERY: VERBAL COMMUNICATION

W e now turn to the second half of delivery dynamics: verbal communication. This chapter will cover five key elements to keep in mind: style, sound, speed, signal, and silence. Then I will offer some suggestions regarding rehearsing prior to the delivery of your sermon.

Delivery Element 1: Style

Many young preachers that have taken my preaching courses in seminary often emulate the style of their favorite preachers. In fact, you'd be surprised how many times Tim Keller and John Piper have preached in my classes! What these students often do, however, is copy the external style of their favorite preachers without learning the internal substance. Furthermore, this prevents them from discovering and developing the unique preaching "voice" or style that God has given to them. While there is much we can learn from great preachers, past and present, we also need to recognize the unique ways God has gifted and trained us to herald his Word.

Some might argue that being a herald means simply getting the message across without paying attention to style. In fact, they would say, any attention given to "style" would be considered contrary to the high calling of heralding God's Word. In response to this, I would argue first that being preoccupied with style to the point of subverting content is certainly not proper. However, God has created individual preachers to know, use, and enjoy the beauty of language and communication. Thus, a delicate balance must be present when a preacher is discovering and developing his style: speaking with authority but also with genuineness. Let me explain.

On the one hand, preachers need to faithfully represent God and present the authoritative message that he gives. On the other hand, preachers also need to communicate God's message in a way that reveals their honest and real persona — that is, their genuine and authentic personality and character. What makes this challenging, however, is that much preparation and thought must go into not only *what* is said but also *how* it is said. Authenticity in preaching style does not equate to being unprepared and extemporaneous.

In contrast to interpersonal conversations that are intimate and can naturally come across as authentic and genuine, preaching sermons requires what Bryan Chapell helpfully calls a "heightened conversational" style.[1] While much preparation is given over to the content and communication of a sermon, it must be delivered with a style that doesn't come across as forced or fake.

Admittedly, discussions on communication styles are subjective and conditioned by cultural norms and expectations. As such, preachers must discover and develop their own style, or "voice," one that is genuinely their own and that does not hinder the communication of God's truth, goodness, and beauty. This frankly will require much practice, experience, patience, and time. Furthermore, each preacher needs to find people in their congregation that can help evaluate and offer constructive criticism.

Delivery Element 2: Sound (Volume, Pitch, and Clarity)

The second area of verbal communication skills to consider is sound, more specifically, the volume, pitch, and clarity of your words.

---

1. Bryan Chapell, *Christ-Centered Preaching: Redeeming the Expository Sermon*, 2nd ed. (Grand Rapids: Baker Academic, 2005), 330–31.

Volume: Preachers must speak with enough volume to be heard by everyone present. While this may sound obvious, it's surprising how audiences often need to strain to hear the preacher. Your volume must not only be comfortable to listen to but also loud enough so that when you vary your volume for emphasis, it can be distinguishable. Many potential problems with volume can easily be solved with good amplification systems (microphones and speakers). But when electronic systems are not available to help offset potentially soft voices, you need to be sensitive to volume and respond accordingly. While appropriate volume is important at every stage of a sermon, it is especially important at the beginning and end of your sermon. Generally, start your introduction confidently, with a clear volume. Likewise, finish your conclusion maintaining good volume. Let me offer some words of advice regarding volume.

- Minimize the amount of distractions and distance that may hinder your voice from being heard by everyone present. Use common sense to remove sounds that will compete with your voice, and make sure your audience is close enough to hear you.
- Maximize your ability to project your voice. Your goal is to speak with more resonance, not merely be loud. Make sure to stand upright, leaning slightly forward. Good posture will support your body's ability to breathe right and project your voice. As you fill your lungs with air, your throat muscles will relax, providing a better foundation for speaking with resonance — what I call "good" volume. When you breathe properly, your abdomen will expand and not your chest.
- Finish each sentence strongly. Trailing off at the end of a sentence with a lower volume is a common problem for speakers. This is usually due to speakers looking down at their notes and not thinking about their volume.
- Vary your volume so as to signal changes of meaning and emotion. This will not only create more interest but will also keep your hearers from falling asleep due to your speaking in the same volume for an extended period of time.
- Don't be too loud. While being too loud is an uncommon

problem, some will struggle with this. Not only can you come across as offensive and bullying, but an overly loud volume will strain and potentially damage your throat and vocal chords.

- Take care of your throat before preaching. Drinking warm water and herbal teas is best. Avoid certain drinks before you speak: milk or creamy drinks can gum up the throat and increases phlegm; alcohol can constrict and dry out your vocal cords; and coffee can tighten and restrict the throat muscles.

Pitch: This refers to the sound of your words as found on a musical scale. While each preacher will have a unique timbre and tone of voice, using pitch appropriately can help convey shades of meaning and signal changes in emphasis. In fact, most of us use changes in pitch intuitively. Think, for example, of how you change the pitch of your voice to distinguish a statement from a question. Thus, preachers can intentionally and strategically use variations in pitch to convey different meanings — in your syllables, words, and sentences. There are two problems associated with pitch that you will want to avoid.

- Avoid monotony, which is speaking in one pitch or with very little changes in pitch. While you will generally use the natural intonations you use in everyday conversation, you want to ensure that there are clear variations in pitch throughout your sentences and the sermon. My experience of reading stories to my young children helped me develop appropriate and different uses of pitch to signify shades of meaning and changes in emphasis. Avoid monotony.
- Avoid repetitious patterns in pitch. This is speaking in such a way so that the pitch rises and falls according to the same pattern for each successive sentence. This is essentially another form of monotony, in which a repetitious form of pitch can create fatigue and indifference in your hearers. Again, use common sense to find and use an applicable and appropriate range of frequencies without sounding forced and fake.

Clarity: Articulation of your words will increase your ability to project your sound and be heard. Pronunciation refers to the way words are commonly spoken in a given culture. Enunciation is the way those words are pronounced with clarity. Making sure your consonants, vowels, and words are spoken with clarity forces the sound away from your throat and into your face, which causes your voice to project. Use all the God-given tools at your disposal: your jaws, lips, and tongue. One easy way to help you articulate better is to practice talking in a whisper. To be heard well in that low volume, you need to speak intentionally using the front of your mouth, lips, teeth, and tongue. This exercise can teach you how to speak with more clarity. Clarity also increases when you avoid the common mistake of using vocalized pauses and other unnecessary filler words or phrases.

- Vocalized pauses are the nondictionary words like "um" or "uh" that are often used to fill in the silence when no words are spoken in a sermon. In everyday conversation, we don't usually notice how often these terms are used. But in a more formal situation like preaching a sermon, vocalized pauses can be detrimental to the clarity of your sermon as well as to your credibility as a speaker. Also, be careful of certain words or phrases that you may use regularly and repetitively without recognition. For some preachers, using seemingly innocuous words or phrases such as "I think that" or "basically" can undermine the sermon's reception, especially if overused.
- Like kicking a bad habit, the use of vocalized pauses and filler words and phrases can be curtailed with practice and replacement. Practice speaking without the use of vocalized pauses and filler words in your daily normal conversations. Replace them with pauses or with more intentional words. At first it will be difficult and seem unnatural, but over time you will become a more clear and articulate speaker without sacrificing naturalness.

Delivery Element 3: Speed

As there are various timbres and tones of voice, people speak at various rates: some swift, some slow, some steady. Sources state that the average American English speaker in a normal conversation speaks at a rate of approximately 110–150 words per minute. Compare this to the average reading rate of the same group: 200–300 words per minute. Speed can change, however, because of circumstances such as emotion, time, and setting. While research continues on whether or not the speed of one's speech influences persuasion, one particular study demonstrated that a slower rate of speaking (about 144 words per minute) was helpful when the audience was already predisposed to the topic, whereas a faster rate of speaking (200+ words per minute) increased persuasion when the audience's attitude was hostile.[2]

Whatever your natural speaking speed, beware of the following that may cause your listeners to dismiss you because of discomfort. First, beware of using a constant speed, whether too fast or too slow. This sameness of speed, like the tedium of monotony, will undermine the reception of your sermon. Second, beware of speaking too rapidly since you can easily trip over your words and come across as unnecessarily nervous and lacking in control. Third, beware that you will probably not speak slowly enough. While it is possible to speak too slowly, the tendency will be to speak too rapidly. The key is to speak slowly enough to engage your hearers and then pick up speed at intentional moments of the sermon to signal emphasis.

Delivery Element 4: Signal (Variation)

As has been mentioned before, a variety of vocal techniques such as volume, pitch, and speed in the sermon should be used at strategic locations to signal emphasis and critical moments. Good speakers signal the audience when to "lean in" and listen more attentively and also signal when it's time to "lean out" and relax, conserving their energy to maintain attention and retention. This presupposes that you have prioritized your content, choosing what you will emphasize in light of the limited amount of your hearers' capacity to listen with purpose.

---

2. Steven M. Smith and David R. Schaffer, "Celerity and Cajolery: Rapid Speech May Promote or Inhibit Persuasion through Its Impact on Message Elaboration," *Personality and Social Psychology Bulletin*, vol. 17, no. 6 (December 1991): 663–69.

Bad speakers give no signals to show the relative importance of their material. They force the audience to work too hard to sift out what they think is important—which is highly improbable.

Unfortunately, some preachers emphasize too much in their sermon, making everything they say seem important. With this high degree of emphasis and not enough variation, preachers will unknowingly wear down their hearers, who will be unable to determine what is actually important. On the opposite end of the spectrum, some preachers will deliver their sermon with a low degree of emphasis, again making it impossible for hearers to figure out what they need to pay more attention to. <u>What you want is to have a variety of places where there are both lean-in and lean-out moments.</u> Emphasize key words or sentences by utilizing various sound techniques. The key is to vary your delivery, be it loudness or softness. Whispering or speaking in slow staccato can often be just as effective in signaling emphasis as speaking loudly or in rapid-fire phrases. Furthermore, try to reflect the emotional traits of your content by varying your delivery. When you reach a pastoral moment in your sermon when you need to share a particularly difficult truth for your hearers, lower your volume and slow down. On the other hand, when you are relating a dramatic story, you can escalate your volume and speed, building to the climax.

Delivery Element 5: Silence (Pauses)

Much the way punctuation marks in books signal to the reader critical moments to stop, pause, and experience the emotional value of the moment in a story, <u>intentional moments of silence in a sermon not only help hearers identify key ideas but also provide spaces of cognitive rest.</u> Research in neuroscience has revealed that using strategic pauses in your sermon increases the likelihood of retention. Pausing benefits both speaker and hearer. For the speaker, using pauses elevates the feeling of control, relaxes the body, provides spaces to breathe, and adds variety and interest. For the hearer, it heightens comfort, provides time to rest, offers time to reflect and draw conclusions, and increases retention. As with general conversation and storytelling, you will want to use pauses before and after transitions, main points, and key insights.

Rehearsing

After the sermon has been written and the preaching outline has been formed, the right kind and right amount of rehearsal is critical. Some of the goals of rehearsing are to refine, remember, and relax.

- Refine: Even at this stage, refining your content is a good goal. Every time you run through your sermon is an opportunity to edit and modify your content and communication. Often the best adjustments to a sermon, though seemingly minor, will happen at this stage of the process as you are becoming more and more familiar with the truth, goodness, and beauty of the text for your people. You are now engaging in the final stages of cutting; all the rough cuts have been done, leaving the polishing stage, in which the small facets are refined so as to produce the maximum clarity and color.
- Remember: Another goal of rehearsing is to increase the amount of retention to achieve effortless articulation. The more you retain the rational content of your sermon, the more you can concentrate on the emotional content. While spontaneity has value, most speakers are not capable of choosing the best possible ways to phrase their ideas extemporaneously. Besides, audience members will know when you are unprepared.It not only decreases your credibility, but also increases your stress and anxiety. Spend the time to remember what you've prepared. Some practical advice on how best to memorize your sermon is given below.
- Relax: The last goal of rehearsing is to help calm your nerves and relax. As you practice, the serotonin levels in your brain increase, yielding more confidence and less fear. Nerves can still be present, however, and that's normal. In fact, the increase of adrenaline is unavoidable, but you can use it to your benefit.

When your adrenal glands are working, you can use that rush to make you more focused, alert, and sharp. For this to work, however, you need to breathe well, know your material, and remember your role as a herald of the King of Kings.

Here is some practical advice on rehearsing.

- Try to simulate the situation in which you will be speaking. Stand up, use a podium, speak aloud with inflection and emphasis, and try intentional gestures. If possible, have trusted friends and/or family members evaluate you. Don't practice in front of a mirror or videotape yourself unless it's a live situation.
- Run through your sermon three or four times aloud. Your goal is to increase familiarity, flow, and control—all of which boost confidence and clarity. Start with your manuscript, and then as you get to know your material better, use your preaching outline to rehearse.
- Focus proportionately on the priorities of the sermon. That is, you will most likely not have the time to memorize 100 percent of the sermon. Frankly, it is not a wise use of your time, and it may lead to unnatural delivery as you try to recall that "perfect" word or phrase. Rather, focus on memorizing the "core 25" percent of the critical content: the introduction and conclusion, main points, main insights, transitions, and pastoral applications and moments. After spending time on these priorities, then move onto the other parts of the sermon.

Again, does all of this guarantee success? Many things remain out of your control—like the work of the Spirit. So that's a good thing. But you can control much of what you do by way of design and delivery. Do your best, as unto the Lord, as you represent him as his herald, faithfully, accurately, and clearly presenting the gospel of grace with truth, goodness, and beauty, for maximum attention, retention, integration, and hopefully transformation.

CONCLUSION

So you want to be a herald of the King? This is the question I pose to first-year preaching students on the first day of classes. It's not meant to be facetious or combative. Before discussing all the theoretical and practical components regarding the art and science of preaching, I want to make sure that these students have counted the cost. I remind them of the enormity of the task—of not only becoming an expert in multiple subjects (two ancient languages; the content of the entire Bible; the loci of systematic theology; and the major ideas, movements, and people in church history), but also combining all of these subjects into a coherent and consistent whole in order to preach, teach, counsel, discipline, shepherd, pastor, evangelize, and so on.

As if that isn't enough, I remind them of the warnings related to the task. Jesus stated unequivocally in Luke 17:2, "It would be better for him if a millstone were hung around his neck and he were cast into the sea than that he should cause one of these little ones to sin." Being a herald is a serious calling. You sure you want to be a preacher?

Usually by this moment in the lecture, a hush falls over the entire room. Most if not all of the students who hear this lecture have come from far distances, sacrificing much to be able to train for gospel ministry. They have given up on the promises of fame and fortune to give their lives in service of their King. They need to be reminded of the glory of that King and of his calling.

I remind them that there is no greater calling than serving our King as his herald. Only a few are chosen and only a few are up to the task. But for those who are, there is no greater honor and no greater glory than to be involved in representing the King of Kings as he marches forward to inaugurate and establish his kingdom through means that many in the world consider foolishness. But as Paul rightly says, "For the word of the cross is folly to those who are perishing, but to us who are being saved it is the power of God" (1 Cor 1:18). For from this seemingly foolish act—preaching Christ and him crucified—lives are transformed as people come to faith, marriages are healed, and conflicts are resolved. In what other job can you write on your resume, "I am involved in resurrection ministry, where dead people come back to life"?

Yes, being a herald is not easy, but it is glorious. This is why we preachers take time every day and every week to pray, select, read, and meditate on the text. Why we discover the truth of the text according to the human author. Why we discern Christ in the text according to the Divine Author. Why we design sermons that are true, good, and beautiful. Why we deliver sermons for attention, retention, integration, and transformation. Because we are heralds, called and appointed by God, united to the Son, anointed by the Spirit, to proclaim the whole counsel of the triune God so that all who hear would be forever transformed by the grace and glory of the gospel.

> Him we proclaim, warning everyone and teaching everyone with all wisdom, that we may present everyone mature in Christ. For this I toil, struggling with all his energy that he powerfully works within me (Col 1:28–29).

Soli Deo gloria.

BIBLIOGRAPHY

Achtemeier, Elizabeth. *Creative Preaching: Finding the Words*. Nashville: Abingdon, 1980.

_____. *Preaching the Hard Texts of the Old Testament*. Peabody, Mass.: Hendrickson, 1998.

Adams, Jay E. *Preaching with Purpose: The Urgent Task of Homiletics*. Grand Rapids: Zondervan, 1982.

_____. *Pulpit Speech*. Grand Rapids: Baker, 1971.

Alter, Robert. *The Art of Biblical Narrative*. New York: Basic Books, 1981.

Ambrose, Susan A., et al. *How Learning Works: Seven Research-Based Principles for Smart Teaching*. San Francisco: Jossey-Bass, 2010.

Anderson, Kenton C. *Preaching with Conviction: Connecting with Postmodern Listeners*. Grand Rapids: Kregel, 2001.

Aristotle. *The Art of Rhetoric*. Trans. by J. H. Freese. Boston: Harvard University Press, 1967.

_____. *The Poetics*. Trans. by W. H. Fyfe. Boston: Harvard University Press, 1973.

Augustine. *On Christian Doctrine*. New York: Macmillan, 1958.

Azurdia, Arturo G., III. *Spirit-Empowered Preaching: Involving the Holy Spirit in Your Ministry*. Ross-shire, Scotland: Christian Focus, 1998.

Bar-Efrat, Shimon. *Narrative Art in the Bible*. London: T&T Clark, 2004.

Barker, William, and Samuel Logan. *Sermons That Shaped America: Reformed Preaching from 1630 to 2001*. Phillipsburg, N.J.: P&R, 2003.

Bauer, Walter, W. Arndt, and Frederick W. Danker, eds. *A Greek-English Lexicon of the New Testament and Other Early Christian Literature*. 3rd ed. Chicago: University of Chicago, 2000.

Beale, G. K., ed. *The Right Doctrine from the Wrong Texts? Essays on the Use of the Old Testament in the New.* Grand Rapids: Baker, 1994.

Benedikt, Michael. *For an Architecture of Reality.* New York: Lumen, 1987.

Bergsma, Derke P. *Redemption: The Triumph of God's Great Plan.* Lansing, Mich.: Redeemer, 1989.

Berkhof, Louis. *Systematic Theology.* Rev. ed. Grand Rapids: Eerdmans, 1996.

Berlin, Adele. *Poetics and Interpretation of Biblical Narrative.* Winona Lake, Ind.: Eisenbrauns, 1994.

Berlo, David. *The Process of Communication: An Introduction to Theory and Practice.* New York: Holt, Rinehart & Winston, 1960.

Berner, Timothy A. "Preaching with the Brain in Mind: Can Neuroscience Enhance Biblical Preaching?" DMin project, Luther Seminary, 2008.

Bettler, John F. "Application." In *The Preacher and Preaching*, ed. by Samuel T. Logan. Phillipsburg, N.J.: P&R, 1986.

Blackwood, Andrew. *Expository Preaching for Today.* Nashville: Abingdon, 1953.

Blomberg, Craig L. *Interpreting the Parables.* Downers Grove, Ill.: InterVarsity, 1990.

_____. *Preaching the Parables: From Responsible Interpretation to Powerful Proclamation.* Grand Rapids: Baker, 2004.

Bonzo, J. Matthew, and M. R. Stevens. *Wendell Berry and the Cultivation of Life: A Reader's Guide.* Grand Rapids: Brazos, 2008.

Bridges, Jerry. *The Discipline of Grace: God's Role and Our Role in the Pursuit of Holiness.* Colorado Springs: NavPress, 1994.

Brilioth, Yngve. *A Brief History of Preaching.* Philadelphia: Fortress, 1965.

Broadus, John A. *On the Preparation and Delivery of Sermons.* Nashville: Broadman, 1944.

Bromiley, Geoffrey, ed. *The International Standard Bible Encyclopedia.* Rev. ed. 4 vols. Grand Rapids: Eerdmans, 1979–1988.

Brooks, Phillips. *Lectures on Preaching Delivered before the Divinity School of Yale College, 1877.* New York: E. P. Dutton, 1894.

Brown, F., S. R. Driver, and C. A. Briggs, eds. *A Hebrew and English Lexicon of the Old Testament.* 1907. Reprint, Oxford: Clarendon, 1978.

Brown, Michael, and Zach Keele. *Sacred Bond: Covenant Theology Explored.* Grandville, Mich.: Reformed Fellowship, 2012.

Brueggemann, Walter. *Finally Comes the Poet: Daring Speech for Proclamation.* Minneapolis: Fortress, 1989.

Buttrick, David. *Homiletic: Moves and Structures.* Philadelphia: Fortress, 1987.

Calvin, John. *Institutes of the Christian Religion.* 2 vols. Trans by F. L. Battles, ed. by J. T. McNeill. Philadelphia: Westminster, 1960.

BIBLIOGRAPHY

Camery-Hoggatt, Jerry. *Speaking of God: Reading and Preaching the Word of God*. Peabody, Mass.: Hendrickson, 1995.

Carr, Nicholas. *The Shallows: What the Internet Is Doing to our Brains*. New York: W. W. Norton, 2011.

Carrick, John. *The Imperative of Preaching: A Theology of Sacred Rhetoric*. Carlisle, Penn.: Banner of Truth, 2002.

Carson, D. A. "Challenges for the Twenty-First-Century Pulpit." In *Preach the Word: Essays on Expository Preaching in Honor of R. Kent Hughes*, ed. by Leland Ryken and Todd Wilson. Wheaton, Ill.: Crossway, 2007.

_____. *Exegetical Fallacies*. Grand Rapids: Baker, 1996.

_____, ed. *Telling the Truth: Evangelizing Postmoderns*. Grand Rapids: Zondervan, 2000.

Carson, D. A., Douglas J. Moo, and Leon Morris. *Introduction to the Old Testament*. 2nd ed. Grand Rapids: Zondervan, 2005.

Chabris, Christopher, and Daniel Simons. *The Invisible Gorilla: And Other Ways How Our Intuitions Deceive Us*. New York: Broadway, 2009.

Chan, Francis. *Crazy Love: Overwhelmed by a Relentless God*. Colorado Springs: David C. Cook, 2008.

Chapell, Bryan. *Christ-Centered Preaching: Redeeming the Expository Sermon*. 2nd ed. Grand Rapids: Baker, 2005.

_____. *Christ-Centered Sermons: Models of Redemptive Preaching*. Grand Rapids: Baker 2013.

_____. *The Hardest Sermons You'll Ever Have to Preach*. Grand Rapids: Zondervan, 2011.

_____. *Using Illustrations to Preach with Power*. Wheaton, Ill.: Crossway, 2001.

Childers, Jana, and C. Schmidt, eds. *Performance in Preaching: Bringing the Sermon to Life*. Grand Rapids: Baker, 2008.

Cicero. *De Inventione; De Optimo Genere Oratorum; Topica*. Trans. by H. M. Hubbell. Boston: Harvard University Press, 1968.

Clowney, Edmund P. *Called to the Ministry*. Phillipsburg, N.J.: P&R, 1964.

_____. *CM: Christian Meditation*. Nutley, N.J.: Craig, 1979.

_____. *The Church*. Contours of Contemporary Theology. Downers Grove, Ill.: InterVarsity, 1995.

_____. *How Jesus Transforms the Ten Commandments*. Ed. by R. Clowney Jones. Phillipsburg, N.J.: P&R, 2007.

_____. *Preaching and Biblical Theology*. Grand Rapids: Eerdmans, 1961. Reprint, Phillipsburg, N.J.: P&R, 2002.

_____. "Preaching Christ from All the Scriptures." In *The Preacher and Preaching: Reviving the Art in the Twentieth Century*, ed. by Samuel T. Logan. Phillipsburg, N.J.: P&R, 1986.

BIBLIOGRAPHY

_____. *Preaching Christ in All of Scripture*. Wheaton, Ill.: Crossway, 2003.

_____. *The Unfolding Mystery: Discovering Christ in the Old Testament*. Phillipsburg, N.J.: P&R, 1988.

Clowney, Edmund P., and Timothy Keller. *Preaching Christ to a Post-Modern World*. Unpublished syllabus, Reformed Theological Seminary.

Colquhoun, John. *A Treatise on the Law and the Gospel*. Ed. by Don Kistler. Morgan, Penn.: Soli Deo Gloria, 1999.

Cook, Jeff Scott. *The Elements of Speechwriting and Public Speaking*. New York: Macmillan, 1989.

Copi, Irving. *Introduction to Logic*. 13th ed. Upper Saddle River, N.J.: Prentice Hall, 2008.

Cox, Richard H. *Rewiring Your Preaching: How the Brain Processes Sermons*. Downers Grove, Ill: InterVarsity Press, 2012.

Craddock, Fred B. *Preaching*. Nashville: Abingdon, 1985.

Crouch, Andy. *Culture Making: Recovering Our Creative Calling*. Downers Grove, Ill.: IVP Books, 2008.

Cuddy, Amy. "Your Body Language Shapes Who You Are," *TEDGlobal* (June 2012); http://www.ted.com/talks/amy_cuddy_your_body_language_shapes_who_you_are.

Cunningham, David, ed. *To Teach, To Delight, and To Move: Theological Education in a Post-Christian World*. Eugene, Ore.: Cascade, 2004.

Dabney, Robert L. *Lectures on Sacred Rhetoric*. Carlisle: Banner of Truth, 1979.

Dargan, Edwin C. *A History of Preaching*. Vol. 1, *From the Apostolic Fathers to the Great Reformers, A.D. 70–1572*. New York: Burt Franklin, 1968.

Davidson, Richard M. *Typology in Scripture*. Berrien Springs, Mich.: Andrews University, 1981.

Davis, Mark H. "Measuring Individual Differences in Empathy: Evidence for a Multidimensional Approach." *Journal of Personal Social Psychology* 44 (1983): 113–26.

Dawn, Marva J. *Reading Out without Dumbing Down: A Theology of Worship for the Turn-of-the-Century Culture*. Grand Rapids: Eerdmans, 1995.

De Graaf, S. G. *Promise and Deliverance*. 4 vols. St. Catherines, Ont.: Paideia Press, 1977–1981.

Dennison, James T., Jr. "Building the Biblical-Theological Sermon," parts 1 and 2, *Kerux* 4, no. 3 (1989): 30–43; 5, no. 1 (1989): 32–46.

DeYoung, Kevin, and T. Kluck. *Why We Love the Church: In Praise of Institutions and Organized Religion*. Chicago: Moody Press, 2009.

_____. *Why We're Not Emergent (By Two Guys Who Should Be)*. Chicago: Moody Press, 2008.

Dillard, Raymond B. *Faith in the Face of Apostasy: The Gospel according to Elijah and Elisha*. Phillipsburg, N. J.: P&R, 1999.

Dillard, Raymond B., and Tremper Longman III. *An Introduction to the Old Testament*. Grand Rapids: Zondervan, 1994.

Dodd, C. H. *According to the Scriptures: The Sub-Structure of New Testament Theology*. London: Nisbet, 1952.

_____. *The Apostolic Preaching and Its Developments*. London: Hodder & Stoughton, 1936.

Doriani, Daniel M. *Getting the Message: A Plan for Interpreting and Applying the Bible*. Phillipsburg, N.J.: P&R, 1996.

_____. *Putting the Truth to Work: The Theory and Practice of Biblical Application*. Phillipsburg, N.J.: P&R, 2001.

Driscoll, Mark. *The Radical Reformission: Reaching Out without Selling Out*. Grand Rapids: Zondervan, 2004.

Duarte, Nancy. "The Secret Structure of Great Talks." TEDxEast (November 11, 2010); http://www.ted.com/talks/nancy_duarte_the_secret_structure_of_great_talks.

Duduit, Michael, ed. *Communicate with Power: Insights from America's Top Communicators*. Grand Rapids: Baker, 1996.

Duguid, Iain M. *Living in the Gap between Promise and Reality: The Gospel According to Abraham*. Phillipsburg, N.J.: P&R, 1999.

_____. *Living in the Grip of Relentless Grace: The Gospel in the Lives of Isaac and Jacob*. Phillipsburg, N.J.: P&R, 2002.

Duhigg, Charles. *The Power of Habit: Why We Do What We Do in Life and Business*. New York: Random House, 2012.

Edwards, O. C. *A History of Preaching*. Nashville: Abingdon, 2004.

Estelle, Bryan D. *Salvation through Judgment and Mercy: The Gospel according to Jonah*. Phillipsburg, N.J.: P&R, 2005.

Eswine, Zach. *Preaching to a Post-Everything World: Crafting Biblical Sermons That Connect with Our Culture*. Grand Rapids: Baker, 2008.

Fant, Clyde, and William Pinson, eds. *20 Centuries of Great Preaching*. Waco: Word, 1971.

Fee, Gordon D., and Douglas Stuart. *How to Read the Bible for All Its Worth*. Grand Rapids: Zondervan, 1982.

Ferguson, Everett. *Backgrounds of Early Christianity*. 3rd ed. Grand Rapids: Eerdmans, 2003.

Ferguson, Sinclair B. *Kingdom Life in a Fallen World: Living Out the Sermon on the Mount*. Colorado Springs: NavPress, 1986.

Fischer, David. *Historians' Fallacies*. New York: Harper, 1970.

BIBLIOGRAPHY

Foer, Joshua. *Moonwalking with Einstein: The Art and Science of Remembering Everything.* New York: Penguin, 2011.

Fokkelman, J. P. *Reading Biblical Narrative.* Louisville: Westminster John Knox, 1999.

France, R. T. *Jesus and the Old Testament: His Application of Old Testament Passages to Himself and His Mission.* Downers Grove, Ill.: InterVarsity, 1971.

Freytag, Gustav. *Technique of the Drama: An Exposition of Dramatic Composition and Art.* 6th ed. Trans. by E. J. MacEwan. New York: B. Blom, 1968.

Futato, Mark D. *Interpreting the Psalms: An Exegetical Handbook.* Grand Rapids: Kregel, 2007.

_____. *Transformed by Praise: The Purpose and Message of the Psalms.* Phillipsburg, N.J.: P&R, 2002.

Gamble, Richard M. *The Great Tradition: Classic Readings on What It Means to Be an Educated Human Being.* Wilmington, Del.: Intercollegiate Studies Institute, 2007.

Gamble, Teri Kwai, and Michael W. Gamble. *Interpersonal Communication: Building Connections Together.* Thousand Oaks, Calif.: Sage, 2014.

Gilmore, James H., and B. Joseph Pine. *Authenticity: What Consumers Really Want.* Boston: Harvard Business School Press, 2007.

_____. *The Experience Economy: Work Is Theatre and Every Business a Stage.* Boston: Harvard Business School Press, 1999.

Gladwell, Malcolm. *Blink: The Power of Thinking without Thinking.* New York: Back Bay, 2007.

_____. *Outliers: The Story of Success.* New York: Little, Brown & Co., 2008.

_____. *The Tipping Point: How Little Things Can Make a Big Difference.* New York: Back Bay, 2000.

Goldsworthy, Graeme. *Gospel and Kingdom: A Christian Interpretation of the Old Testament.* Exeter, U.K., Paternoster, 1994.

_____. *Preaching the Whole Bible as Christian Scripture: The Application of Biblical Theology to Expository Preaching.* Grand Rapids: Eerdmans, 2000.

Goppelt, Leonhard. *Typos: The Typological Interpretation of the Old Testament in the New.* Trans. by Donald H. Madvig. Grand Rapids: Eerdmans, 1982.

Gordon, Ernest. *Through the Valley of the Kwai.* New York: Harper, 1962.

Gordon, T. David. *Why Johnny Can't Preach: The Media Have Shaped the Messengers.* Phillipsburg, N.J.: P&R, 2009.

_____. *Why Johnny Can't Sing Hymns: How Pop Culture Rewrote the Hymnal.* Phillipsburg, N.J.: P&R, 2010.

Greidanus, Sidney. *The Modern Preacher and the Ancient Text: Interpreting and Preaching Biblical Literature.* Grand Rapids: Eerdmans, 1988.

_____. *Preaching Christ from the Old Testament: A Contemporary Hermeneutical Method.* Grand Rapids: Eerdmans, 1999.

_____. *Sola Scriptura: Problems and Principles in Preaching Historical Texts.* Toronto: Wedge, 1970.

Hale-Evans, Ron, and Marty Hale-Evans. *Mindhacker: 60 Tips, Tricks, and Games to Take Your Mind to the Next Level.* Indianapolis: Wiley, 2007.

Hall, Christopher A. *Reading Scripture with the Church Fathers.* Downers Grove, Ill.: InterVarsity, 1998.

Hallinan, Joseph. *Why We Make Mistakes: How We Look without Seeing, Forget Things in Seconds, and Are All Pretty Sure We Are Way Above Average.* New York: Broadway, 2009.

Heath, Chip, and Dan Heath. *Made to Stick: Why Some Ideas Take Hold and Others Come Unstuck.* London: Random House, 2007.

Hobson, R. Peter. *The Cradle of Thought: Exploring the Origins of Thinking.* New York: Macmillan, 2002.

Holladay, William L. *A Concise Hebrew and Aramaic Lexicon of the Old Testament, Based upon the Lexical Work of Ludwig Köhler and Walter Baumgartner.* Grand Rapids: Eerdmans, 1971.

Horton, Michael S. *A Better Way: Rediscovering the Drama of God-Centered Worship.* Grand Rapids: Baker, 2002.

_____. *The Christian Faith: A Systematic Theology for Pilgrims on the Way.* Grand Rapids: Zondervan, 2011.

_____. *Christless Christianity: The Alternative Gospel of the American Church.* Grand Rapids: Baker, 2008.

_____. *Covenant and Eschatology: The Divine Drama.* Louisville: Westminster John Knox, 2002.

_____. *God of Promise: Introducing Covenant Theology.* Grand Rapids: Baker, 2006.

_____. *The Gospel Commission: Recovering God's Strategy for Making Disciples.* Grand Rapids: Baker 2011.

_____. *The Gospel-Driven Life: Being Good-News People in a Bad-News World.* Grand Rapids: Baker 2009.

Humphrey, Nicholas. *The Inner Eye: Social Intelligence in Evolution.* Oxford: Oxford University Press, 2003.

Hunter, Marsha, and B. K. Johnson. *The Articulate Advocate: New Techniques of Persuasion for Trial Attorneys.* Prescott: Crown King, 2009.

Hurley, Patrick. *A Concise Introduction to Logic.* 12th ed. Boston: Cengage Learning, 2014.

Jackman, David, and C. Green, eds. *When God's Voice Is Heard: Essays on Preaching Presented to Dick Lucas.* Leicester, U.K.: InterVarsity Press, 1995.

BIBLIOGRAPHY

Jacks, G. Robert. *Getting the Word Across: Speeech Communication for Pastors and Lay Leaders.* Grand Rapids: Eerdmans, 1995.

_____. *Just Say the Word! Writing for the Ear.* Grand Rapids: Eerdmans, 1996.

Jensen, Eric. *Teaching with the Brain in Mind.* 2nd ed. Alexandria, Va.: Association for Supervision and Curriculum Development, 2005.

Jeremias, Joachim. *The Parables of Jesus.* 2nd rev. ed. New York: Scribner's Sons, 1954.

Johnson, Dennis E. *Him We Proclaim: Preaching Christ from All the Scriptures.* Phillipsburg, N.J.: P&R, 2007.

_____. *Let's Study Acts.* Edinburgh: Banner of Truth, 2003.

_____. *The Message of Acts in the History of Redemption.* Phillipsburg, N.J.: P&R, 1997.

_____. *Triumph of the Lamb: A Commentary on Revelation.* Phillipsburg, N.J.: P&R, 2001.

_____. *Walking with Jesus through His Word: Christ-Centered Bible Study.* Phillipsburg, N.J.: P&R, 2015.

Johnson, Dennis E., ed. *Heralds of the King: Christ-Centered Sermons in the Tradition of Edmund P. Clowney.* Grand Rapids: Crossway, 2009.

Jones, Peter R. *Capturing the Pagan Mind: Paul's Blueprint for Thinking and Living in the New Global Culture.* Nashville: B&H, 2003.

_____. *The Gnostic Empire Strikes Back: An Old Heresy for a New Age.* Phillipsburg, N.J.: P&R, 1992.

_____. *Spirit Wars: Pagan Revival in Christian America.* Mulkiteo, Wash.: WinePress, 1997.

Kahneman, Daniel. *Thinking, Fast and Slow.* New York: Farrar, Straus and Giroux, 2011.

Kaiser, Walter C., Jr. *Preaching and Teaching from the Old Testament: A Guide for the Church.* Grand Rapids: Baker, 2003.

_____. *Toward an Exegetical Theology: Biblical Exegesis for Preaching and Teaching.* Grand Rapids: Baker, 1981.

Keller, Timothy. *Center Church: Doing Balanced, Gospel-Centered Ministry in Your City.* Grand Rapids: Zondervan, 2012.

_____. *Counterfeit Gods: The Empty Promises of Money, Sex, and Power, and the Only Hope That Matters.* New York: Dutton, 2009.

_____. "A Model for Preaching," parts 1, 2, 3, *The Journal of Biblical Counseling* 12, no. 3 (Spring 1994): 36–42; 13, no. 1 (Fall 1994): 39–48; 13, no. 2 (Winter 1995): 51–60.

_____. *The Prodigal God: Recovering the Heart of the Christian Faith.* New York: Dutton, 2008.

_____. *The Reason for God: Belief in an Age of Skepticism*. New York: Dutton, 2008.

Kennedy, George. *Classical Rhetoric and Its Christian and Secular Tradition from Ancient to Modern Times*. Chapel Hill: University of North Carolina Press, 1980.

Kittel, Gerhard, and Gerhard Friedrich, eds. *Theological Dictionary of the New Testament*. Trans. by G. W. Bromiley. 10 vols. Grand Rapids: Eerdmans, 1964–1976.

Kline, Meredith G. *By Oath Consigned: A Reinterpretation of the Covenant Signs of Circumcision and Baptism*. Grand Rapids: Eerdmans, 1968.

_____. *Images of the Spirit*. Grand Rapids: Baker, 1980.

_____. *Kingdom Prologue*. Eugene, Ore.: Wipf and Stock, 991.

_____. *The Structure of Biblical Authority*. 2nd ed. Grand Rapids: Eerdmans, 1972.

_____. *Treaty of the Great King: The Covenant Structure of Deuteronomy: Studies and Commentary*. Grand Rapids: Eerdmans, 1963.

Köstenberger, Andreas, and R. Patterson. *Invitation to Biblical Interpretation: Exploring the Hermerneutical Triad of History, Literature and Theology*. Grand Rapids: Kregel, 2011.

Kuruvilla, Abraham. *Privilege the Text! A Theological Hermeneutic for Preaching*. Chicago: Moody, 2013.

Larson, Craig Brian. *Preaching That Connects: Using the Techniques of Journalists to Add Impact to Your Sermons*. Grand Rapids: Zondervan, 1994.

Larson, David L. *The Anatomy of Preaching: Identifying the Issues in Preaching Today*. Grand Rapids: Baker, 1989.

_____. *The Company of Preachers: A History of Biblical Preaching from the Old Testament to the Modern Era*. Grand Rapids: Kregel, 1998.

_____. *Telling the Old, Old Story: The Art of Narrative Preaching*. Grand Rapids: Kregel, 1995.

Lawrence, Michael. *Biblical Theology in the Life of the Church*. Wheaton, Ill.: Crossway, 2010.

Lawson, Steven J. *The Expository Genius of John Calvin*. Lake Mary, Fla.: Reformation Trust, 2007.

LeDoux, Joseph. *The Emotional Brain: The Mysterious Underpinnings of Emotional Life*. New York: Simon and Schuster, 1996.

Léon-Dufour, Xavier, ed. *Dictionary of the New Testament*. Trans. by P. Joseph Cahill. New York: Seabury, 1973.

Lepore, Ernest. *Meaning and Argument: An Introduction to Logic through Language*. 2nd rev. ed. Hoboken, N.J.: Wiley-Blackwell, 2012.

Lewin, Roger. *Human Evolution: An Illustrated Introduction*. 4th ed. Oxford, U.K.: Blackwell Science, 1999.

Lewis, C. S. *An Experiment in Criticism.* Cambridge, U.K.: Cambridge University Press, 1961.

Lints, Richard. *The Fabric of Theology: A Prolegomena to Evangelical Theology.* Grand Rapids: Eerdmans, 1993.

Lischer, Richard. *A Theology of Preaching: The Dynamics of the Gospel.* Eugene: Wipf & Stock, 2001.

_____. *Theories of Preaching: Selected Readings in the Homiletical Tradition.* Durham: Labyrinth, 1987.

Litfin, Duane. *St. Paul's Theology of Proclamation: 1 Corinthians 1–4 and Greco-Roman Rhetoric.* Cambridge, U.K.: Cambridge University Press, 1994.

Lloyd-Jones, D. Martyn. *Preaching and Preachers.* Grand Rapids: Zondervan, 1971.

Logan, Samuel T., Jr., ed. *The Preacher and Preaching: Reviving the Art in the Twentieth Century.* Phillipsburg, N.J.: P&R, 1986.

Long, Thomas G. *Preaching and the Literary Forms of the Bible.* Philadelphia: Fortress, 1989.

_____. *The Witness of Preaching.* Louisville: Westminster John Knox, 1989.

Long, V. Phillips. *The Art of Biblical History.* Foundations of Contemporary Interpretation, vol. 5. Grand Rapids: Zondervan, 1994.

Longman, Tremper, III. *How to Read the Psalms.* Downers Grove, Ill.: InterVarsity, 1988.

_____. *Literary Approaches to Biblical Interpretation.* Foundations of Contemporary Interpretation, vol. 3. Grand Rapids: Zondervan, 1987.

Louw, Johannes P., and Eugene A. Nida, eds. *A Greek-English Lexicon of the New Testament: Based on Semantic Domains.* 2nd ed. 2 vols. New York: United Bible Societies, 1988.

Lowry, Eugene L. *The Homiletical Plot: The Sermon as Narrative Art Form.* Rev. ed. Louisville: Westminster John Knox, 2001.

Lucas, Sean Michael. *On Being Presbyterian: Our Beliefs, Practices, and Stories.* Phillipsburg, N.J.: P&R, 2006.

Lucas, Stephen E. *The Art of Public Speaking.* 6th ed. Boston: McGraw-Hill, 1998.

Mathewson, Steven D. *The Art of Preaching Old Testament Narrative.* Grand Rapids: Baker Academic, 2002.

Matsumoto, David., ed. *The Handbook of Culture and Psychology.* New York: Oxford University Press, 2001.

Mawhinney, Bruce. *Preaching with Freshness.* Grand Rapids: Kregel, 1997.

Mayer, Richard E. "Multimedia Learning: Are We Asking the Right Questions?" *Educational Psychology* 32, no. 1 (1997): 1–19.

_____. *Multi-Media Learning.* Cambridge, U.K.: Cambridge University Press, 2001.

McCartney, Dan, and Charles Clayton. *Let the Reader Understand: A Guide to Interpreting and Applying the Bible.* Wheaton, Ill.: Victor, 1994.

McGaugh, James, C. McIntyre, and A. Power. "Amygdala Modulation of Memory Consolidation: Interaction with Other Brain Systems." *Neurobiology of Learning and Memory* 78 (2002): 539–52.

Medina, John. *Brain Rules: 12 Principles for Surviving and Thriving at Work, Home and School.* Seattle: Pear Press, 2008.

Metaxas, Eric. *Bonhoeffer: Pastor, Martyr, Prophet, Spy; A Righteous Gentile vs. the Third Reich.* Nashville: Thomas Nelson, 2010.

Meyer, Jason. *Preaching: A Biblical Theology.* Wheaton, Ill.: Crossway, 2013.

Miller, C. John. *The Heart of a Servant Leader: Letters from Jack Miller.* Ed. by B. Miller Juliani. Phillipsburg, N.J.: P&R, 2004.

_____. *Outgrowing the Ingrown Church.* Grand Rapids: Zondervan, 1986.

Mitchell, Margaret M. *Paul and the Rhetoric of Reconciliation: An Exegetical Investigation of the Language and Composition of 1 Corinthians.* Louisville: Westminster/John Knox, 1991.

Moss, Jessica. "Right Reason in Plato and Aristotle: On the Meaning of *Logos.*" *Phronesis* 59 (2014): 181–230.

Myers, Kenneth A. *All God's Children and Blue Suede Shoes: Christians and Popular Culture.* Wheaton, Ill.: Crossway, 1989.

Niles, D. T. *The Preacher's Task and the Stone of Stumbling.* New York: Harper, 1958.

Nouwen, Henri J. M. *In the Name of Jesus: Reflections on Christian Leadership.* New York: Crossroad, 1989.

Old, Hughes Oliphant. *The Reading and Preaching of the Scriptures in the Worship of the Christian Church.* Vols. 1–5. Grand Rapids: Eerdmans, 1998–2004.

Ophira, Eyal, Clifford Nass, and Anothony D. Wagner. "Cognitive Control in Media Multitaskers." *PNAS* 106, no. 37 (August 24, 2009): 15583–87.

Panksepp, Jon. *Affective Neuroscience: The Foundations of Human and Animal Emotions.* Oxford, U.K.: Oxford University Press, 1998.

Parker, T. H. L. *Calvin's Preaching.* Louisville: Westminster John Knox, 1992.

Pasquarello, Michael, III. *Christian Preaching.* Grand Rapids: Baker Academic, 2008.

Paul, Ian, and David Wenham. *Preaching the New Testament.* Downers Grove: IVP Academic, 2013.

Peterson, Eugene H. *Five Smooth Stones for Pastoral Work.* Grand Rapids: Eerdmans, 1980.

_____. *Working the Angles: The Shape of Pastoral Integrity.* Grand Rapids: Eerdmans, 1987.

BIBLIOGRAPHY

Piper, John. *God Is the Gospel: Meditations on God's Love as the Gift of Himself.* Wheaton, Ill.: Crossway, 2005.

———. *The Supremacy of God in Preaching.* Rev. ed. Grand Rapids: Baker, 2004.

Pitt-Watson, Ian. *A Primer for Preachers.* Grand Rapids: Baker, 1986.

Plantinga, Cornelius, Jr. *Reading for Preaching: The Preacher in Conversation with Storytellers, Biographers, Poets, and Journalists.* Grand Rapids: Eerdmans, 2013.

Poirier, Alfred. *The Peacemaking Pastor: A Biblical Guide to Resolving Church Conflict.* Grand Rapids: Baker, 2006.

Pollard, Tim. *Oratium: Mastering the High-Stakes Presentation.* Billings, Mont.: Oratium, 2011.

Postman, Neil. *Amusing Ourselves to Death: Public Discourse in the Age of Show Business.* New York: Viking, 1985.

Powlison, David. "Idols of the Heart and Vanity Fair." *Journal of Biblical Counseling* 13, no. 2 (Winter 1995): 35–50.

Poythress, Vern S. *Logic: A God-Centered Approach to the Foundation of Western Thought.* Wheaton, Ill.: Crossway, 2013.

———. *The Shadow of Christ in the Law of Moses.* Phillipsburg, N.J.: P&R, 1990.

Pratt, Richard L. *He Gave Us Stories: The Bible Student's Guide to Interpreting Old Testament Narratives.* Phillipsburg, N.J.: P&R, 1990.

Premack, David, and A. Premack. *Original Intelligence: Unlocking the Mystery of Who We Are.* Boston: McGraw Hill, 2003.

Prutow, Dennis J. *So Pastor, What's Your Point?* Philadelphia: Alliance of Confessing Evangelicals, 2010.

Quintillian. *Institutio Oratorio of Quintillian.* Vol. 1. Trans. by H. E. Butler. Boston: Harvard University Press, 1958.

Rasch, Björn, et al. "Odor Cues during Slow-Wave Sleep Prompt Declarative Memory Consolidation." *Science* 315 (2007): 1426–29.

Restak, Richard. *Think Smart: A Neuroscientist's Prescription for Improving Your Brain's Performance.* New York: Riverhead, 2009.

Ridderbos, Herman. *The Coming of the Kingdom.* Philadelphia, N.J.: P&R, 1962.

———. *Paul: An Outline of His Theology.* Trans. by John R. de Witt. Grand Rapids: Eerdmans, 1975.

Robertson, O. Palmer. *The Christ of the Covenants.* Phillipsburg, N.J.: P&R, 1981.

Robinson, Haddon W. *Biblical Preaching: The Development and Delivery of Expository Messages.* 2nd ed. Grand Rapids: Baker, 2001.

Rock, David. *Your Brain at Work: Strategies for Overcoming Distraction, Regaining Focus, and Working Smarter All Day Long.* New York: HarperBusiness, 2009.

236

Rosenzweig, Phil. *The Halo Effect: And Eight Other Business Delusions That Deceive Managers*. New York: Free Press, 2007.

Runia, Klaas. *The Sermon under Attack: The Moore College Lectures, 1980*. Exeter, U.K.: Paternoster, 1983.

Ryken, Leland, James C. Wilhoit, and Tremper Longman III, eds. *Dictionary of Biblical Imagery*. Downers Grove, Ill.: InterVarsity, 1998.

Ryken, Leland, and Todd Wilson, eds. *Preach the Word: Essays on Expository Preaching; In Honor of R. Kent Hughes*. Wheaton, Ill.: Crossway, 2007.

Sande, Ken. *The Peacemaker: A Biblical Guide to Resolving Personal Conflict*. 3rd ed. Grand Rapids: Baker, 2004.

Sayers, Dorothy L. *The Lost Tools of Learning*. New York: National Review, 1961.

_____. *The Mind of the Maker*. New York: Living Age, 1956.

Sereno, K. K., and C. D. Mortensen, eds. *Foundations of Communication Theory*. New York: Harper, 1970.

Shannon, Claude, and Warren Weaver. *A Mathematical Theory of Communication*. Chicago: University of Illinois Press, 1949.

Siegal, M., and R. Varley. "Neural Systems Involved in the Theory of Mind." *National Review of Neuroscience* 3 (2002): 463–71.

Silva, Moisés. *Biblical Words and Their Meanings: An Introduction to Lexical Semantics*. Grand Rapids: Zondervan, 1983.

Sinek, Sam. "How Great Leaders Inspire Action." *TEDxPuget Sound* (September 2009); http://www.ted.com/talks/ simon_sinek_how_great_leaders_inspire_action?language=en.

Smith, Steven W. *Dying to Preach: Embracing the Cross in the Pulpit*. Grand Rapids: Kregel, 2009.

Smith, Steven, and D. Schaffer. "Celerity and Cajolery: Rapid Speech May Promote or Inhibit Persuasion through Its Impact on Message Elaboration." *Personality and Social Psychology Bulletin* 17, no. 6 (December 1991): 663–69.

Spurgeon, Charles Haddon. *Lectures to My Students*. Grand Rapids: Zondervan, 1980.

Stott, John. *Between Two Worlds: The Art of Preaching in the Twentieth Century*. Grand Rapids: Eerdmans, 1982.

_____. *The Preacher's Portrait: Some New Testament Word Studies*. Grand Rapids: Eerdmans, 1961.

Stuhlmacher, Peter, ed. *The Gospel and the Gospels*. Grand Rapids: Eerdmans, 1991.

Sweet, Leonard. *Giving Blood: A Fresh Paradigm for Preaching*. Grand Rapids: Zondervan, 2014.

Tracy, Jennifer, and David Matsumoto. "The Spontaneous Expression of Pride and Shame: Evidence for Biologically Innate Nonverbal Displays." *PNAS* 15, no 33 (August 2008): 11655–60.

BIBLIOGRAPHY

Trimp, C. *Preaching and the History of Salvation: Continuing an Unfinished Discussion*. Trans. by N. D. Kloosterman. Scarsdale, N.Y.: Westminster Book Service, 1996.

Tripp, Paul David. *Dangerous Calling: Confronting the Unique Challenges of Pastoral Ministry*. Wheaton, Ill.: Crossway, 2012.

_____. *Instruments in the Redeemer's Hands: People in Need of Change Helping People in Need of Change*. Phillipsburg, N.J.: P&R, 2002.

Um, Stephen, and J. Buzzard. *Why Cities Matter: To God, the Culture, and the Church*. Wheaton, Ill.: Crossway, 2013.

Vanhoozer, Kevin J. *Is There a Meaning in This Text? The Bible, the Reader, and the Morality of Literary Knowledge*. Grand Rapids: Zondervan, 1998.

Veith, Gene Edward, Jr. *The Gift of Art: The Place of the Arts in Scripture*. Downers Grove, Ill.: InterVarsity Press, 1983.

_____. *State of the Arts: From Bezalel to Mapplethorpe*. Wheaton, Ill.: Crossway, 1991.

Vickers, Brian. *In Defense of Rhetoric*. Oxford: Oxford University Press, 1988.

Visscher, J. "Redemptive-Historical Preaching Revisited." In *Unity in Diversity: Studies Presented to Professor Dr. Jelle Faber on the Occasion of His Retirement*, ed. by Riemar Faber. Hamilton, Ont.: Senate of the Theological College of the Canadian Reformed Churches, 1989.

Vitruvius: De Architectura. Trans. by Frank Granger. Boston: Harvard University Press, 1931.

Vitruvius: Ten Books on Architecture. Trans. by Ingrid Rowland. Cambridge, U.K.: Cambridge University Press, 1999.

Vos, Geerhardus. *Biblical Theology*. Grand Rapids: Eerdmans, 1975.

_____. *Grace and Glory: Sermons Preached in the Chapel of Princeton Theological Seminary*. Edinburgh: Banner of Truth, 1994.

_____. *The Pauline Eschatology*. Grand Rapids: Eerdmans, 1952.

_____. *Redemptive History and Biblical Interpretation: The Shorter Writings of Geerhardus Vos*. Ed. by R. B. Gaffin Jr. Phillipsburg, N.J.: P&R, 1980.

Weiner, David. *Reality Check: What Your Mind Knows, But Isn't Telling You*. Amherst, N.Y.: Prometheus, 2005.

Welch, Edward T. *Blame It on the Brain? Distinguishing Chemical Imbalances, Brain Disorders, and Disobedience*. Phillipsburg, N.J.: P&R, 1998.

Westminster Confession of Faith, Larger and Shorter Catechisms (1646).

Willhite, Keith, and Scott M. Gibson, eds. *The Big Idea of Biblical Preaching: Connecting the Bible to People*. Grand Rapids: Baker, 1998.

Willimon, William H. *Peculiar Speech: Preaching to the Baptized*. Grand Rapids: Eerdmans, 1982.

BIBLIOGRAPHY

Willimon, William H., and Richard Lischer. *Concise Encyclopedia of Preaching.*
Louisville: Westminster John Knox, 1995.

Wilson, Douglas. *The Case for Classical Christian Education.* Wheaton, Ill.:
Crossway, 2003.

_____. *Recovering the Lost Tools of Learning: An Approach to Distinctly Christian Education.* Wheaton, Ill.: Crossway, 1991.

Wilson, Paul S. *A Concise History of Preaching.* Nashville: Abingdon, 1992.

_____. *The Practice of Preaching.* Nashville: Abingdon, 1995.

Wirzba, Norman, ed. *The Art of the Commonplace: The Agrarian Essays of Wendell Berry.* Emeryville, Calif.: Shoemaker & Hoard, 2002.

Witherington, Ben, III. *New Testament Rhetoric: An Introductory Guide to the Art of Persuasion in and of the New Testament.* Eugene, Ore.: Cascade, 2009.

Witmer, Timothy Z. *The Shepherd Leader: Achieving Effective Shepherding in Your Church.* Phillipsburg, N.J.: P&R, 2010.

Wright, Christopher J. H. *Knowing Jesus through the Old Testament.* Downers Grove, Ill.: InterVarsity, 1992.